KITCHEN SINK REALISMS

Studies in

THEATRE HISTORY

AND CULTURE

Edited by Heather Nathans

DOROTHY CHANSKY

KITCHEN SINK REALISMS

DOMESTIC LABOR, DINING, AND DRAMA IN AMERICAN THEATRE

UNIVERSITY OF IOWA PRESS

Iowa City

University of Iowa Press, Iowa City 52242

Copyright © 2015 by the University of Iowa Press

Printed in the United States of America

Design by Richard Hendel

www.uiowapress.org

The University of Iowa Press is a member of Green Press Initiative
and is committed to preserving natural resources.

Printed on acid-free paper

Library of Congress Cataloging-in-Publication Data
Chansky, Dorothy.
Kitchen sink realisms : domestic labor, dining, and drama in
American theatre / Dorothy Chansky.
    pages   cm. — (Studies in theatre history and culture)
Includes bibliographical references and index.
ISBN 978-1-60938-375-6 (pbk), ISBN 978-1-60938-376-3 (ebk)
1. Theater—New York (State)—New York—History—20th
century. 2. Domestic space in the theater—New York (State)—New
York. 3. Women in literature. 4. Labor in literature. I. Title.
PN2277.N5C46   2015
792.09747'1—dc23   2015005039

In memory of

EDNA AGRANOVITCH CHANSKY,

ELLEN BENNETT, *and* EDITH KERN

CONTENTS

ACKNOWLEDGMENTS

In the decade that went into writing this book, I depended on the kindness of strangers (many of them librarians), friends, family, colleagues, and grant-giving institutions. I am grateful to Philip Auslander, Chris Bennion, John Calhoun, Faedra Carpenter, Jonathan Chambers, Edward Chansky, Joel Chansky, Pamela Cobrin, the College of Visual and Performing Arts at Texas Tech University, Tracy C. Davis, the Five College Women's Studies Research Center, Helene Foley, Anne S. Hrobsky, the late Carolyn Hailey, Louise Martzinek, Jeremy Megraw, Koritha Mitchell, Elizabeth Reitz Mullenix, Paul D. Naish, the Office of the Provost at Texas Tech University, the Office of the Vice President for Research at Texas Tech University, Jorgelina Orfila, Jorge Ramirez, Cecelia Riddett, Kristen Rogers, Cindy D. Rosenthal, Charles Starke, Carolyn Tate, Marvin J. Taylor, Rob Weiner, E. J. Westlake, Ann Folino White, Edye Wiggins, Brian Withers, Aaron Wood, and W. B. Worthen. My editors Catherine Cocks and Heather Nathans were consistently helpful, generous, and living proof that the cheerleading squad can come from the ranks of the intellectuals holding the line. They bucked up my spirits and watched my back where credibility was concerned. My mother played a large role in my circuitous route to this project. She kept a clean, orderly house, but I learned little about cooking and cleaning from her, as her mantra was "get the M.A. with dots before you get the one without dots." So long as the dishes were washed and the beds made, she was happier seeing me in the library, and for that I am in her debt. Foremost, I thank my husband, Terry A. Bennett, who spared me more domestic labor than I will probably ever realize, to enable me to focus on writing.

Part of chapter 1 appeared in an earlier form as "Kitchen Sink Realisms: American Drama, Dining, and Domestic Labor Come of Age in Little Theatre," in the *Journal of American Drama and Theatre* (Spring 2004), published by Martin E. Segal Theatre Center Publications. Part of chapter 2 appeared as "Dialectic of Domesticity: Homemaking and Its Discontents in 1920s American Drama," in a special issue of *Women and Performance: A Journal of Feminist Theory* (November 2006) devoted to domesticity. Parts of chapters 6 and 7 appeared as "Retooling the Kitchen Sink: Representing Domestic Labor in American Performance after 1963," in *Working in the Wings: New Perspectives on Theatre History and Labor* (Southern Illinois University Press, 2015).

ACKNOWLEDGMENTS

KITCHEN SINK REALISMS

INTRODUCTION
REALISM AND ITS DISCONTENTS

"Kitchen sink realism" can polarize theatre workers and audiences. It is used by critics, ticket buyers, acting teachers, directors, and designers to denote plays trafficking in the domestic everyday, reveling in the use of household objects, often depicting people of limited financial means, and frequently featuring intense showdowns that favor psychologically credible acting, rather than, say, abstract, consciously poetic, or athletically physical styles. Some love its grittiness, literal-minded representational practices, and emotional intensity. Designers can have a field day with brand-names, vintage clothing, and working appliances; actors can invoke their deepest affective memories. Others roll their eyes at its mimetic naiveté. Playwright John Guare went so far as to title a 1996 anthology of his early plays *The War against the Kitchen Sink*.[1]

Coined to describe a new kind of post–World War II British realism, "kitchen sink" was also known as "angry theatre" or "committed theatre." John Osborne's *Look Back in Anger* (1956) enjoyed pride of place in the repertoire. In that strategically rebellious work "the well-furnished elegance of the middle-class stage gave place to kitchens and attics, with all their sordid paraphernalia of cooking stoves and ironing boards and beds."[2]

The notion of an ironing board or a stove as sordid (ignoble, vile, squalid, wretchedly poor, run-down) strains credulity, unless one imagines realism as a genre delimited by drawing room conventions or policed by the privileged critic. That Arthur Miller considered *Look Back in Anger* the only modern British play worth seeing suggests that kitchen sink realism was long overdue, at least in England. American plays had been depicting food preparation, ironing, the hovels of the destitute and the criminal, working-class homes, small-town families around the dinner table, and farm kitchens since the end of the nineteenth century. American audiences are particularly attached to realism, and permutations of that genre are almost relentlessly marshaled to reveal relationships and problems in the domestic realm.[3]

This book begins in 1918, a key year for several reasons. It was the first year that the Pulitzer Prize was given for drama, and the winning play, *Why Marry?*, addressed in a frothy way the very questions that would be central in many middlebrow dramas and comedies of the 1920s: What do intelligent, energetic women get out of marriages that tease with the promise of romance but close with the guarantee of a life of domesticity? The 1918 one-act *Tickless Time*, my first case study, was a product of the Little Theatre Movement's most famous company: the Provincetown Players. Playwrights Susan Glaspell and George Cram Cook's humorous look at the drudgery required to maintain even a small, childless home says as much about the awakening audience for this kind of kitchen sink realism as it does about its topic—going overboard with fads. The Little Theatre Movement fostered an audience for plays about the everyday concerns of "average" Americans who did not see themselves as stereotypes.[4]

One can also read 1918 as a capstone year for a style of theatre that then faded into nostalgic memory. The 1918 hit *Lightnin'*, with its rambling, corny joke–driven dramaturgy, was, as Ethan Mordden argues, the last hurrah of an era, with 1919 the start of a forty-year period anchored by Eugene O'Neill, the Theatre Guild, the star duo of Alfred Lunt and Lynn Fontanne, the rise of realism as we now recognize it in acting, and musicals with serious themes.[5]

The 2005 end point of this study is the year that *The Clean House* was a finalist for the Pulitzer Prize. It named as shortsighted, cold, unfair, and selfish the expectation that a housekeeper of color could be treated as a commodity to relieve a white career woman of having to do her own housework.[6] This play came on the heels of *Caroline, or Change*, which placed an African American domestic center stage in a Broadway musical interrogating not only racism but also the status of domestic workers as laborers and citizens. *Caroline* joined other twenty-first-century plays considering domestics, domestic labor, and the impossibility of keeping house on minimum wage, including *Living Out* and *Nickel and Dimed*.

The term "kitchen sink realism" has proven useful far beyond its original context. It is now applied to theatre produced both before and well after its mid-1950s heyday. Critics use it loosely to describe dramas with domestic settings rendered in detail and performed with an eye to plausibility. Part of the flexibility of the label and also the popularity of the genre can be attributed to what might be called its failures. Kitchen sink drama, despite its originators' desire to dispense with tradition, never overcame an affinity for the structure of the well-made play with a conventional emotional climax. Nor did kitchen sink drama attract a working-class audience. It provided instead a look at domestic life in a way that appealed to traditional theatregoers. New subject matter was mitigated by old dramaturgy.

There is more to kitchen sink realism, however, than even its supporters suggest or perhaps want to see. By pluralizing the descriptor— kitchen sink *realisms*—I look at the ways that food preparation (sometimes feigned, sometimes actual), domestic labor (including sewing, knitting, ironing, dusting, sweeping, floor scrubbing, vacuuming, bathing and dressing children, caring for the elderly, and doing laundry), dining, serving, entertaining, and cleanup saturate the lives of dramatic characters and situations even when the kitchen-related activities do not take center stage. I am also interested in the daily realities repressed by realism—the genre—in the interest of keeping the audience coming back for more: for example, What is the servant thinking? Where did that roast originate before arriving in the suburban kitchen in butcher paper? Who maintains those immaculate, starched, pressed garments? Who is minding the children, so carefully sequestered offstage? While one could obviously answer that these lacunae are necessary to put the focus where the playwright wants it, such an explanation requires major excisions from the realm of what fits in realism.

My project is hardly just to expose what is ignored in the interest of a saleable dramaturgy, or simply to show how drama, theatre, and performance "reflect" domestic actualities, although I do this, too. Rather, this book "concentrates on the forms, patterns, and symbols which largely middle-class America used" to deal with the home that William Dean Howells saw as the locus of our "main human interest" in American drama.[7] The repeated, reworked usage suggests something unresolved, which is exactly where I want to put pressure on the texts and productions I examine.

As *feminist* history, *Kitchen Sink Realisms* investigates the unremittingly gendered nature of virtually all domestic labor portrayed on the American stage. I want to explore how domesticity—what Carol

Shields once called the "shaggy beast that eats up 50 percent of our lives"[8] — is "reproduced across generations," with an eye to the "inextricable interconnectedness and mutual constitution of psyche, society, and culture."[9] Theatre, drama, and performance played an important role in both supporting and contesting the idea that the home is "naturally" women's sphere, especially since the multiple, simultaneous tracks of a play production (text, performance, mise-en-scène, soundscape) may do both—support and contest—at the same time.

Although virtually all American plays with domestic settings reproduce the household with an individual, private kitchen and the said household's repetitive and often offstage work, spectators may well have derived and continue to derive from performances—originals and revivals—something other than satisfaction in recognizing a version of a mediated status quo. The cohort perhaps most likely to experience a disconnect comprises women, and all studies and surveys of American audiences from the 1910s through 2003 have shown a majority of playgoers and ticket buyers to be women.[10] Theatre critics until very recently have been preponderantly men.[11] Although much has changed in the nearly nine decades covered here, women are still overwhelmingly responsible for housework, and the idea that women "belong" in the home persists.[12]

Because domestic labor appears in a variety of genres including dramas, drawing room comedies, domestic comedy, domestic tragedy, performance art, and musicals, the idea of *realisms* is a nod to how many kinds of signifiers can point to a shared set of referents. How, then, do I propose to use my plural? What does it have to do with exposing and exploring both what Betty Friedan famously called "the problem that has no name" and some of the joys and skills that make the domestic sphere a site of delight and creativity?[13]

"Realism" is a richly fraught term covering the work of writers whose ideas of what they are doing differ widely.[14] Excerpts from Émile Zola's "Naturalism in the Theatre" (more to come on how this both overlaps and differs from realism) and August Strindberg's preface to his one-act play *Miss Julie* frequently serve as introductions to the term. The former argues for the inexorable, ineradicable effects of economic and environmental forces in determining the lives and actions of individuals, and the necessity of representing these accurately. The latter stands pat on individual psychology, albeit with some deterministic ideas about sexual difference, again with an eye to revealing truth. Bertolt Brecht—typically offered as an arch-opponent to realism—insisted it was the right term for his own work. "Realism is not a mere question of form," he wrote in opposing Georg Lukács's assertion that it was the genre par excellence for representing the true "relations between appearance and essence without the need for any external commentary."[15] Explaining that Lukács was too invested in the fusty forms of the nineteenth-century novel, Brecht declared:

> Realistic means: discovering the causal complexes of society / unmasking the prevailing view of things as the view of those who are in power / writing from the standpoint of the class which offers the broadest solutions for the pressing difficulties in which human society is caught up / emphasizing the element of development / making possible the concrete, and making possible abstraction from it.[16]

Because my project involves exposing causalities and ironies in the behaviors and assumptions that go with domestic labor and dining, Brecht's concern for realism as unmasking is pertinent. Because mimeticism has been so relentlessly popular on the American stage, Zola's concerns—at least at the level of objects, spaces, and assignment of social tasks—are sometimes the base on which a Brechtian superstructure is erected. And Strindberg's interest in the individual psyche remains a bedrock of much compelling acting—acting generally associated with some version of realism—whether or not a particular script calls for it explicitly.

Pam Morris offers "a useful way of understanding part of the artistic impulse behind realism: a complex, ambivalent responsiveness towards, rather than repulsion from, the tangible stuff of reality. Realism is committed to the material actuality we share as embodied creatures."[17] That material actuality, of course, is hardly identical across cultural space. Since writers and readers vary in their social situation, "what is seen as 'reality' depends on the social position of the perceiver."[18] Both Zola and Strindberg are right. Literary realism is not a mirror but a synecdoche, as Brian Richardson observes—a shorthand for the social world.[19] Literary representation is never identical to its object.[20] These arguments refer to realist novels, but the insights are equally valuable regarding plays, especially since the realities encountered in the theatre are not just textual and may resonate visually even when rankling verbally, or vice versa. In this way, more or less realistic theatre productions may precisely, in Brecht's words, "unmasking the prevailing view of things" in the eyes of spectators who don't totally share, or who share uneasily, the "view of those who are in power."

Morris repeatedly makes clear that "the form of realism is necessarily protean, but the commitment of the genre to historical particularity is non-negotiable."[21] The sometimes bad rap that realism gets in theatre is largely the result of its being misrecognized as *not* being protean.[22] This point yields two additional insights. First, examining the spread of photography from the mid-nineteenth century onward, Morris points out that despite the infinite possibilities and myriad actual images the camera made available, "there was not a concomitant expansion in the variety. Increasingly, photography established and adhered to generic protocols for classifying, posing, shooting and naming its subject matter."[23] The analogue in theatre would be the commitment to such things as character types, predictable plots, favored types of closure, familiar settings, and so on. In other words, the possibilities of this genre—realism—are often constrained by the needs of the marketplace, resulting in a limited use of, and therefore a limited understanding of, something potentially much more malleable.[24]

Morris's second insight is drawn from David Harvey's point that phenomena look different "when analyzed at global, continental, national, regional, local, or household/personal scales."[25] Readers or spectators have the capacity to do conceptually what a photographer does in adjusting a lens. We can zoom in, zoom out, adjust the relation between background and foreground, decide which is to be which, crop, edit, pan, imagine in another context, or otherwise interpret the selected material. And realism itself is nothing if not selective. The same artwork may be viewed differently in the company of one's daughter than how it is viewed in the company of one's employer, or differently as part of an outing when the tickets are gifts than how it is read if one is writing a critique for a school assignment. Most obviously, it may look different on a second viewing.

Not only are individual spectators capable of reading and thinking from multiple perspectives, but various contingents within an audience may read a shared cultural phenomenon differently. Cultural sign systems such as plays are always ambiguous. While most cultural texts have a "preferred meaning," they do not have a "fixed or inexorable meaning," Justin Lewis notes, even though much audience research has presumed commonality of meaning that can be the result of sources that manifested consensus. "So, if something meant the same to X, Y, and Z, it remained uninterrogated. Only when X, Y, and Z responded differently were questions asked."[26] When our historic sources for responses to plays are newspaper critics and people affiliated with professional theatre, X, Y, and Z may agree, but A, B, and C—conceivably women spectators—are eliminated from the discussion. As Tracy Davis so trenchantly states, "[S]ilence is not absence."[27]

Audience research need not literally involve asking spectators questions or monitoring how they express themselves. We can reasonably and responsibly posit responses by analyzing the culture in which audiences experienced plays. "Cultural forms do not drift through history aimlessly. They are grounded in an ideological context that gives them their historical significance."[28] Yet even the most rigid ideologies have visible, vocal resistors. Consider the oft-presumed ubiquity of Cold War containment and the ideal of the suburban home, complete with commuting dad and homemaking mom. Then recall that two of the most often studied iconographic endeavors from the 1950s are the poetry of the Beats and the film *Rebel Without a Cause*. One did not need to be called to testify before the House Un-American Activities Committee to see cracks in the ideological facade, nor even to have resistant opinions on some subjects.

Theatre is different from literature in that theatre proceeds on simultaneous, multiple tracks, all of which are available to the audience, and does so in real time. Hence, realism in the theatre is not just the product of the text. In historicizing the late nineteenth-century advent of realism as America's favorite genre, Brenda Murphy notes that innovations in plays emerged *after* innovations in stagecraft, meaning that the hyperrealistic mise-en-scène (settings, props, costumes, physical arrangements) preceded the earliest recognized realistic play texts by nearly a generation. Murphy uses an inverted and slightly relabeled version of Aristotle's criteria for tragedy to name the features that American playwrights worked with to write dramas falling under the rubric realism. The category "stagecraft"—roughly analogous to spectacle—was sixth of six for Aristotle, first for emerging realist playwrights. American playwrights began to stipulate and comment on detailed settings with the idea that these were not just decoration or backdrop but were important to understanding character and theme.

Playwrights also expected actors to bring to life specific, individuated characters, and to facilitate this, they provided nuanced, particularized ways of talking that (presumably) went beyond stereotypes, with the goal of invoking specific classes, neighborhoods, ethnicities, and personalities. This commitment to verisimilitude as an ordinary way of doing business allowed audiences to trust playwrights' introducing them to new or strange milieus. In this study, I am also interested in how playwrights used realistic milieus and dialogue to upset understandings of the everyday. Stage realism might be a part of a package of literary and design genres that delivered accuracy in one or two ways (typically clothing, props, and language) while experimenting in other ways (settings, soundscapes, asides, masks, or dramatic structure).[29]

If realism frequently gets a bum rap, naturalism is sometimes dismissed altogether—when the pair aren't simply being loosely applied interchangeably—as "radical realism," which seeks to "present a slice of life instead of a carefully constructed plot."[30] For Bruce McConachie, writing in 2006, what characterizes most naturalist plays—relegated in his reading to a now-dead avant-garde thriving between 1880 and 1914—are "banality, cynicism, sentimentality, and violence."[31] Is there any reason for a contemporary theatre scholar to seek to recuperate this putative absence of plot (the critique seems to assume that only a certain kind of emplotment really counts) coupled with banality and surface detail? Or, if the answer is no, is there anything about naturalism that goes beyond this blunt-edged understanding?

Jennifer Fleissner offers an original feminist reading of naturalism that recuperates it for my project and does so regardless of concern for literary genre.[32] Fleissner notes that naturalist plots feature "neither the steep arc of decline nor that of triumph, but rather . . . an ongoing, nonlinear, repetitive motion . . . that has the distinctive effect of seeming also like a stuckness in place."[33] In the late nineteenth- and early twentieth-century novels she examines, characters begin to look quite modern, like our own contemporaries, as they obsess on constructing themselves for public consumption as acceptable products of the marketplace, ready to be admired, to be hired, and to fit in.

Characters in naturalist texts make visible the negotiations between nature and culture "in the elaborations of the smallest details of ordinary bodily upkeep that psychologists would later term *compulsions*: cleaning, eating, locking the doors."[34] Their compulsions are efforts at fitting in, at being modern, indeed at being women. Such compulsion renders "this individual stuckness . . . tied to a stuckness at the broader level of history as well."[35] Fleissner argues for the superiority of naturalism for revealing the unhappiness of women as consumers over the predetermined aims of the well-made realist play for closure and authority. Compulsive housekeeping becomes, in this schema, a creative attempt at wholeness on the only terms available to the compulsive (woman). If the terms drive the individual woman crazy or wear her down or make her a bore, it is not for her lack of trying. It is precisely because of the system in which she is caged.

The plays I examine depict domestic labor in varying amounts but nearly always with the same metonymic purpose: This work is pleasant in its effects, perhaps, but it is also repetitive and laborious; it is generally treated with circumspection in much dialogue or is handled offstage or in the background, while other concerns are driving the plot. In other words, the *clean, orderly* house is a lovely backdrop for retreat or romance, a symbolic guarantor of harmony and even Americanness, but the *cleaning and ordering* are drudgery and not a worthy backdrop (much less topic) for anything. When housework is depicted, it is nearly always capably handled by a poor woman, often, although not always, a paid domestic, who ironically is often fully able to get the job done while also handling emotional and political problems— sometimes including the problem of finding a way for the next generation to be able to focus on emotional and political problems without having to expend energy on housework.

Like realism, the kitchen bears discussing, as it has a history that is economic, technological, and social and since it is the location most readily identified with domestic labor. Indeed, the earliest American homes were all kitchen, to the extent that they were one- or two-room dwellings with most household and social activities taking place around the fire, as this was the only place that was warm. The woman tending this fire multitasked as she cooked, washed, watched children, spun, wove, made or mended clothing, and possibly participated in a craft business. In the beginning of the nineteenth century large houses in developing cities had separate rooms as kitchens, which might be staffed with servants but still had open hearths. Stoves appeared in the middle third of the nineteenth century and became common after the Civil War. Only the extremely wealthy woman could divorce herself entirely from daily housework. More middling householders differentiated themselves from whatever help they had by the particular work they did (e.g., sewing but not laundry; cooking but not chopping firewood) and by maintaining a hierarchy of authority.[36]

"Help" was not necessarily a full-time phenomenon, as many women used paid workers for some heavy tasks—laundry being the most common—or for seasonal or special event work such as spring cleaning, help with a new baby, or assistance with a feast or party. In keeping with the traditional division of labor in the pre-twentieth-century household, housewives were responsible for apportioning tasks. Children might help with chores requiring the least organizational skill or judgment (fetching or mending), while servants did the most arduous or messy work (scrubbing floors, laundry, ironing, or blacking the stove), leaving the tasks requiring the most organizational skill, creativity, or judgment (cooking meals or fine sewing) to the housewife herself.[37] The percentage of households with what could truly be called servants was always small. In the twentieth century it was one in fifteen in 1900 and one in forty-two in 1950.[38]

While many modern Americans imagine they do without servants or even "help," they are in fact making use of the labor of people in industry or service to do things that household workers would previously have done. Obvious examples include dry cleaning, food processing, serving fast food, factory labor to produce clothing and other household goods, or even hair care in beauty salons. Moreover, household help was not always a maid in a uniform. Sometimes it was a poor relation working for room and board or a poorly paid teenager earning a small amount of money before marrying and setting up her own household. Part of my project is to consider the invisible labor that makes possible the household depicted on the realistic stage, whether this labor is invisible because frequently exiting stage left or because it is part of a national or global economy screened out of consciousness in the consuming household. As Amy Bentley notes, it is not possible to understand consumption properly without an attendant understanding of the conditions of production, and production for modern household consumption takes place to a large extent outside the home.[39] In plays, it usually takes place outside the entire dramatic realm.

Where does the kitchen sink fit into these evolving "realisms"? The sink is not a casual choice for defining a genre originally associated with the "sordid." If there is a single kitchen item that can be connected with backbreaking, sweaty, greasy, dirty, repetitive domestic labor, it is the sink, which, like everything else in the American household, can be historicized. The sink has always had a use value, but it can also be assessed as a product and an indicator of consumer status. The earliest American homes had no running water and no built-in sinks. Basins or tubs for washing utensils or clothing were portable. Piped household water was introduced in eastern cities before the Civil War but was hardly ubiquitous. Susan Strasser, a historian of American housework, points out that kitchens with built-in sinks were unusual for urban industrial workers and most rural people even at the start of the twentieth century.[40]

Only by the 1920s did indoor plumbing leave the luxury category, and even then this did not extend to many rural households even if they were reasonably well-off.[41] Kitchens dedicated only to cooking and washing were not part of every house. One-room cabins lasted beyond the colonial era, especially among homesteaders. Well into the first third of the twentieth century, in urban apartments as well as the shacks of the rural poor, with large numbers of people housed in small numbers of rooms, daybeds and worktables shared the same four walls as cookstoves and washtubs. The familiar one-bedroom apartment in present-day cities often has no separate dining room, and if the kitchen is large enough, that is where its lessee or owner may have a table at which to eat her meals, pay bills, work at her computer, sit a child down to do homework, play cards, set up her sewing machine, or read.

In the 1924 *Outward Bound*, popular on Broadway and later with amateur theatre groups, passengers on a mysterious ship turn out to be headed for the afterlife, where the snooty rich are punished, the troubled middle class are given another chance, and a hardworking char (cleaning lady) is rewarded with a cottage by the sea about which her single question is, "'As it got a good sink?"[42] Audiences were expected to know that such an amenity would be special for a woman born into poverty in the nineteenth century and perhaps identify her as a mother figure, since she is actually the mother of the man who is the audience's proxy in figuring out the situation. When the 1959 musical *Gypsy*'s Mama Rose was depicted as a willing eater of canned dog food under some circumstances, audiences were to understand that her transgression was not poverty per se but spending too little time in the kitchen and too much time as a wannabe mother of vaudevillians on the road where, if necessary, bathroom sinks doubled as kitchen sinks for washing filched flatware. A concern for "'aving" a kitchen sink signified good mothering; indifference might mean daughters who jump ship either to elope as teenagers or to become strippers.

The same people who were wooed as ticket buyers were also advised and targeted regarding their own kitchen sinks. Washing dishes or doing laundry depended on both male and female work prior to the late eighteenth and into the nineteenth centuries, when household labor was gendered but shared. Men chopped and carried firewood while women hauled and heated water for washing dishes and doing laundry in tubs men had made. The biggest domestic and economic change in the nineteenth century was, for middling families other than pioneers and ranchers, the separation of home and gainful employment. Men went out to work for wages, the household now bought more than it produced, and women became purchasers and managers within their "separate sphere."[43]

This familiar view depends on accepting an economy in which women's labor within the consuming household (cleaning, mending, nursing, organizing, entertaining, educating, supervising, cooking) is read as not "real" work because it does not directly generate income. The plays I examine point to the fact that housework is real work in the sense of being tiring and necessary, but too often read as "not real" in the sense of earning little respect and less independence outside the charmed family circle. In plays where servants do the work of cooking and cleaning, it rarely even earns the spoken respect of the employing family. The latter chapters take up the too-often unquestioned equating of work for money with worthy citizenship and posit domestic labor as a crucial part of the economy as traditionally understood.

Although onstage families may dismiss or ignore the servants who facilitate searches for soul mates and fulfillment in love or work, many American audience members come from families with members who do know about housework, in part because they have been indoctrinated by experts publishing to relatively wide circulations for close to two centuries. In this context, one of the best-known early American texts was Catharine Beecher's (sister of Harriet Beecher Stowe) 1841 *Treatise on Domestic Economy*, which discoursed on efficiency and thrift to a particular emerging audience. Regarding kitchens, Beecher advised designing new homes with a single room for eating and some cooking, thereby dispensing with the separate dining room. Still, the sink was to be located in a small adjoining room to keep "the most soiling employments" out of the family's sight.

Beecher gave specific directions regarding dishwashing itself, for which dishwater was to be reused with progressively greasier and dirtier items. The overall task required two tin tubs, one for washing and one for rinsing, as well as a tray on which to drain the dishes, two water pails, several dishrags, and hard soap.[44] Dishwashing flakes (never mind liquid) were decades away; making the soap was understood as a household task. The idea that dishwashing and scrubbing out the kitchen sink could be used as an indicator of a woman's skills and worthiness was clearly in effect. Beecher's predecessor Lydia Maria Child had issued in 1832 the no-nonsense dictum that "there is no need of asking the character of a domestic, if you have ever seen her wash dishes in a little greasy water."[45]

Readers of these and successors to such treatises who were "respectable" theatregoers were not necessarily expected to wash dishes, but they were supposed to know how to supervise those who did. These two famous homemaking manuals were hardly the only ones of their sort, nor did the genre die out in the nineteenth century. Cheryl Mendelson's hefty 1999 *Home Comforts: The Art & Science of Keeping House* provides explicit instructions on everything from the proper cleaning of cutting boards to the uses of different kinds of towels and rags in the kitchen. Jolie Kerr's 2014 *My Boyfriend Barfed in My Handbag . . . and Other Things You Can't Ask Martha* includes instructions on how to wash dishes and clean burned food from the bottom of a pot, how to wash floors and walls, and how to clean dishwashers, microwaves, and refrigerators.

Strasser notes that "water tasks were considered primarily women's work," and the labor of hauling water into the kitchen—whether from a stream or later from an outdoor pump or a common faucet in an urban apartment building—fell, despite the strength it required, to women, unless they could cajole men or boys into helping, which happened only if the males were not engaged in other tasks in their own domain. Seeking help with laundry before anything else is, therefore, easy to understand. A single wash, boiling, and rinse—the pre–washing machine procedure—requires about fifty gallons of water, representing four hundred pounds to be carried back and forth in buckets and boilers that could themselves weight forty or fifty pounds.[46] Even when pumps delivered water to the back door of farmhouses, women still had to haul it inside. Houses with indoor pumps or faucets—early incarnations of the latter sometimes delivering water from large barrels or cisterns—still required carrying the water to the stove to be heated, from the stove to the dishpans, and then outside for disposal. Ruth Schwartz Cowan, in her history of household technology, asserts that the stove was the first labor-saving device to enter the household because the labor it saved was male; the stove halved the amount of work that men had to do in cutting, hauling, and splitting wood.[47] So, another kitchen sink realism is that saving women's labor may have occurred only as it was directly legible to men and made sense to them.

It did make sense to them as businessmen. Jane Smiley notes that nineteenth-century household contrivances were in part the product of the new value attributed to the setup of women presiding over households in which they did not literally produce their own food, goods, and clothing. Maintaining this setup required "conveniences," which did not actually shorten the domestic workday but enabled it to enter the realm of consumer competition for status. Smiley argues that in the long run feminism depends on consumerism, particularly in the domestic sphere. "The freedom . . . to earn money, to have a vocation, to have an avocation, to engage in all the useful and useless activities of our historical moment, depend on the lightening of the domestic load through contrivance, technology, and the use of nonhuman, non-animal power."[48] Smiley suggests that household advice manuals can be read as feminist to the extent that they are concerned with women's health, longevity, contentment, and authority. Proper household management in previous centuries tied knowing how to prevent a smoky or cold house, chronic aches and illness, fatigue, indigestion, unnecessary smelliness, and spoiled food to a sense of worth and self-respect.

Household advice took on an additional component toward the end of the nineteenth century, as the home economics movement turned to laboratory science and empirical studies with an eye to improving nutrition as well as the circumstances and methods of household labor. A cohort of privileged, activist, educated women made it their mission to overhaul the domestic habits of poor women with regard to everything from sanitation and ventilation to menu planning, adequate protein, and children's dietary needs. Domestic scientists' projects extended from work in settlement houses to founding eateries for working women to starting domestic training programs, and they created college and university programs.[49]

By the 1920s, the first full decade in my study, concern for a well-balanced diet with an adequate supply of vitamins and calories was an ordinary matter for any who had learned about it in high school or could read about it in popular magazines. (This is not the same as being able to afford it, but choice did and does play a role in nutrition at all but the very poorest levels.) In Martin Flavin's 1929 play *The Criminal Code*, set largely in a prison run by sadistic and opportunistic authorities, the secretary of the Prison Commission brags that the prisoners get "[s]paghetti, coffee, bread—all the bread they want. . . . It's better grub than most of them ever had. Good wholesome food, plenty of vitamins and calories and all that stuff."[50] His cynical reading of a diet based on starch and caffeine and missing any protein, fruit, or greens puts a cruel spin on the very concerns with which loving homemakers and mothers were supposed to be occupied, but it did so in precisely the scientific nutritional vocabulary of the day.

Readers may be questioning my sometime skirting and sometime vaguely defined use of the term "middle class" to describe households, housewives, consumers, and theatre audiences. It bears discussion and analysis. Cowan asserts that in nineteenth-century American cities, the possession of servants was "virtually the only sure way of defining who was a member of the middle class."[51] To assess early twentieth-century families, though, she avoids the usual labels of middle, upper, lower, and working, because these refer either to the employment category or the income of the male head of household. Rather, she sees two groups of Americans, whom she calls roughly rich and poor—an insightful way of thinking for considering the kitchen sink realisms of actual women and dramatic characters. Poor households comprised not merely the destitute but any whose household income from employment was not enough to achieve a socially accepted idea of the "decent" or "comfortable" standard of living of its day. The line between the two was drawn on female employment. In "rich" households, women did not need to seek paid employment to maintain the family's standard of living. In actuality, women worked throughout the twentieth century to maintain "rich" (read middle-class, but arguably in many instances lower-middle-class) standards, but not until the latter part of the century did the two-income family come to be ordinary even among the already "rich" (read middle class, and increasingly, as the century drew to a close, upper middle class).

Plays of the 1920s through 1950s regularly depicted wives and mothers who were not employed outside the home. This statement is complicated by the fact that many plays from these decades— especially the first two—depict two- or three-generation households in which young, unmarried daughters may work outside the home, thereby acquiring the wardrobes, contacts, and worldliness to "marry up" and leave their jobs. Accordingly, older women sometimes assume the status of servants in plays depicting Cowan's "rich" families. That is, they serve the gainfully employed members of the family but have minimal help of their own. Tensions around class status and the actual responsibility for scrubbing out the kitchen sink abound in plays of the 1920s, a decade of social growing pains during which—to use the indices drama, dining, and domestic labor—Broadway saw more openings than in any other decade, even as the talkies put the last nail in the coffin of the live play as mainstream narrative entertainment.

A burgeoning white-collar labor force ate lunch in inexpensive restaurants rather than go home or carry a lunchbox, while, as the first widely accepted ethnic cuisine, Italian food "went from being marginal to mainstream";[52] and iceboxes and electric refrigerators were marketed side by side (until the end of the decade, when electricity won out); while domestic help, for those who had it, was for the first time more likely to be African American than immigrant white throughout the Northeast and Midwest as well as the South.[53]

After World War II, government-supported housing, mortgages, and road building sent thousands of American families into suburban developments, where women were "rewarded" with appliances (the favorites were washing machines with spin cycles that did the equivalent of wringing, and refrigerators with freezers), televisions, and frozen foods. They were simultaneously isolated from cities and daily contact with the many store proprietors and service workers with whom their mothers had had social interaction, and increasingly obligated to chauffeur their children, for whom public transportation was not part of the American Dream as built by developers with generous loans and tax breaks from the federal government.

Perhaps only at this point did it become clear who was really "middle class" (by Cowan's rich/poor division as well as by garden-variety income and consumption standards) and who was not, and some of this had to do with who worked for a salary rather than for wages as well as who owned a house. Ironically, following the passage of the Taft Hartley Act in 1947, organized labor became more like the middle class, as it was legally restrained from certain kinds of strikes and organization and as both membership and leaders focused on pay scales more than on an idea of a laboring class or identity.[54] In other words, starting in the 1950s, even labor behaved and consumed like management, in kind if not quantity or even quality, and the American Dream was packaged in varying price ranges.[55]

One readily recognizable index to the blurring of representational boundaries between actual working-class and middle-class people is the fact that other than *The Honeymooners,* a television sitcom whose main characters are two housewives and their bus driver and sewer worker husbands, most television shows depicting domestic life featured the families of white-collar or professional workers. Prime examples include the much-storied *Father Knows Best, Ozzie and Harriet Show, Donna Reed Show,* and *Leave It to Beaver.* Theatre largely, although not completely, followed suit. *Pajama Game*'s (1954) factory workers, the switchboard operator in *Bells Are Ringing* (1956), and *Bus Stop*'s (1955) waitress, bus driver, and rodeo cowboy were popular characters depicted in lower-middle-class or working-class worlds, but they were increasingly exceptions to a new rule. Two of the three heroines who achieve closure through marriage in these shows marry "up." Only *Bus Stop*'s bar singer accepts life with a rancher, achieving financial security but not social cachet, except to the extent that she will no longer be regarded as a possible prostitute.

Whether because of the continuing frustration of suburban isolation or because of other cultural phenomena and attendant anxieties, a focus on houses, kitchens, and kitchen appliances has only escalated in the decades since suburbia took hold as a kind of norm. Designer kitchens and high-end appliances remain out of the reach of most people, but lower-end brands mimic their styles and try to offer cachet and a means to scratch the itch of envy.[56] The two hundred thousand-dollar kitchen is the province of the filthy rich, but commodity fetishism can inspire designs made to fit niche markets and knock-offs to soothe the green-eyed monster. A 2003 *New Yorker* cartoon featured a grumpy couple in their small kitchen. With their backs to each other, she stares into a full refrigerator and he sits at the table eating an apple and looking at the newspaper, uttering the caption line: "I don't care if everyone else is getting one—we are not buying a refrigerator with a learning curve."[57]

Quotidian household devices may spell boredom or they may spell creativity, and shifting demographics may spell new opportunities or a terrifying loss of the familiar. Little about the sink, however, promises even the relative fun of easy-to-make waffles, the two-in-one function of the steam iron, or the snob appeal of a stove that can multitask without soot. A dishwasher can relieve a lot of the labor, but whatever is left for the kitchen sink is usually the grubbiest part of post-cooking cleanup. Accordingly, the sink itself, even if it is not mentioned in drama—but especially when it is—nearly always signals drudgery and tension (although actual onstage working sinks usually delight audiences when the faucets are turned on). Also, the kitchen sink, along with the devices beside which it plays ugly duckling, spells female territory. The popular press of the twentieth century traditionally depicted kitchen work as "'naturally' rewarding to a woman both emotionally (she nourished the ones she loved) and aesthetically (she was encouraged to delight in the artistic pleasure of building a quivering molded tower out of Jello and canned fruit . . .)."[58] No matter that much kitchen work is laborious and mind-numbing or that new devices eliminated only drudgery but neither the hands-on involvement nor the time suck of housework.

The increased ease of performing tasks related to cooking and cleaning only upped the stakes with regard to the complicatedness of what was considered acceptably nutritious, clean, or simply indicative of caring.[59] In the popular imagination women "belong" in the kitchen. That so many dramas depict them in the living room or even the office does not so much challenge this as underscore it by showing the problems that ensue for women outside their "proper" domain or the challenges of trying to please or avoid the men who would enable or stand in the way of their having their own kitchens, while ignoring the routine and lack of power that go with said kitchens.

It would be easy to treat this problem diachronically, which my study does, and to assume that pre–*Feminine Mystique* plays situated women in the home craving their era's version of the refrigerator with the learning curve, and that afterward female characters were "liberated"—a teleology I try to avoid. Twentieth-century Broadway plays have always depicted women who work outside the home in capacities other than as domestics, albeit usually unmarried women and often in glamorous careers. Blanche DuBois, famous for her desperation and sexual needs, is a college-educated English teacher, on the lam for private problems, not because of any overarching desire to stop working. *South Pacific's* Nellie Forbush is a nurse, as are all the other American women in the musical. Even the show's Bloody Mary is an entrepreneur making money on grass skirts and excursions to Bali Hai.

Bus Stop features a waitress and a singer. Women in mainstream plays of the forty-plus years following Betty Friedan's exposé are not demographically totally different from their older sisters. Many are housewives or are in pre-marriage jobs, sometimes as secretaries (*Promises, Promises*; *How to Succeed in Business Without Really Trying*), flight attendants (*Company*), or librarians (*Music Man*). Sometimes women are depicted in traditionally female jobs, as teachers (*The Primary English Class*; *Stop Kiss*) or nurses (*Whose Life Is It Anyway?*; *Wit*). Women characters with careers often have glamorous or at least high-paying ones (most of Wendy Wasserstein's creations). The nonemployed, privileged with servants still seek fulfillment (Tina Howe's stage families) and resemble some of the independent women in works from the 1920s and 1930s by Philip Barry, S. N. Behrman, and Robert E. Sherwood.

This is hardly to say that domestic representations did not change over the course of eighty-seven years. This book investigates the ways in which they did. Perhaps the biggest change is that the "invisible" laborers facilitating the interesting careers attached to glamorous Broadway characters finally, on occasion, took center stage themselves in plays intended for Broadway and/or major regional theatre audiences. As early as Lorraine Hansberry's 1959 *A Raisin in the Sun*, a family of domestic servants (a chauffeur and two housecleaners) are the hero and heroines.[60] The Latina nanny in Lisa Loomer's 2003 *Living Out* is a counterpoint to her lawyer employer—both working women struggling to balance paid labor and child care. And in a vibrant, historically rich, and poignant depiction of the American household and its domestic help writ large, the music theatre piece *Caroline, or Change* (first workshopped in 1999 and opening in 2003), set in 1963, an African American maid embodies not only the blight of racism on unrepresented as well as organized labor, but also the economic evils of the feminine mystique—including the cruelty and blind spots of liberalism. Both the latter show's workers and their very means of production—the (singing) washer and dryer—are characters who merit stage time. Note, too, that this short list is a quick survey of largely *Broadway* work.

Experimental pieces and plays written for particular niche audiences also morphed over the course of the last century, something that is abundantly clear when one compares the one-acts written by and for African Americans in the 1920s and 1930s with the Broadway and Off-Broadway plays by and about African Americans created later in the century, or in comparisons between the frustrations of the 1910s white wife with those of her 1990s or 2000s analogues. Ambiguity replaces polemic in some instances; rage replaces accepting a status quo in others.

While the representations changed, however, the central issue has not: American society offers no practical and affordable way for most adults to combine gainful employment with child rearing and housekeeping. Not every play about domestic pressures and problems pushes the issue to its limits, but few escape suggesting it, even when they represent a bliss that depends upon just this division and its attendant silence concerning the economic inequality and fragile security it underwrites. One of my main points is that whether or not plays with domestic labor and its frustrations actually spell out the problem in so many words—and many do—audiences bring their own awareness of cultural norms and problems to the theatre with them and can read in the margins and between the lines of the stories, characters, and activities they witness onstage. Present-day audiences who eat takeout, restaurant meals, or fast food and whose cell phones are almost prostheses cannot watch scenes of families sitting down to dinners prepared by mom and consumed absent any television or telephone accompaniment and read them as literal representations of an historical everyday reality. Retreats into idealized domesticity represent neither a solution nor an economically viable response to this overriding issue, except for the very wealthy. I contend that audiences know this and that at least some part of them, some of the time, knew it in the past.

The readings I offer of plays, musicals, and performance pieces are sometimes resistant and frequently differ from what newspaper critics had to say about the shows when they opened, but I believe they depend on ordinary information rather than sophisticated psychoanalytic or high-level economic theory and are legible in the sense that they examine these cultural products in light of ideas that are neither esoteric nor really revolutionary, as they mostly call for revision, not overthrow, of social arrangements determined by money and gender prejudice. My readings fit both of Justin Lewis's categories of media criticism: the "speculative and literary" and the "overtly political." For Lewis the literary critic is "an intellectual free agent" whose interpretations need not be validated by audiences (theatregoers) to be legitimate, contra the examination of plays for specific audiences, which requires attention to a particular cultural and semiotic environment.[61]

The readings I present do draw on particular cultural environments to offer interpretations that may not have appeared in published reviews but that can responsibly be proposed as possible responses on the part of spectators who did not see women as eternally, naturally, and inevitably linked to kitchens, romance, and economic dependence. The few women critics who have worked for daily papers suggest that alternative responses to popular plays may arise precisely based on the sex (read cultural situatedness) of the viewer.[62] So, I claim the speculative as well as the political and do so as "intellectual free agent." I also claim that my readings would be largely legible to the domestic workers whose labor and interests they seek to recuperate.

Plays are not, of course, ethnographies, and the final authority on their viability as social documents is an audience, not an editor or specialist checking for historiographic methodology. As discourse, theatre productions falling under my broad *kitchen sink realisms* rubric resemble advertising. Both theatre and ads refer to an "American Dream" that creates "inarticulate longings," and both help construct this dream by interpellating an imaginary ideal consumer who resembles but is not identical to the people who see the ad or attend the performance.

This (actual) person is often paying for the privilege of being so addressed, either by purchasing a magazine, admission to a movie theatre, or a theatre ticket, although part of the power of these media's persuasion depends on the reinforcement of their purchased images in outlets that are accessible (perhaps a better word is "unavoidable") for free, such as billboards or radio in the early part of the century and, later on, these plus television and the Internet.[63]

Jennifer Scanlon borrows the phrase "inarticulate longings" in her study of *Ladies' Home Journal* (*LHJ*) to name the feelings of dissatisfaction the magazine sought (and seeks) to stir up to sell itself and the products whose advertisers keep it in business. Scanlon contends that *LHJ* reached a fairly broad demographic by addressing a fictional ideal reader who was prettier, more happily married, healthier, and financially better off than many who bought the magazine.[64] Her argument is applicable to many other mainstream, middlebrow women's magazines such as *McCall's*, *Redbook*, and *Good Housekeeping*, to name only a very few.[65]

LHJ's construction of the ideal reader was propped up by a nexus of truisms parsed by Roland Marchand in his study of American advertising in the 1920s and 1930s. Foremost among these is that American advertisements in those decades rarely depict working-class people who look different or have different concerns from their wealthier or better-educated compatriots.[66] Maids, when they used to appear in advertisements, were as slim and well groomed as their mistresses. Poorer women in ads may emerge from smaller houses than the supposed average, but their hairdos and children resemble those of the fictional ideals they presumably strive to emulate. Marchand argues that in the third and fourth decades of the last century, advertising delivered its most sophisticated messages via its design, where it could readily embrace new trends in art. Its mimetic representation of individual consumers and their social relations was often conservative. The succeeding decades have continued to display sophisticated design in the service of recuperative values in most mainstream advertising.

It is fair to ask why a look at American theatre's representation of domestic labor and dining in the years from 1918 to 2005 is of cultural significance. Since the period covered in this study includes a massive output of movies, wouldn't that be a better place to look for middlebrow fiction about household relations?[67] Doesn't television tell us more? Here I want to focus on the audience for theatre, especially, although not exclusively, in New York. Films and television have bigger budgets and reach bigger audiences, but they cannot stake a unique claim on the particular segment of our society that supports theatre. Popular commercial theatre can tell us much about how a city brands itself and what it seeks to offer tourists in the way of special, unusual, memorable experience.[68] But even American theatre with more rarefied material and more limited appeal has, as David Savran notes, since the 1920s largely been the province of the middlebrow—cultural strivers embracing the intellectually validating so long as it is neither unduly difficult or confusing nor delivered without explanatory critical apparatus.[69] In other words, self-aware aspirants to the socially and aesthetically prestigious or worthwhile have sought this at commercial theatre over the last century.

Why is it useful to think about the dramatic fictions that appeal to the particular demographic who attend theatre, particularly theatre in New York? Studies of American theatre audiences repeatedly show the same things: they are more educated, more interested in the other arts, and better off financially than their fellow citizens who are not theatregoers. This is stale news. More informative is a consideration of theatregoers in terms of the blend of anxiety, self-satisfaction, and habit underpinning the desire to attend plays repeatedly. Theatregoers are not the only people with education and money, but a particular cohort within that demographic. Roger Angell's description of the emerging *New Yorker* reader in the 1920s also captures the emerging, in-the-know but ultimately middlebrow theatregoer. Discussing Helen Hokinson's cartoons (often of theatregoers), Angell says, "Her overdressed suburban matrons and club ladies were foolish but gallant, and encouraged *New Yorker* subscribers, a middle-class and increasingly suburban bunch, to laugh at themselves a little, even as they felt the sophisticate's kick of superiority."[70]

The "sophisticate's kick of superiority" should not be underestimated as reflective of a way of seeing that informs the professional and consumer decisions of this powerful class viewed in microcosm in the mainstream theatre audience. The *New Yorker*'s founder, Harold Ross, stated in the magazine's prospectus that it would eschew the "radical or highbrow. It will be what is commonly called sophisticated . . . not edited for the old lady in Dubuque . . . a magazine avowedly published for a metropolitan audience."[71] This audience, courted by magazine and theatre alike as intelligent, is also understood by those who market to it successfully to be conventional as well.[72] Theatre, as Soyica Diggs Colbert notes, unites and shores up its audiences' sense of security and worth, because it "can approximate the psychic reassurances of home by creating a safe space of belonging," even "mimic[king] the feeling of a house . . . through the enfranchisement property rights create."[73]

A key observer of the New York theatregoing audience as cohort was Burns Mantle. For twenty-eight of the first thirty years covered in this study (starting in 1920), Mantle edited and wrote the introduction to the annual *Best American Plays* volume from which many of my examples are drawn. Mantle (1873–1948), who was born in Watertown, New York, began his career as a drama critic in 1898 and worked in Denver and Chicago. He moved to New York, where he started as a drama critic for the *Evening Mail* in 1911, then spent twenty-two years a theatre critic for the *New York Daily News*. His invaluable volumes contain redacted versions of ten plays deemed "best" and, with one exception, the 1920 *Miss Lulu Bett*, always include the Pulitzer Prize winner, along with cast lists, lengths of run, design and production personnel, and thumbnail summaries of every show opening on Broadway during the previous season.

The ongoing series has had a number of editors since Mantle's death in 1948, but none spent as much time and ink as he did trying to discuss the slippery ideas of "typical" audiences, "taste," and "excellence." In doing so, he provided a wonderful collage of the interwoven sophistication and provincialism that made, and still make, New York audiences tick.[74] It is a combination very much like the one that Marchand outlined in his examination of the advertisers who created the ads that generated the longings and fictions to keep Americans buying. The early advertisers had little contact with people unlike themselves; they regarded rural people as not very worthy; they didn't bother to address people who were poor; and they measured their own worth in terms of keeping up with others in the same world of art and commerce.

My point is that theatregoers in New York came together to enjoy a world created by and for those who imagined themselves both distinct within and largely in advance of most other Americans, yet at the same time "average." To the extent that the plays this cohort supported were exported to and imported by producers in other cities (amateur and professional) and thereby helped build their own sense of themselves, the New York audience is of interest. That this audience also consumed other forms of entertainment does not mean that its interest in theatre qua theatre cannot be isolated and examined.

■ ■ ■

The next four chapters focus on Broadway plays, many of which toured large US cities after their initial runs. Chapters 5 and 6, covering years in which television, then video and, later, DVDs and the Internet became widely available, include more Off-Broadway and Off-Off-Broadway work, as these domains are not only the Little Theatre of our time, but, like Broadway, they capture an audience looking for alternative, possibly experimental or avant-garde versions of aestheticized reality. Also, since second-wave feminism and the creation of a culture in which a two-earner family is a middle-class norm, the domestic either/or of the earlier decades is far less of an option. Accordingly, the latter two chapters are thematically rather than primarily chronologically organized. The concluding section of four of the chapters moves the "typical housewife" to the margins, upending her "normalcy" to focus on plays featuring servants, domestic labor in African American or Latino/a homes, or both.

Chapter 1 looks at one-act plays written just after World War I and on the cusp of the decade that brought electricity to most middle-class American homes.[75] Most of these plays were originally intended to be performed by amateurs in Little Theatres or schools, and they were written in an era in which "household efficiency"—the expertise claimed by domestic science and consumer guru Christine Frederick—was a scientific watchword and a cultural yardstick. *Tickless Time* (1918) by Susan Glaspell and George Cram Cook, *The Unseen* (1918) by Alice Gerstenberg, and *Thursday Evening* (1921) by Christopher Morley all air the anxieties of middle-class women who are trying to find fulfillment while negotiating the imperatives of "Domestic Science." Meanwhile, live-in help was leaving in droves for jobs in industry. The final two plays in the chapter, Alice Dunbar-Nelson's 1918 *Mine Eyes Have Seen* and Mary P. Burrill's 1919 *Aftermath* are representative of a genre by and for African Americans that depicted women performing domestic labor with more on their minds than boredom or stylishness.

Chapter 2 examines domestic labor as a central topic in comedies, tragedies, and one expressionist play in the 1920s; it takes its title, "Ambushed," from a play that has next-door neighbors with opposite views regarding whether keeping house oneself is desideratum or drudgery. Guy Bolton's 1923 comedy *Chicken Feed* stages a housewives' strike, predicated on a precise understanding of the dollar value of their labor. In George Kelly's 1924 *The Show-Off*, everything from sewing patterns to car insurance makes an appearance in a gestalt acknowledging that the everyday minutiae of keeping a house are part of the American Dream. *Miss Lulu Bett* (1920) and *Machinal* (1928) are hopeful and dark versions of the plight of ordinary women seeking to escape a routinized daily grind. Finally, in Georgia Douglas Johnson's 1926 *Blue Blood*, domestic labor is neither an ordeal nor an ideal but rather a skill set and business as usual in an African American house where women have far larger challenges than feathering nests and staving off ennui.

Chapter 3 considers theatrical representations of domesticity and domestic labor during the Depression through 1939. Some of the most famous plays of the 1930s, including Clifford Odets's *Waiting for Lefty* and *Awake and Sing* (both 1935), make it clear that domestic labor is *work*. Even Broadway comedies such as *Her Master's Voice* (1933) show that getting meals and keeping a house clean require physical exertion and scheduling. The chapter concludes with an assessment of Langston Hughes's lampoon of whites' blindered views of African American domestics in his 1938 skit *Limitations of Life*.

Chapter 4 shows how domestic labor as patriotism played out in plays produced between 1940 and 1947. From Robert E. Sherwood's *There Shall Be No Night* (1940) in which actress Lynn Fontanne dons an apron and learns both how to do her own cooking and how to shoot a rifle, to the soldier who is expert at ironing his own uniform in Ruth Gordon's 1944 *Over 21*, performing household chores was portrayed as doing the right thing for the times. The plays of this era also policed boundaries of propriety regarding domestic labor, blaming women who worked outside the home for juvenile delinquency (Elsa Shelley's 1944 *Pick-Up Girl*), while lauding those who work for pay at home. By the end of the period, black domestics had been shown a few times doing more than serving as decoration or plot devices, even in Broadway plays. The 1946 *On Whitman Avenue* was about civil rights, but it also spoke to the sorts of questions about housing for nuclear families that would link the dystopia of the Kowalskis' close quarters in the 1947 *A Streetcar Named Desire* with the suburban ideal exploded in the following chapter.

Chapter 5 explores plays that use domesticity as a baseline for critiquing problems hidden by the chipper *Ozzie and Harriet* veneer of the postwar years. As Off-Broadway gained a serious foothold in American theatre by the end of the era, a full-blown critique of domestic "normalcy" became a trope of its own. Plays in this chapter include *Death of a Salesman* (1949); *Come Back, Little Sheba* (1950); *The Member of the Wedding* (1950); and 1959's *A Raisin in the Sun*. The chapter concludes with Edward Albee's black comedy of 1961, *The American Dream*. In this period African American domestics were finally given stage time as leading ladies with problems and desires of their own, albeit still in modified Mammy mode. Never again would women of color or domestics be considered beyond the pale (pun sort of intended) of mainstream theatre as central figures.

Chapter 6 covers the years bookended by *The Feminine Mystique* (1963) and Susan Faludi's *Backlash* (1991)-cum-"Nannygate." Faludi's prize-winning book exposed the ways in which American women were being urged to return to the domestic realm; Nannygate refers to President Clinton's two attempts to appoint women to the position of attorney general, both scuttled by controversies over child care and paid domestic labor. As Off-Broadway and feminist theatre companies' experimentalism took hold in the 1960s and 1970s, artists increasingly resisted the supposed inevitability and "appropriateness" of domestic labor for women. Exemplars include Martha Rosler's 1975 *Semiotics of the Kitchen*; Marsha Norman's *'night, Mother* (1983); Neil Simon's *The Prisoner of Second Avenue* (1971); Israel Horovitz's *Park Your Car in Harvard Yard* (1991); Sam Shepard's *True West* (1980); and Karen Finley's 1988 *The Theory of Total Blame*.

Chapter 7 turns to domestic labor in the new millennium. Household workers appeared center stage in such plays as Joan Holden's 2001 *Nickel and Dimed* and Lisa Loomer's 2003 *Living Out*. In these plays women perform domestic labor for pay and are clearly depicted as earning too little for giving up too much. The 2003 musical *Caroline, or Change* presents an African American domestic worker grappling with her professional and social status in 1963. Sarah Ruhl's *The Clean House* (2005), the final work in my study, exposes the stifling nature of domestic labor but couples this ironically with demonstrations of the valuable expertise and the comfort housekeeping offers to some.

Whether ideas of fairness or the value of domestic labor can escape the stalemate of necessary drudgery versus the pleasures of staying home with money remains an open question and the DNA of many of the works in the final chapter of *Kitchen Sink Realisms*. If drama and performance have not offered solutions to large cultural problems manifest in the unremittingly gendered status of domestic labor, they have provided some of the most provocative, unforgettable, and multi-faceted renderings of the problem. My project here is to examine the multiple ways in which a too-often belittled but perennially popular realm of American theatre can be fruitfully and seriously reassessed.

1 THE FIRST YEARS
1918–1921

The first Pulitzer Prize for Drama was awarded in 1918 to Jesse Lynch Williams's *Why Marry?* To a present-day reader, the piece smacks of second-rate Shavianism, with its lengthy, prolix debate about whether marriage is a domestic trap or a fulfilling obligation for women. Williams employs stock characters of the period: the wealthy businessman, John; his browbeaten wife; the poor-relation clergyman literally working his wife to death; the New Woman, Helen, who resists marriage; and her whiz-kid scientist boyfriend, Earnest. John, Helen's older brother, knows that Earnest cannot support a wife on a scientist's meager earnings. John also knows that Helen values her own work in science but that she would need to work if she married Earnest. He puts the problem to his sister:

> [W]ho'll take care of your home when you're at work? Who'll take care of your work when you're at home [?]. Look at it practically. To maintain such a home as he needs on such a salary as he has— why, it would take all your time, all your energy. To keep him in his class you'll have to drop out of your own, become a household drudge, a servant.[1]

Helen agrees. A married Earnest would have a poor home, "morbid meals," and a wife concerned with everything she didn't have. An unmarried Earnest could take his meals at the university club, "at slight expense compared with keeping up a home, upon the best food in the city with some of the best scientists in the country."[2] Helen will, therefore, follow Earnest to Europe as a single woman, keep up her own research, and bypass the piece of John's equation that would make her a household drudge: marriage. Other characters weigh in. Ultimately, the couple is tricked into saying "I do," although we gather that

29

they still head for Europe and the life of the lab. The setting is John's weekend country house, where no actual domestic labor is depicted, although a butler and footman appear sporadically. The problem is clear and meant to address women who are smart and independent. Is domestic labor a worthwhile lifetime commitment? For that matter—especially in plays that answer "yes" to the question—is it worth looking at onstage?

Domestic labor had not always been portrayed in American drama as a potential trap. Nor had it been something to avoid onstage and hand off to invisible help. In *Shore Acres*, James A. Herne's hit of 1893, a full act (of four) is devoted to the preparation and consuming of an anniversary dinner, complete with roasting a turkey in the onstage oven, a discussion of recipes for cranberry sauce and mashed potatoes, and several family members, including an elderly uncle, participating. The scene does nothing to further the plot. But watching a couple of generations in a farm family cook on a woodstove was satisfying theatrical fare in the 1890s, even if the next act's ship passing a lighthouse on a stormy night was more thrilling. Melodrama, spectacle for the sake of fireworks, and meandering storytelling were, however, going the way of the horse and buggy by 1918.[3]

In their stead, plays began to question the value of housework, positioning it as trap or career. Packaged with questions about domestic labor were questions about marriage and food. Between 1918 and the advent of the Depression, domestic labor was front and center in American theatre across genres as a topic in its own right. The plays in this chapter come from the earliest years of the period and are one-acts crafted for noncommercial theatres in which audiences and performers were understood to come from the same social group. United under the rubric Little Theatre, these companies' audiences included people who were participant members—some with aspirations to professionalism, many with the goal of social uplift—as well as like-minded friends from outside the companies.[4] Little Theatre was a national phenomenon that started in the mid-1910s. By 1926 a writer for *Variety* claimed there were five thousand Little Theatres.[5] Their workers and supporters were virtually all white collar. Accordingly, the kitchen sink realisms their plays favored tell a great deal about the concerns and expectations of their members.

The first three plays in this chapter feature various middle-class white characters; in the final two, written by black playwrights for black audiences, domesticity serves larger, racial questions about citizenship. All grapple—sometimes humorously or indirectly—with three American institutions that changed dramatically by 1918 and that sparked debate and consumer interest throughout the 1920s: food, theatre, and housework. A brief look at the broad nature of the changes serves as a prelude to examining plays and productions.

Food historian Harvey Levenstein locates the arrival of a "Newer Nutrition"—one based on a scientific understanding of the values of food groups, vitamins, and minerals—around 1915.[6] The originators of the earlier "New Nutrition"—"domestic scientists" and largely women—wanted improved efficiency, sanitation, and nourishment. They were also "Americanizers," hoping for a nation built on WASP thriftiness and a bland diet.[7] The Newer Nutrition had similar goals and benefited from improved laboratories, the discovery of and work on several vitamins beginning in 1911, and alliances with food processors and advertising.[8] Its principles as well as a nationally homogenized way of eating were consolidated in the 1920s, when mass-produced foodstuffs began to shape the eating habits of all but the most isolated rural Americans and when ideas about healthful, modern eating came to saturate women's magazines aimed at readers from almost all income levels.

Theatre of the same era underwent major changes as a result of the Little Theatre Movement. The goal of this national, grassroots phenomenon was to make theatre less frivolous, more personally meaningful to audiences and to amateur participants, and to combat what Little Theatre reformers saw as the trivialities of both commercial theatre and the increasingly "threatening" movies. As Douglas McDermott notes, in the 1910s and 1920s American theatre "became an image of reform, struggling against a conservative corporate society. . . . [L]ive theatre persists because it offers an alternative image of society to an audience that desires one."[9] Thus, American theatregoers after the late 1910s cannot be understood as representatives of the body politic writ small. They were, and remain, a self-selected cohort.[10]

Little Theatre values and styles infiltrated Broadway, so this sense of specialness is appropriate to the examination of most post–World War I American Theatre audiences.[11] David Savran has argued that American drama critics after World War I worked to make their subject taken seriously so they themselves would be taken seriously, using, among others, Eugene O'Neill to shore up the intellectual and "high art" components of their field.[12] Theatregoers did come to take seriously published criticism, which was applied to any and all theatre, not only the most difficult. Accordingly, theatregoers who read criticism by critics understanding themselves as specialists became, in turn, a cohort who saw theatregoing and drama as salutary and important, even when scripts or genres might suggest otherwise.

The third American institution, housework, changed radically after World War I for two reasons. First, uneducated young women who needed to work for wages became much more likely to chose manufacturing occupations. Those in domestic labor increasingly ceased to "live in," preferring day work.[13] Even when employed in manufacturing or service industries, though, they often contributed to household labor in ways that became invisible to many families: wage earners facilitated the production of processed foods or became waitresses in the many lunch counters and restaurants that began to cater in the 1920s to diners who were not wealthy.[14] Second, housework was marketed to middle-class women by schools and advertising as serious, important, and even creative work that would make them better citizens and more desirable wives if they did it right.

Concomitant with the exodus of the live-in maid was a social and political retrenchment on the part of radical "New Women" of the "bohemian" 1910s, and the arrival of a popular ideal of female fulfillment residing neither in marriage as a retreat into family service (a Victorian ideal) nor in careers or independent living (a bohemian ideal), but in a companionate marriage to the right man. Theorists of modern marriage posited a union in which sexual intimacy and an intense psychological bond held the couple together; one in which the couple had a right to privacy and to use birth control to guide the spacing and number of children; and one in which wifely subservience was replaced with respect for her intellectual and emotional equality.[15] In this context, the plays treated in the following discussion negotiated a new terrain in which public and private overlapped through advertising, electricity, and increased access to education, putting people previously divided by class, sex, or national origin into increasingly shared social space.

SELF (AND) HELP

Susan Glaspell and George Cram Cook's *Tickless Time*, staged by the Provincetown Players, cofounded by the two authors, in 1918, features two main female characters adamant that they do not belong in the kitchen. *Tickless Time* captures the anxieties and pieties of a particular segment of American theatregoers even as it goes about deflating these. As Greenwich Village "bohemians," Provincetown audience members were rebelling against the mores of Victorian Protestantism; a number were émigrés from the Midwest and had a push-pull relationship with the small towns they had left behind. They chafed at moral and social strictures even as they recalled fondly some of the values of a "simpler" way of life.[16] Virtually all did white-collar work, and many were writers. Few had any background in theatre or much interest in popular entertainments, so the drama they wrote and the theatre they created satisfied their need to see themselves reflected on a stage of their own devising.[17] At worst, their plays were self-indulgent and unpolished. At best the group was part of a new movement that made theatre a locus of social commentary and expression for and by a changing middlebrow citizenry.

The small theatre in which they presented their works was set up as a private membership organization to circumvent fire codes.[18] The Provincetowners sought publicity and reviews virtually from the outset, but the membership requirement as well as the location outside New York's main theatre district generated a self-selected audience for the productions. In the first season, members of the well-heeled New York Stage Society purchased a block of subscriptions.[19] The Stage Society's members had an interest in theatre and followed the latest in European avant-garde work. Between these aesthetically progressive elites and the Provincetowners an audience profile emerges of a group that was interested in new ideas but hardly willing to give up personal comfort, whatever their responses to depictions of social inequality might be. They emblematized an American theatregoing public that would emerge over the next few years and continue to refine itself over the twentieth century. The extent to which plays were legible and attractive to this cohort would have much to do with what was seen as "real" (even if not always classed as "realist") on the American stage.

Tickless Time is set in Provincetown, Massachusetts, where Ian and

Eloise Joyce, a young couple who consider themselves superior to most of their culture, neighbors, and friends, have decided to do away with their mechanical clocks and live by a sundial Ian has constructed. The action occurs in the yard where the sundial stands; the playing space includes access to the house itself and the gate through which visitors arrive. Invigorated by the chance to "refuse to be automatons" (133) and live in "a first-hand relation with truth" (131), the Joyces prepare to bury their regular clocks. They are contrasted to their friends the Knights, described in the list of characters as Eddy, "a Standardized Mind," and Alice, "a Standardized Wife." Eddy inquires how, if the Joyces "cast off standard time," they are going "to connect up with other people" (145), and Alice answers Ian's disappointed observation that the cook "would rather have a clock than grow" by asking why one can't do both (152). Burying the clocks, say the Knights, is a bad idea, and Eloise realizes that minus a watch, she will have trouble with things like getting to the train or the dentist on time.

The Knights' intervention regarding the clocks, however, is not nearly as dramatic as their intervention regarding the impending departure of the cook, Annie. Other than the jokey sense that the spoiled Joyces will be unable to function without her, much of the domestic reality related by the incidents involving Annie is hard for a present-day audience to grasp. It is precisely these domestic realities, however, that would have made the play thematically and ideologically immediate for its viewers.

The cook herself would have been read as Irish for a number of reasons. Her name was almost as familiar as Bridget or Maggie for cooks in literature or plays. The fact that Edna St. Vincent Millay, who first played the role, had red hair would have added to the impression. But Irish live-in maids and cooks were on their way out the door long before Millay's character departed in frustration mid-scene over the loss of her kitchen clock. That migration would have been a familiar phenomenon to those accustomed to Irish live-in household help. In New England, where the play is set, American-born women preferred Irish and Scandinavian maids, according to a 1910 study. First-generation Irish immigrant women workers frequently entered domestic service, but by the turn of the century their daughters had other aspirations. In 1900, 54 percent of all *Irish-born* working women in the United States were servants. In the same 1900 study, only 18.9 percent of Irish women *born in the United States* were in household service. By 1920, only 7 percent of native-born and 20 percent of immigrant women wage earners made their livings as servants.[20] The fictional Annie, therefore, was part of a breed headed for extinction. She would be replaced by electrical appliances or black domestics who would live in their own homes and work an eight-hour day rather than on demand.

The Joyces' and Knights' anxiety about Annie's threatened departure plays out in a spoof of the silliness of the "servant problem." Alice grabs a shovel and begins to dig up the clocks as Eddy cries out, "Come home, Annie! Clock! Clock!" Ian, knowing exactly which clock Annie wants, disinters the timepiece and runs after her with it. Their return is described with "Annie triumphantly bearing her alarm clock, Ian — a captive at her chariot wheels — following with suitcase, shawl-strap, and long strings of bag around his wrist" (159, 160). The "servant problem," as David M. Katzman observes, "was always a middle-class one, since the upper class could always command the hire of whatever servants they needed. The expansion of the middle class . . . occurred more rapidly than the growth of the servant pool," and the fact that American values promoted equality meant that most eschewed the label "servant." This became increasingly viable as vocational training and compulsory education affected the lives of most Americans. Both Glaspell and Cook were born in the 1870s and were, therefore, able to see how domestic service and servants had changed. By 1920 only about half as many American families or individuals had servants as would have been the case in 1870.[21] Even bohemians who came from comparatively modest circumstances (Glaspell's profile) would have been accustomed to some household help. *Tickless Time* strikes at the intersection of pretensions and progressiveness regarding household servants.

The play also reveals how the playwrights and their presumed audience saw food, its preparation, and eating habits. The codes invoked would speak to rebellious, forward-thinking Protestants in ways that would have little meaning for immigrants, non-WASPS, or many present-day readers. When Annie first rushes in, she is peeling an onion and trying to calculate time by the sundial: "Starting the sauce for the spaghetti. Fry onions in butter three minutes" (148). Although Italian food would gain broad acceptance after World War I, it was hardly a staple in 1918. Glaspell and Cook's audience would certainly have recognized it, though, since Greenwich Village was one of the first places to have Italian restaurants staffed by Italians but targeting non-Italian customers.[22] Accordingly, what might look simply economical to a present-day audience would have been stylishly "alternative" to those in the know in 1918.

Annie's recipe reveals something else about the Joyces. She is cooking the onions in butter, not olive oil, suggesting an accommodation to a WASP palate. Also, she says nothing about sautéing garlic. Spiciness was routinely tempered throughout the first two-thirds of the twentieth century in recipes for Italian, Mexican, or Chinese food intended for consumption by mainstream Americans. Still, the Joyces want to be thought of as modern. When Eloise waxes sentimental about the clock with which her grandmother started housekeeping (making it roughly a product of the 1870s or possibly earlier), Ian dismisses the grandmother as a "meticulous old woman." Eloise retorts that "you were glad enough to get her pies and buckwheat cakes" (136).

Both these comestibles would have been recognized as high on the list of old-fashioned foods that home economists of the New Nutrition school wanted to discourage. Yeast breads were considered lighter and more sophisticated than buckwheat cakes or cornbread, which had been staples prior to flour becoming largely a commercial rather than a homeground product in the mid-nineteenth century. Pies were the bane of the food reformers' existence, as Helen Campbell, head of home economics at the University of Wisconsin, pointedly noted. She criticized rural women's menus of "fried meat, chiefly pork, and . . . pie and cake three times a day" and regarded such homey symbols of comfort as signs of dangerous, regressive victimhood. "It was one of these victims who told me that with her own hands she had made in one year twelve hundred and seventy-two pies," Campbell reported.[23] Eloise has scored a hit where it really hurts: Ian has a very old-fashioned streak.

Later in the play Annie announces that the liver she is cooking has to soak for five minutes, suggesting that meat would be the main course. The choice of liver reveals their social status. Very poor Americans would, when they could afford meat at all, choose beef. Organs were less expensive so less special. The Joyces may be economizing, but they are not embarrassed to do so (bohemians!) even on a night when they have invited friends for dinner. They are also willing to eat stylishly (Italian!) but still temper that stylishness to fit the familiar.

That the Joyces' live-in cook is both timing her cooking and preparing unfamiliar food offers two other indicators that this is a progressive household. Had Annie been cooking foods of her own choosing in a manner she had learned at home, the clock might have been irrelevant. Rather, she is cooking in a way that home economists had been encouraging for a quarter of a century by 1918, a way codified and popularized by Fannie Farmer, known for stressing precise measurements and timing and whose *Boston Cooking-School Cook Book*, first published in 1896, continued to be printed in batches of 50,000 after having sold 360,000 copies by the time of the author's death in 1915.[24] If Annie attended any kind of school in the United States, she might have learned the rudiments of cooking in home economics, which entered high school curriculums in the early twentieth century, following its arrival in adult education programs (largely for immigrants) and in a handful of universities, and was considered important training for future housewives.

However, Ian Joyce suggests that Annie's mastery of cooking along modern lines has been less than complete. "Let her establish a first-hand relation to heat. If she'd take a look at the food instead of the clock—!" (149). He would like her to embody John Dewey's philosophy. For Dewey, merely learning to follow directions did not constitute education; he favored schooling that taught children to grasp principles, thereby enabling them to solve problems based on their understanding of the global laws of science operating in any given situation. Heat in cooking was one of the very examples Dewey used in his writing.[25] The play, then, spoke to progressive thinkers who would have recognized the Deweyite imperative but would also have been able to laugh at Ian's taking it, as well as virtually everything else, to extremes.

Food preparation is not the only realm in which loss of Annie's services seems alarming. When Alice asks, "[W]hat's the difference what's *true* if you have to clean out your own sink?" the stage directions indicate that the line is delivered to Ian, preceded by the stern warning that "Eloise can't do the work! Peel potatoes—scrub" (158). It would be easy to read the anxiety as snobbishness or even laziness and the appeal to the husband as indicative of the wife's protected position, his pride in this, and her exclusion from financial decisions.[26] But Eloise's status regarding her own kitchen sink is ambiguous, and Alice's aggressive role in mobilizing the troops to prevent Annie's departure challenges the idea that her friend is pampered, weak, or spoiled. For instance, it is not clear who earns the money in the Joyce household.

If the Joyces are stand-ins for Glaspell and Cook, both work and are freelancers for whom income arrives irregularly (with Glaspell the more successful of the two in real life). It is also unclear whether they are summer residents of Provincetown seeking simplicity and escape, as many of the Players were. If so, the house in which they find themselves might be more spacious but have fewer conveniences than their Manhattan apartment; part of its appeal as a summer retreat might be the unaffordable-in-Manhattan cook. It would not be surprising if the kitchen in which Annie labors has a pump rather than faucets, an iron or zinc sink, and no electricity, like the Truro, Massachusetts, kitchen that Walker Evans photographed in 1930. Alice might then be referring to a summer luxury (this is part of Eloise's vacation, or part of what enables her to write) rather than old-fashioned values or simple class privilege.

Interpreting Eloise's class privilege is not simple. Her reference to her graduation would, if it refers to a college, put her in an unusual category. Only 3.8 percent of all American women between the ages of eighteen and twenty-one were enrolled in college in 1910, rising to 7.6 percent in 1920 and 10.5 percent by 1930.[27] College-educated women had access to better jobs, but education was no guarantee of a career; in many fields that now require college degrees—journalism and management, for example—talent and opportunity were sufficient if one could get one's foot in the door. Social convention would continue to dictate that women leave the salaried workforce upon marriage or, in the case of more progressive thinkers, upon the birth of their first child, making college a push-pull proposition for bright women. On the one hand, it encouraged intellectual and social development; on the other, except in a few elite universities and at the Seven Sisters, it encouraged conformity and fostered the idea that even the female college graduate would find her greatest fulfillment as a wife and homemaker.[28]

Homemaking and college education were joined at the hip by the mid-1910s. The domestic science movement that had given rise to the New Nutrition in the late nineteenth century gained a solid foothold in the university in the twentieth. Largely founded by Ellen Swallow Richards, the first woman to earn a degree at MIT, domestic science wedded the male domain of research and objectivity to the female do-

Kitchen, De Luze house, Truro, Massachusetts, 1931. Photo by Walker Evans.
The Metropolitan Museum of Art, Walker Evans Archive, 1994 (1994.256.634),
© Walker Evans Archive, The Metropolitan Museum of Art.

main of home and family. Cooking schools, college courses, and consulting for industry all furthered the domestic science agenda, so that
by 1914, over 250 colleges and universities offered home economics
(the movement's modern name, selected by Richards in 1899) courses,
with twenty-eight schools having four-year programs leading to the
BA, twenty offering a master's degree, and a PhD in household administration available at the University of Chicago.[29] Home economics was
considered a "parallel" program to agriculture in midwestern schools, **39**

and historian Laura Shapiro observes that it "enjoyed an unusually fluid position in the university curriculum, so that women ran across it no matter where they concentrated their studies." Chemistry, biology, art, and economics proper were among the fields that "could be studied profitably from the point of view of the home."[30] For all but the most ambitious of women college students, education was a means to an old-fashioned end, albeit with a progressive twist.

Eloise—neither part of the labor force nor a mother—floats in a dramatic limbo that would have been recognizable to many in the original audience of *Tickless Time*. Women members of the Provincetown Players accomplished work as artists as well as in professional capacities in their "day jobs." Yet their artistic work was frequently ignored by both the press and the male members of the group, and they often expressed guilt about neglecting their maternal or wifely "duties."[31] Both the popular press and home economics scholars found ways to link the values of higher education to the imperative to please one's husband and find stimulation in scrubbing the kitchen sink and peeling potatoes. The pressure to fit into this schema was great. Accordingly, Alice's cry may be a plea: Eloise can't perform these tasks if she is to escape living in a realm prescribed by them. The issue is not helplessness but a fear of being (re)defined by the very tasks that would sap her of the energy and time to do other, more creative, and more remunerative work sorely needed by a paycheck-to-paycheck household. The fine—and slippery—line dividing college graduate as beloved wife from beloved wife as de facto scullery maid and cook (the problem in *Why Marry?*) would have been crucial to an educated, urban, progressive audience of independent but not wealthy young women and men. And it would have made sense to working women—albeit white-collar ones—in the audience.

In the 1918 production of *Tickless Time*, two other facts would have underscored the anxiety attendant on falling prey to domestic slavery and women continuing to be seen as belonging in the kitchen. First, Edna St. Vincent Millay, the original Annie, had graduated from Vassar the year before she played this role, here offering an embodied, albeit fictional, conflation of the two kinds of young women. Second, anyone who could read a program could discern the similarity—even the bond of sisterhood—between maid and educated wife, as the role of Eloise was played by Millay's sister, Norma.

Two other Little Theatre one-acts provide insight into what kind of domestic-labor-focused plays amused a certain progressive audience around 1920. Both feature young couples with professional husbands, stay-at-home wives, expectations of upward mobility, and tension surrounding domestic labor. One is set in a city and the other in a suburb, thereby complementing the rural seaside setting of *Tickless Time*.

Alice Gerstenberg's *The Unseen* (1918) had been produced at least three times in the Midwest before its 1921 publication in her *Ten One-Act Plays*, which enjoyed fifteen printings between 1921 and 1959.[32] The play has three characters and is unusual because Hulda, described as "a Swedish servant" (68), has a large role, stands up for herself, and may, depending on one's reading, reveal the shortsightedness and entrapment of the seemingly privileged young wife. Jeffry Baldwin, the husband, is an up-and-coming architect; his wife, Lois, is portrayed as flighty and shallow. She neglects to tell Hulda precisely how to prepare the unfamiliar (to Hulda) foods expected for dinner, admits that she can't think of anything besides the new dress she is making, chides Hulda for failing to serve from the left, and wishes she could go to the theatre more often. Jeffry, irritated over the dismal service Hulda provides, asks Lois, "Why didn't you go into the kitchen yourself and show her? After all it is your job to look after things" (71). When Hulda's failure to deliver a telegram costs Jeffry an important commission, Jeffry turns on Lois, not Hulda. "What's a wife supposed to be to a man? Haven't your slack methods ruined my prospects for life?" (87).

The play may ask what a wife is supposed to be as much as it asks whether the titular "unseen" forces guide our lives more than we recognize. (Hulda's negligence later turns out to be a godsend, as the second-choice architect who receives the commission is killed in an on-site accident that would have claimed Jeffry's life.) Stage directions and dialogue suggest at least a seven-room dwelling for a couple whose live-in servant problem is the result of the fact that "no one else will come for the small price we pay" (70). Lois may or may not have gone to college or be destined for wealth. But as the realm of finger bowls, dressmakers, and breakfast caps—all specified in the play—disappeared for all but the wealthiest Americans, the question of what a wife was supposed to be remained. If she has the privilege of household help, how is she using her time? If she cannot afford help, what kinds of skills does she need?

Home economists, popular culture, and many university programs argued that wives were to be homemakers and that homemaking was vital to national well-being. They claimed it as distinct from mere housekeeping in that homemakers were not just domestic laborers married to their bosses. They were savvy consumers who did house-work and might even acknowledge that it was drudgery. They valued efficiency (appliances and processed foods) because industry's answer to the exodus of household help enabled wives to have more time to make themselves interesting to their husbands and useful to their chil-dren.[33] Homemaking was, according to one household arts professor, a "phase of citizenship," its proper realms the encompassing water supply, concern with suffrage, sanitation, the problems of women and children working in factories, staying "young in body and spirit," and setting an example for the "foreign housewife." Woe be to the "liberal education" that failed to train girls *to do, to think, to vision* and *to sense human needs*," which, for female students, meant to do all of these things predicated on dishwashing, cooking, consumerism, and wifeliness.[34]

Higher education that made girls want to compete in the market-place was suspect to home economists, as Mrs. Max West asserted in 1920. West was well known as the author of the popular *Infant Care* of 1914, the Government Printing Office's best-selling publication of the year, which made her an important member of the home economics world, although her ideas were old-fashioned and derivative.[35] She de-cried "the present miasma [that] pervades [college girls'] minds that the one great purpose of an education is to get them a good job, paying a large salary, preferably, in those economic and other fields where they compete with men." The female student should be steered to courses with a "positive relation to her special needs"—homemaking.[36]

Homemaking, rather than mere housework, was what servants like Annie and Hulda aspired to, as it was rarely the nature of their tasks per se that troubled them. Like their native-born, middle-class, or college-educated sisters, they hoped to leave the workforce upon mar-riage or the birth of their first child and to assert their independence in their own houses or apartments. Unlike their counterparts in other areas of the workforce, they labored in a realm where "the worker her-self was hired rather than just her labor" and were subject to the per-sonal desires of their bosses, which might have as much to do with indolence or the need to lord it over someone as with the option of paying for work.[37] Some domestic servants appreciated a home environment, and receiving room and board enabled them to save their wages. Most queried by researchers (and few were) complained about lack of privacy, the impossibility of having guests, and the difficulty of such things as even taking a bath, since many were denied use of the family's facilities and were interrupted by the housewife's call even if they hauled water to their own rooms. Although they often had ideas about making the kitchen more efficient, they were rarely heeded.

After World War I domestic labor came to be understood as something for which one paid on an hourly, daily, or weekly basis, with the laborer going home at night to her own household. In this context, some progressive American plays wrestled with other kitchen sink realisms. Maids and cooks did not disappear from middle-class protagonists' lives, but they moved offstage as the onstage characters struggled to make sense of new household responsibilities, new ideas about homemaking, new products, and new ambitions.

The Little Theatre one-act *Thursday Evening* by Christopher Morley, first presented in 1921 by the Stockbridge Stocks, a Little Theatre company based in New York City, puts domestic labor at the heart of middle-class aspiration.[38] The title refers to the stereotyped servants' night off,[39] and the action is set in "a small suburban kitchen in the modest home of Mr. and Mrs. Gordon Johns" (457) following a dinner that the twenty-three-year-old wife, Laura, has prepared. The couple are parents of a ten-month-old baby. Both their mothers have unexpectedly joined them for dinner, but Gordon and Laura refuse offers of help with cleanup and start to do the dishes themselves. Fatigue, personal preferences, and each spouse's desire to praise mother over mother-in-law have them bickering in short order. The plot resolves when the couple storm out in opposite directions and the two mothers-in-law take over, recognize the sources of the conflict, and stage an argument of their own in which each calculatedly criticizes the other's child. They know their offspring are eavesdropping, and the mothers quietly exit to allow the couple to reconvene, apologize, and shake their heads over the audacity of the mothers trying to set them against each other.

The entire physical activity of the play involves clearing, scraping, washing, drying, and putting away dishes, along with disposing of garbage, emptying the icebox tray, and inspecting the baby clothes drying near the stove. The stage directions specify the layout of the kitchen fixtures, and dialogue reinforces the details: an oil stove, open-shelved cabinets, a sink with separate dishpan, a kettle in which the dishwater must be heated, and a cracked platter that upsets Gordon because it was a wedding gift from his mother. The centrality of consumer savvy to modern wifedom appears in Laura's disparaging retort that Copenhagen is "a stock pattern. You can get another at any department store" (461). Throughout the play the two take turns complaining about the absent African American maid, Ethel (a sign of the changing times in the northern suburbs). The couple's irritations are familiar: Ethel doesn't cook to their taste, she is careless of their personal treasures, and she can't accommodate herself to the particular technologies by which they define themselves. Gordon complains that he never saw a cook who could remember to empty the icebox pan, whereupon he empties it into the sink, cooling off the dishwater to the point that the dishes washed in it come out greasy. Laura's reminder that he should wash "the silver first, while the water's clean" (459) could have come straight from Catherine Beecher's 1841 treatise (see introduction).

Laura is caught in a world where women were expected to be housewives in homes that no longer conferred special claims to cultural influence as they had in the nineteenth century. She is embarking on her homebound career in the decade that probably gave birth to the apologetic phrase "just a housewife."[40] In the mothers-in-law's fake fight, Mrs. Johns laments "that Gordon should have to entrust his son to amateur care when it needs scientific attention" but responds to the suggestion that he participate in the household with the observation that "Gordon is too intellectual to be bothered with these domestic details." Mrs. Sheffield, in turn, says, "I think the way Laura runs her little house is just wonderful. See how she struggles to keep her kitchen in order—this miserable, inconvenient little kitchen, no gas, no pantry, no decent help. . . . A husband, a home, and a baby—it's enough to ruin any woman" (478–79).

In the reconciliation, although Gordon promises to be less obstinate and less obsessed with saving leftovers, it is Laura whose anxiety comes through. She refuses a nurse for the baby and defends herself as "scientific" and "*not* an amateur," since she weighs the baby every week and keeps a chart (481). We also know she follows some of the latest ideas about housework because she sits to dry the dishes, a strategy recommended by home-efficiency expert Christine Frederick. Scientific and competent or not, Laura reminds Gordon that he's all she has.[41] Tellingly, Laura has no interest in giving up the cook, and, once they are in a better mood, Gordon expansively notes that Ethel is "all right" and that they are "lucky to have her" (482). Order is restored, and Gordon invokes his favorite nickname for Laura: Adorable Creature.

Maintaining "adorableness" and being "scientific" make up Laura's understanding of how to hold on to all she has. Laura is a character built almost wholly on clichés of wifedom; we know little of her past, her aspirations, or her skills, except that she is a knowledgeable shopper. After World War I shopping would be presented relentlessly to housewives as the way to fulfill their duties as homemakers and citizens. Advertisers played into anxieties about practicality, adorableness, and duty with such lines as, "Are you keeping up with your husband?" as a lead for selling appliances. "Are you still the attractive, alert, up-to-date woman he married? Are you keeping up with the interesting things in life as he is, or are you devoting all your time, strength and thought to housework?" reads a 1918 ad for the Simplex Ironer, warning that men "progress mentally" through their contacts at work, while wives who subsist without household aids are forced into "the narrow sphere of housework," a situation that is bad economy in terms of both finances and companionship.[42] The answer for the fatigued housewife is a more modern product. Unlike Cook and Glaspell's Eloise, who "can't" scrub out the kitchen sink because she has intellectual or professional goals, or Gerstenberg's social-climbing Lois, who won't, Morley's Laura lives in a world that revolves around the kitchen sink and, with her absent maid and budget-conscious husband, is the model target for such ads.

It would be easy to read American plays of the 1910s and early 1920s featuring domestic settings with an eye to how female characters capitulate to the lures of advertising and how male characters expect their women to do precisely that. It would likewise be easy to see plays themselves as commodities meant to allay anxieties about fitting into a rapidly changing postwar economy by giving audiences models to follow. But neither advertising nor plays, no matter how predictably melodramatic or ethnographic they may seem from a distance, can be read as sets of directions eagerly gobbled up by wholly gullible consumers. As Ed Schiffer notes, consumer advocates base their activism on the belief that consumers need not be passive in consuming advertising. When Schiffer speaks of the genius of successful commercials, he might also be speaking of the genius of successful plays, which "lies in their ability to negotiate between . . . two views of its [*sic*] audience, either by appealing to one in the name of the other, or by using an appeal to one to legitimate the other."[43]

Even the most cynical theatre producer or playwright cannot stipulate precisely how audiences might make use of what they see and feel while or after attending a play. In some of the most popular and memorable (not always the same thing) plays of the 1920s, the frisson between advertisers' or psychologists' norms and characters' or audiences' desires concerning domestic labor, food, and wifedom would have been palpable. Recall Brian Richardson's observation that literary (or here dramatic and theatrical) realism is synecdoche rather than mirror, and in its status as representation, realism of any sort is never identical with what it presents.[44] Accordingly, the whole summoned by the part may be incongruous or dialectical. It certainly may register differently in the eyes of varying beholders.

DOMESTIC LABOR IN BLACK AND WHITE

When African American playwrights presented domestic settings and domestic labor in the 1910s and 1920s, both their stated topics and their use of stage time and space were of a wholly different order than what was usual in such plays by and for whites. African American women characters were routinely depicted engaging in domestic labor in their own homes, but their labor fulfilled both commercial and familial functions. They were frequently scripted washing or ironing clothes to be delivered to white customers as well as preparing, serving, or cleaning up after meals for their own families. More important, these women were depicted performing household tasks while grappling with problems deriving from culture-wide political issues, such as the racism with which black soldiers returning from World War I were met, miscegenation, or lynching.[45] Women characters in these plays protect their children by finding ways to escape mobs; seek help from authorities if they know trustworthy white men; hide an accused man from attackers; or arrange marriages to keep their families together and avoid reprisal—the latter often anticipated in the form of murder at the hands of an angry white man or mob if a black man has attempted to protect his sister or wife's honor. Occasionally an eldest daughter steps in when her mother is defeated by overwork and poor health, suggesting that the problems women work to solve are ongoing rather than individual or isolated.[46] But they do all of this while keeping house.

The respect for housewifedom and domestic labor in these plays serves two purposes. Historically, although they worked for money, most post–Civil War black women prioritized family life. Jacqueline Jones notes that "motherhood, not job status, served as their primary source of self-definition. . . . [T]he singleminded devotion to industry that only personal drive could instill was merely a useless expenditure of energy among workers automatically denied any chance of advancement."[47] Accordingly, these plays' emphasis on housework reflects the real concerns and activities of real black women. The display of domestic propriety was also an assertion of worthiness in a predominantly white world whose prevailing view of blacks was that they were "animalistic," beset by "moral putridity," and unable to maintain a stable family life.[48] Indeed, as black audiences were the exclusive target for most of these plays with domestic settings and civic concerns, Koritha Mitchell argues that they offered assurance to blacks of being not crazy, irresponsible outsiders but worthy citizens whose community needed strength, self-respect, and confidence.[49]

Two early African American one-acts with domestic settings and featuring domestic labor are Alice Dunbar-Nelson's *Mine Eyes Have Seen* (1918) and Mary P. Burrill's *Aftermath* (1919). Burrill's play could be seen as a resistant answer to Dunbar-Nelson's, since *Mine Eyes Have Seen* exhorts black families to see service in the US military as the obligation of a male citizen, while *Aftermath* shows the racism awaiting the black soldier when he returns from war.[50] Both plays are straightforward polemics, but they depict political questions as having direct impact on the home, refusing to erase domestic labor to foreground something more traditionally understood as "political." That one play is set in an apartment in the urban North and the other in a cabin in the South suggests that race, and not class or geography, is the basis on which both the arguments and the ideas about domesticity are erected.

Dunbar-Nelson (1875–1935) was a teacher, and she presented *Mine Eyes Have Seen* with her students at Howard High School in Wilmington, Delaware, in 1918. She also gave permission to Dunbar High School in Washington, D.C. (where Mary Burrill was head of English and dramatics), to present the play concurrent with its publication in *Crisis* magazine. Affiliation with *Crisis*, house organ of the National Association for the Advancement of Colored People (NAACP), and a major, socially progressive African American magazine with a circulation of seventy-four thousand, meant an investment in "respectability" and "uplift."[51] Accordingly, readers of plays published in *Crisis* were socially analogous to the white theatregoers who embraced drama as "worthwhile." In 1915, the NAACP had set up a Drama Committee to encourage black writers to pen plays for blacks about black experiences.

The setting of *Mine Eyes Have Seen* is a tenement kitchen.[52] "All details of furnishing emphasize sordidness—laundry tubs, range, table covered with oil cloth, pine chairs" (4). The presence of laundry tubs either means that the woman of the house is taking in washing or that the family cannot afford to send theirs out. Certainly in the absence of hot water—ordinary in the 1910s in poorer apartment buildings—or perhaps even the absence of any piped-in water, "sordid" is a value judgment as much as anything else. In this apartment, twenty-year-old Lucy starts the play "bustling about the range preparing a meal" (4) for her older brother, Dan, crippled years earlier in a factory accident, while they wait for their younger brother, Chris, to return from work. As they worry about Chris's whereabouts, Lucy and Dan reminisce about "the old days . . . in the little house with the garden, and you and father coming home nights and mother getting supper. . . . [W]e didn't have to eat and live in the kitchen then" (5).

For the first fifth of the play, Lucy's hands are busy with lunch, even as Dan recalls that the idyllic house of their youth was burned "because niggers had no business having such a decent house" and their father was shot "for daring to defend his home" (5). When Chris enters, Lucy serves him. Only when Chris announces that he has been drafted does her domestic competence lapse, as she "drops plate with a crash" (6). Domestic labor is suspended for the remainder of the play as an array of neighbors (an Irish widow, a Jewish man of Chris's age, Chris's light-skinned black girlfriend, a white social worker) enter to underscore the importance of Chris's doing his patriotic duty. But that suspension in the face of national crisis is precisely the point. Presumably normal domesticity will be resumed only as African Americans step up to the plate to fight the good fight.

This family's experience would not have been entirely "average" in 1918. The Great Migration of blacks from the South to northern cities peaked between 1916 and 1921. This family moved earlier. (Lucy recalls doing her homework in their southern house, suggesting that she was a child when their lives were disrupted. Their mother died after the move north.) Their move was not an odyssey from rural poverty to the often-dashed hope of urban, industrial opportunity but a flight from small-minded southern whites. For many blacks who moved north, the tenements for which they paid too much (in Harlem, at least) offered the wonders of electricity, indoor plumbing, and access to commercially prepared versions of foods they would previously have had to grow or butcher or can themselves.[53]

The former privilege of this family allows the kitchen–cum–dining room in the northern city—a normal setup in the homes of many rural blacks and poor whites in the South—to be coded as "sordid." Certainly that reflects the feeling of the characters for their surroundings. It would also have spoken to the most privileged of Harlemites—the doctors, lawyers, and other professionals living on the elite block commonly called Strivers Row, certainly among the readers of *Crisis*—and would have been recognizable as characteristic of many less desirable buildings just a few blocks away. At the same time, it would have been too ordinary to notice and hardly sordid for many residents of Harlem. The playwright cleverly manages to have her domesticity both ways.

Mary Burrill's (1884–1946) *Aftermath* was published in 1919 in the *Liberator*, a monthly socialist magazine established by (white) siblings Max and Crystal Eastman.[54] Burrill attended Emerson College of Oratory (later Emerson College) in Boston and then taught English in Washington, D.C., for thirty-nine years. The South Carolina cabin in which her play is set may or may not have been drawn from first-hand experience. It fit, however, with the sorts of folk plays that were encouraged by both black and white believers in the social value of drama.[55] The characters speak in dialect, and the elderly Mam Sue— likely the grandmother, but possibly a great aunt of the young brother and sister—is superstitious. Here, a "soft afterglow" of light pours in the window as Millie, a sixteen-year-old girl, is ironing in the main room of a two-room cabin. A "great stone hearth blackened by age" is at one end of the room, and a Bible rests on the mantel over the hearth. There is no question of electricity, as a kerosene lamp is prominent on the set and is lit as darkness descends. A clotheshorse is laden with the ironing. In this play, the kitchen table, situated in the center of the room, is described as well scrubbed.[56] The ironing is being done for wages, and early in the play Millie gets ready to take the fresh clothes to her client.

As in *Mine Eyes Have Seen*, domestic labor is showcased at the start of the play, here to indicate a family member caring for others or labor undertaken for income, or possibly both, as Millie may be assisting the elderly Mam Sue with the laundry. When Millie's soldier brother arrives, she immediately offers him a meal and starts to serve it. The latter part of this play, like the latter part of *Mine Eyes Have Seen*, features suspended domestic labor as the major issues, lynching and the mistreatment of black soldiers, are aired and action is finally taken by the central male figure. Significantly, neither of these plays depicts a husband and wife: The families in both plays have been victims of lynchings, leaving the household itself decapitated.[57] Such families are not the only ones that might have more on their minds than whether wives are fulfilled as homemakers, but by taking romance out of the equation, other ways of seeing domestic labor in the context of familial love and everyday routine come to the fore.

In many ways these plays are opposites. One is pro-military service for blacks; the other critiques it. One is set in an urban Black Belt ghetto; the other, in a southern cabin. One has black characters speaking almost stiffly proper, declamatory English; the other lays on the dialect thick and fast. One sees a kitchen/living room as a hardship; the other figures this arrangement as cozy. In both cases, however, women are featured performing domestic labor *and* participating in serious discussions about citizenship, social action, and responsibility. One endeavor does not obviate the other. It would be more than a decade before plays by, for, and about whites featured an analogous combination of domestic labor and political awareness. That would have to wait for the advent of the Great Depression.

2 AMBUSHED

1920–1929

In the 1920s, American women moved into ever more elaborate kitchens even as they claimed more places as university students; the way experts and advertisers addressed "average" women and the way they were depicted in the theatre only increased the irony of this combination. The feminine mystique started not in the 1940s or 1950s but squarely in the 1920s, when housework and consumerism came to be seen as expressions of women's fulfillment, keeping women who could afford to be there at home and encouraging the belief that unmarried women were suspect and female camaraderie old-fashioned.[1]

Domestic drama of the 1920s, whether its overt theme is love, personal advancement, intergenerational disagreement, the battle of the sexes, religious hypocrisy, isolationism, or urban anomie, is ghosted by and often staged on the battlefield of doing, avoiding, or paying for domestic labor. Discussions of domesticity and its discontents were an obvious component of at least half of the decade's most popular and important Broadway productions, using Burns Mantle's *Best Plays* series as an index.[2] Close to two-thirds of the plays on Mantle's lists feature domestic settings for at least a single act, even when the main topic and theme foreground something else.[3]

Frank Craven's popular *The First Year* (1920) shows a young, suburban, newlywed housewife so frustrated with cooking that she says she'd willingly eat cabbage—something she hates—if she could only go to a restaurant for dinner. *Ambush* (1921) by Arthur Richman features next-door neighbors, one happy to darn socks but weary of social climbing, the other exhausted by housework and eager for her daughter to do all the social climbing she can. Guy Bolton's 1923 comedy *Chicken Feed* has middle-class, midwestern wives going on strike and charging each others' husbands for domestic labor to reinforce the monetary value of their household work. One of the young wives challenges her father directly when he borrows against an insurance policy without telling his wife. Half the money, asserts the daughter, is her mom's: "Hasn't she worked for you and kept house for you? What do you think you'd have to pay for all she's done for you for twenty-five years? Why, even at servant's wages you owe Mother thousands of dollars."[4] (By 2009 standards, a stay-at-home mom did the work equivalent of $122,732 per year.[5])

The heroines of the 1924 *Desire Under the Elms* (Eugene O'Neill) and *They Knew What They Wanted* (Sidney Howard) marry men almost old enough to be their grandfathers because housekeeping is the only profession that can guarantee them a home. They also enjoy the autonomy and ownership that homemaking offers them over being in service to others. In the Pulitzer Prize–winning drama *Craig's Wife* by George Kelly (1925), a controlling woman loses husband, family, servants, and friends over her obsessive need to keep a perfect house. Even Christ is not exempt from weighing in on the specifics of domestic organization. In Channing Pollock's 1922 *The Fool*, a modern Jesus, a minister named Daniel, allays his fiancée's fears that she'll end up washing dishes in a three-room flat in a side street in midtown Manhattan. He tells her: "I don't think we shall come to a three-room flat. . . . We'll have five or six rooms, and our books, and each other."[6] Even the Christian messiah had to bow to middlebrow domesticity for the sake of ticket sales.

While most of the plays with this subject and these settings could be classified as realism, not all are. And the literary category into which a play fell was only one part of how its production spoke to audiences about domesticity. A meal served from an offstage kitchen, for instance, even if only mentioned in passing, is a metonym for the labor required to produce it and for the kitchen as a site of ongoing work. A character's activity, such as sewing or reading, whether or not the character is speaking, conveys information and stimulates response. Moreover, plays categorized as experimental, expressionist, or otherwise not realist frequently deploy realistic props and activities. How these were read depended on hegemonic values, but the values shaping the mainstream theatre audience also provide the very tools for understanding gaps, fissures, and resistance. What people read or the social groups they belonged to spoke to the same needs as did the plays they saw.[7] Shared reading and rituals among a theatregoing class, how-ever, hardly made the audiences monolithic. Most male theatregoers of the era worked outside the home, while many females did not, giving rise to the probability of differing magazine subscriptions, daily top-ics of conversation—especially with friends of the same sex—club af-filiations, relations to children's lives, and spending patterns coexisting under one roof. As Barbara Ehrenreich summarizes, "[A] class is never of one mind."[8]

DOMESTIC DYSTOPIAS

While many 1920s plays that air questions about domesticity are comedies, or at least dramas with recuperative endings, the decade beginning with the 1919–20 Broadway season was bookended by two pairs of plays that saw little hope for happiness in ordinary housewife-dom. "Ordinary" here included homemaking in a midwestern town, on a New England farm, in a Greenwich Village apartment, and in transition from an outer borough (Brooklyn, Queens, or the Bronx) lower-middle-class apartment to a wealthy, perhaps suburban home. *Beyond the Horizon* and *Miss Lulu Bett* present two different domestic dystopias, in each of which a nonurban woman who does not work out-side the home is constrained and punished by a male-headed family with no interest in her needs, even when these needs are to be a re-sponsible housekeeper. Roughly a decade later, the heroines of *Gypsy* and *Machinal*, both city women, fail to find satisfaction in either the domestic realm or paid work.

These plays expose the drudgery of most employment available to women at the time, unsettling the idea of home as de facto haven. All four plays offer the possibility of reading domesticity against the then-mainstream critical grain, if one gives attention to the implica-tions of the naturalist compulsion as well as the realist drive for closure and, perhaps more important, if one considers the possible response of female playgoers for whom the domestic activities represented had recognizable everyday referents. That these connections rarely showed up in mainstream criticism does not mean audience members did not make them. It may mean that the frisson just under the surface in many plays was a component that kept viewers coming back for more, even as it escaped the notice of professional male critics.

Beyond the Horizon, which opened in February 1920, winning that

year's Pulitzer Prize, charts a male dreamer's disappointment leading to his death—literally from tuberculosis but metaphorically from
a broken spirit. Robert, a farmer's son who has always wanted to go
to sea, marries Ruth in a moment of mutually mistaken passion; his
brother, Andrew, who loves farming and had always thought he would
marry Ruth, ships out in Robert's stead. The play traces Ruth and
Robert's slide into bitterness and indifference, but virtually all reviewers and most later critics view the tragedy as Robert's and the agon as
between the brothers. Ruth comes to resent Robert's lack of order, his
reading, being late for meals, and their child's constant crying. Robert,
while he recognizes his failure as a farmer, is only intermittently interested in how he might also be failing as a husband and father; Andrew
calls Ruth, who admits her mistake, "the cause of all this."[9] Had she
married a more successful man, O'Neill seems to suggest, a life of domesticity would presumably have been her dream come true.[10]

O'Neill's text traces Robert's decline scenographically via his wife's
slackening housekeeping. By the final act, the main room of the farmhouse, "seen by the light of the shadeless oil lamp with a smoky chimney which stands on the table, presents an appearance of decay, of dis-
solution. . . . The whole atmosphere of the room, contrasted with that
of former years, is one of an habitual poverty too hopelessly resigned to
be any longer ashamed or even conscious of itself" (175). Attention to
the visual and active world of the play, and to what characters say about
themselves and what O'Neill tells us about them in his novelistic de-
scriptions, can suggest another reading: one in which domesticity itself,
not Ruth, is the villain, and in which Ruth has also been denied agency
and fulfillment.[11] *Beyond the Horizon* has three acts, each featuring
an indoor and an outdoor scene. The outdoor scenes depict the road
Robert wishes to travel (i.e., his dreams) and a hill where the family enjoys a picnic, but not the farm that Robert fails to manage. The failure
is displayed in the domestic interior—Ruth's domain. Reviewers of the
original production derided the painted backdrops depicting the out-
doors.[12] The interior was supposedly rendered with more credibility,
no doubt in part because the requisite items were a few properties and
limited furniture, arrayed within a box set—something more modern
than the backdrops and also clearly synecdochal.[13]

The props and what the actors did with them—even two years before American actors were exposed to Stanislavskianism during the

Moscow Art Theatre's first American tour—are telling. A list of props at the end of the Dramatists Play Service acting edition of *Beyond the Horizon* shows that the props requiring ongoing or repeated usage are, with one exception, used by the women. Men carry books, pick up a newspaper, tote a doctor's bag, look at a watch, or remove a pair of spectacles—characterological actions rendered quickly and not germane to the play's main action—but women put wood in the stove, knit, serve a meal, read and then hide letters, or negotiate the stage in a wheelchair—actions that are either repeated, take some stage time to execute, or are significant to the play's conflicts. The single exception is Robert's removing his daughter's shoes and stockings for a nap. Tellingly, he neither knows whether the footwear should come off nor where to put the items once they have been removed, although the child is two and he has had twenty-four months in which to master— or at least observe—such things. The metonymic as well as the symbolic worlds for which these properties stand speak volumes, and naturalist repetition as gendered behavior is everywhere evident.[14]

At the start of act 2 Ruth has prepared a lunch for which Robert is late. Robert's mother, who resides with the couple, offers to help with the dishes, but Ruth refuses, noting that it's far too hot in the (offstage) kitchen for the older woman. A New England farmhouse in 1917, the year O'Neill started writing the play, would have had a stove that likely burned either wood or coal. The temperature in the entire house would have risen whenever anyone prepared a hot meal, and during the summer, the kitchen would have been blisteringly hot. Household historian Susan Strasser notes that a farm kitchen needed "a large, six-hole stove with a firebox large enough to hold 'quite big wood.'"[15] Ruth would have been cooking for the help as well as for the family (help hired for Robert's work, not for hers). In the final act, Ruth puts the last of the chopped wood in the onstage (living room) stove to keep her mother warm.

Ruth's mother, the invalid Mrs. Atkins, is confined to a wheelchair and spends the first part of act 2 either knitting or fanning herself, repetitive activities that may or may not lead anywhere but that certainly make known the presence of the person doing them and that speak to the excess energy of a woman removed from domestic labor but not granted any other dominion or independence. Louise Closser Hale, the actress who originated the role of Mrs. Atkins (in a performance one reviewer called "remarkably true and interesting"[16]) added something performative to O'Neill's printed requirements that various other characters wheel her about: she wheeled herself around, too, using the chair as "something to brandish, something wherewith to bridle and emphasize a thought or point a bit of wit."[17] Women need to have skills to negotiate the domestic world, and actresses have to master these skills to succeed in their professional world.

Over the course of the play, Robert fails out of doors while Ruth withers inside; each denies the other access to the other's realm. Robert fails to notice the dinner getting cold and, according to Ruth, would make more of a mess washing the dishes than his "help" would be worth. Rather than explore textually the possibility that domesticity without love or respect is a prison (or even that Ruth might have made a good farm hand—she is described as a "healthy . . . out-of-door girl" [130]), O'Neill silences or immobilizes or redirects Ruth at key moments. When Robert's brother returns and she wants to run to meet him, Robert pushes her away from the door and steers her back into the house toward their child. After learning that Andrew no longer thinks of her, Ruth is written by O'Neill to keep the child in her arms and remain silent. At the end of the scene she takes Robert's hint and says she'll get dinner for the child, though we know the brothers' mother has made a special dinner for Andrew's return.

What might otherwise have been a break from domestic labor (someone else cooked dinner for once) is taken from Ruth so Robert can punish her with a meaningless domestic chore. While Robert is habitually too distracted to care about the food Ruth prepares, Andrew announces that he'd stay for his mother's dinner "if I missed every damned ship in the world" (174). The play's final argument between the two brothers features Ruth sitting silently on the side, her face (according to the stage direction) covered by her hands. The labor she performs is unappreciated; the actions she might perform if given agency by the playwright are proscribed; her participation in the brothers' discussion is headed off at the dramaturgical pass.

In the final act, with both of Robert's parents and little Mary dead, the downtrodden Ruth tends to her cranky mother and, in response to a complaint about the dirty lamp, announces that she has a clean one in the kitchen. Arguably the information provides a reason for her mother to request being wheeled offstage as Ruth goes for the lamp.

But for anyone who had used oil lamps, Ruth's statement suggests she can provide a bit of comfort in her own realm (the kitchen) but has no interest in laboring to provide the same comfort in Robert's part of the house. Kerosene lamps required "daily chimney wiping and wick trimming, weekly washing of chimneys and shades, and periodic rewicking and dismantling for thorough cleaning with soda, inside and out. Unpleasantly sooty and smelly, these tasks had to be done for decent light."[18]

The original production of *Beyond the Horizon* may have tipped the scales in favor of the male characters because actress Helen McKellar, who played Ruth, left the impression with critics that "she had difficulty with the early, joyous, girlish scenes but felt at home with the suffering, complaining, frustrated wife of the last act."[19] Perhaps. But there is no reason not to posit a gendered way of seeing the play—female spectators may have had a different response to the conflicts at its heart. The 1926 revival featured Aline MacMahon as Ruth. Burns Mantle found her characterization "thin," and Percy Hammond perceived Ruth as "shallow."[20] Katharine Zimmermann, in a rare instance of a woman reviewing for a major daily, said that MacMahon "glides with sureness and understanding from the fresh and buxom maiden, who is loved by both brothers, to the pitiful slattern in whom cares and disappointments have killed even the power to feel."[21] Zimmerman imputes to Ruth the characteristic that critic Joel Pfister says drives all of O'Neill's characters: depth.[22] Her review suggests that Ruth, too, has squelched dreams and has made sacrifices.

Sacrifice for the questionable privilege of performing domestic labor is at the heart of the 1921 Pulitzer Prize winner, *Miss Lulu Bett*, by Zona Gale. Based on Gale's popular novel, the play depicts an unmarried woman (Lulu) who keeps house for her critical, self-absorbed sister (Ina) and the sister's pompous, patronizing husband (Dwight) in a small midwestern town. Lulu's mother (Mrs. Bett) also lives in the house, as do Lulu's nieces, an independent teenager (Diana) and a ten-year-old (Monona) who deliberately tries the adults' patience. A neighbor with a piano shop (Neil Cornish) admires Lulu, as does Dwight's long-lost brother (Ninian), who shows up, realizes Lulu is being taken for granted, and marries her. When it turns out that Ninian already has another wife, Lulu returns to the family circle, where Dwight insists she keep quiet about what happened. In the novel's conclusion, Lulu marries Cornish. In the play's original ending, Lulu refused Cornish's proposal in order to strike out for independence and parts unknown. In the revised ending, Ninian returns after discovering that his first wife has died and happily reunites with Lulu.

While the endings of Lulu's story and its narrative closure make differing moral or sociological statements (just wait long enough and someone will see your true worth; the only way out of the trap is to slam the door on the doll house; true love will triumph), the naturalist activities in the play's first two acts remain the same and reinforce the questions the play raises.[23] Lulu does "triumph" in all of the endings, but if she were an actual midwestern woman in 1921, she would doubtless live out her post-triumph days in a world of housekeeping much like that depicted in the first two acts. Most important, if she lived long enough and had children, she might end up like her mother, a key figure in the visual and performative world of the play and a financial and social drain in the other characters' lives. Mrs. Bett offers the chilling observation that after the pain of raising six children and burying four of them, she often feels as though nothing ever happened to her and her life hasn't made much difference.

As the play starts, the dining room table is set for dinner with almost all the food in place. The family enters, and Ina complains about Lulu's appearance. Lulu then enters with a plate of muffins, only to learn that Monona will not eat the main course of creamed salmon.[24] Lulu offers to make her milk toast and leaves to do so.[25] Lulu's mother then enters and also refuses to eat, saying she is not hungry. Lulu offers to make her tea and exits to do that. In less than a dozen pages, all the play's characters save one have been introduced and exited once, except Mrs. Bett and Lulu, who remain onstage at the end of the act. Lulu has meanwhile exited to prepare two alternative dinners and returned to serve them; she has cleared the table in several trips to the kitchen, folded the tablecloth, and thrown away a plant to which her brother-in-law objected. She has also answered Dwight's question about the price of canned salmon, only to be told when she responds with a question about purchasing butter that he wants no conversation about domestic matters. He derides her for jumping from salmon to butter, since there is "not the remotest connection" between the two, with salmon the product of a river and butter of a cow.[26] Not only are Lulu's labor

Carroll McComas as Lulu Bett in *Miss Lulu Bett*, 1920.
Billy Rose Theatre Division, The New York Public Library for the Performing Arts.

taken for granted and her activity ignored, but the very terms on which she manages the household for the others' convenience are censored.

In the play's second scene, Lulu peels and slices apples for pies. Several other characters come and go, notably Ninian, who appreciates her labor, and Monona, who assists with the apples and makes a mess. Publicity stills from the production feature actress Carroll McComas wrapped in a big apron over a plain gingham dress for this scene. In one photo she is wielding a large paring knife and hunching over a bowl of apples, looking lost in thought and decidedly plain and unsmiling, her hair pulled back in a tight bun. Photos from the end of the play show her with a puffier hairdo, curls around her face, and fancier dresses. The final two acts of the play streamline the "business" by which Lulu has been defined in the first act as the focus is put on "what happens" and on escape and clothing.

Miss Lulu Bett ran over two hundred performances on Broadway to positive but not glowing reviews. Most appreciated the play's point but questioned its lack of action. On the road, however, it was a hit up and down the East Coast, in upstate New York, and in the Midwest. Two themes recur in the reviews: the depiction of domestic life seemed "real," and performances by McComas as Lulu and Louise Closser Hale as Mrs. Bett were hailed as riveting—"among the truest and most captivating pictures of American domestic life that have ever come to the stage," according to the Rochester (NY) *Herald*.[27] Reviewers appreciated McComas's ability to deglamorize herself and "sink an attractive personality into an unattractive role that it may stand out in its true colors. . . . The hesitancy of speech, the occasional flash of resentment . . . poignantly . . . index the soul of the woman who symbolizes a social condition that did not end with Lincoln's emancipation proclamation."[28]

Hale, the same actress who played the invalid mother-in-law in *Beyond the Horizon*, impressed Pittsburgh reviewer Fay Templeton Patterson for her detailed rendition of age: "At times her performance [as Mrs. Bett] was so realistic as to be positively uncanny . . . the entire body expressing the ravages of time and suffering . . . depicted with . . . consummate skill."[29] The spasms, lack of control, and suffering noted in Hale's performance lent naturalistic credence to a role that, on the page, is one of pathos mixed with humor but hardly one that would necessarily define the terms of the dramatic world. Here repetitive behaviors encoded in the script and devised by two actresses gave depth and the impression of reality to a play that is clear in its intent but also playable as melodrama or even comedy. To a modern eye, photographs of the 1920 set look stagey at best and amateurish at worst. What resonated for viewers were the credibly naturalist performances of the two actresses portraying recognizable characters mired in an inescapable domesticity.

Escape from domesticity typically figured in plays in terms of either romance or employment, and by the end of the 1920s, it was not unusual for female characters in Broadway plays to work outside the home. Like their real-world counterparts, these characters usually worked prior to marriage, or if married and working, they were—if white and middle class—childless. "Escape" rarely meant a reprieve from household responsibilities, just a dramatic focus away from them. Women's magazines were full of recipes for working wives, targeting women who, despite putting in the same hours as their husbands, were also expected to keep house and provide attractive, nutritious meals.[30] A "happy ending" for such women—when they were characters in

Stage set for *Miss Lulu Bett* by Zona Gale, 1920. Featured: William E. Holden, Catherine Calhoun Doucet, William Robertson, Carroll McComas, Lois Shore, Louise Closser Hale, and Beth Varden. Photo by White Studio, © Billy Rose Theatre Division, The New York Public Library for the Performing Arts, Astor, Lenox, and Tilden Foundations.

plays—would be marriage to a moneyed man or a spousal raise that would enable the wife to stay home full time, since women's jobs were figured as stepping-stones or stopgaps, not careers. Two plays, however, show that work can be dreary and that marriage is not a panacea. Both use domestic labor to make their complicated points.

Sophie Treadwell's play *Machinal* revealed the rotten underbelly of the entire setup. The 1928 "gallery of one woman's soul sojourn" depicts a secretary who feels oppressed by her life, repeatedly crying out that nothing is her own.[31] In nine episodes, the emblematic Young Woman is shown at her repetitive job; at home with her anxious, drab mother; on her loveless wedding night to her well-to-do boss; after giving birth to a baby she doesn't want; going to a speakeasy with a woman from her office; engaging in a tryst; at home with her Babbitt-like husband;

on trial for his murder; and awaiting execution for her crime. Analyses of the play routinely discuss its expressionist techniques, its references to the then-recent trial of Ruth Snyder for the murder of her husband, and its indictment of the mechanized life available to women coming of age after World War I, noting that the protagonist "typifies a hundred thousand of her sex in the Big City; rudderless craft on a turbulent sea. Fed into the greedy maw of the machine, they are ground to atoms."[32]

"Expressionism" was, as Ronald Wainscott notes, "used by artists and critics to identify any kind of theatrical experiment except symbolism" in the 1920s.[33] Robert Edmond Jones's setting was suggestive, adding touches to identify the locale and pressures unique to each episode.[34] Treadwell's text stipulates repetitive ambient sounds to create the oppressive world Young Woman inhabits.[35] The style of acting is harder to identify, in part because, from a present-day perspective, most stage acting still didn't look like the sort of Stanislavskianism we now read as "realistic." In 1928, however, that was exactly the word used for the portrayal of the lead. Treadwell's notes in her original manuscript indicate that Young Woman is to be played "as a straight, realistic performance."[36] The editor of *Theatre* magazine was moved by the play's "aliveness and reality tinctured with poetic pathos."[37]

Machinal, unlike *Beyond the Horizon*, did not use many hand properties or repetitive domestic activities to stake out its connection with an everyday world the audience understood as real. The single stunning exception is the confidence and willingness with which Young Woman puts on a pair of rubber gloves to wash dishes for her mother at the end of episode 2. Rubber gloves were a much-advertised item in the second half of the 1920s, marketed to women as a means of keeping their hands soft and, thereby, themselves sexually desirable.[38] Young Woman's mother responds with derision: "Those gloves! I've been washing dishes for forty years and I never wore gloves! But my lady's hands! My lady's hands!" (194). We know from the previous scene that the boss admires Young Woman's soft hands; she announces to her mother that her hands have won her a husband; in the play's penultimate scene she informs a trial lawyer that she began wearing rubber gloves to bed in the weeks before murdering her husband. While putatively resoftening her hands, she was also creating an alibi for use of something that would eliminate fingerprints on the murder weapon. It would be wrong to say that donning the gloves is a repetitive or even a particularly time-consuming stage activity. It is, however, the one quotidian action in which Young Woman engages with nonchalance and generosity, and dishwashing is arguably the one that links her to her female forebears while also marking her as modern.

If *Machinal*'s Young Woman methodically gives the lie to an ordinary maiden's happiness residing in economic security, a nice house, and an appreciative male, the end-of-the-decade unfulfilled housekeeping wife problem exploded with rather colorful and melodramatic force in Maxwell Anderson's *Gypsy*, which opened in January 1929 and stumbled along for sixty-four performances. Ellen, the free spirit of the title, is a twenty-something wife with a good office job, a devoted husband, and terrific housekeeping skills. She even pays at least half the household expenses from her own earnings. Her problem is that she can't resist taking lovers. Anderson loads the play with devices: Ellen's mother is portrayed as a tramp, and the playwright hints that Ellen's problem is inherited. Act 2 opens with David, the husband, being especially solicitous of Ellen, who has just had an abortion, although the word is never used. She foreshadows the ending of the play by saying she didn't want a baby for fear it would be a girl—therefore like herself and her mother—and for such a person, "there's no way out except dying."[39] On opening night the play concluded with Ellen turning on the gas but opening a window after deciding she would take a telephone call from her current beau. One reviewer told readers that after the failed suicide "you're just plain annoyed."[40] Shortly thereafter the ending was changed to conclude with a successful suicide.

Gypsy might well have sunk out of sight in the annals of theatre history were it not for Burns Mantle's including the play among his "ten best" for 1928–29, telling readers of the yearbook that *Gypsy* is "important in that it represents another American writer's attempt to expose, and thereby help to clear, certain accepted phases of a new feminine psychology that will stand a considerable amount of observation and discussion."[41] Richard Lockridge of the New York *Sun* alone praised unstintingly a play he called a "primer for the moderns" presenting a "truthful" look at the upshot of "offering the only intelligent and thoroughly modern means of escape from the direful restrictions of which we are all so childishly afraid."[42]

Despite Ellen's fears about the restrictions of monogamy, the playwright devotes time and energy to assuring us that she is neither averse to nor incompetent at housekeeping. In the opening scene, she informs her new boyfriend (visiting her apartment while her husband is out working) that she is "a pretty fair sort of housewife for a lady who also works in an office," adding, "I get breakfast, and I get dinner, except when I'm too late at the office, and I wash the dishes—and clean house" (1–13). She also confesses to darning socks.

Audiences are not asked to take Ellen's word. In a bohemian version of *Miss Lulu Bett*'s introductory scene, Ellen makes two trips to the kitchen in a little under five typed pages, serving coffee and sandwiches for three guests as well as herself and her husband in a midnight supper. When another guest arrives, she puts up a fresh pot of coffee. In the play's third act, Ellen has relocated to a one-room furnished apartment in Manhattan's East 40s, moving uptown from Greenwich Village and paying all her own bills. In her husband's plea to her to return, he tells her that being exciting is better than being a housewife, ruefully noting that he himself has become a good housewife in her absence. Being good at housekeeping obviously does not make it good in and of itself.

Domestic competence is the reassurance the playwright offers his audience to blame Ellen's problems on a restlessness born of the age (or of inherited nymphomania) but not as a response to either any drudgery associated with homemaking or to the repetitiveness of much office work. Compared to the novels Ellen's boyfriend writes, the music her husband plays, and the acting their friend does, her office work is not fulfilling (although she never says this in so many words). We see nothing of her professional life, while the play puts Ellen's domestic expertise on display. This concern for the stage actions of domestic labor in an otherwise very talky play suggests nervousness about propriety. While the play can venture abortions and mothers who take lovers into bed with their children, it can't let go of sandwiches, coffee, and offers of jam. These presumably make the other unseen topics permissible at arm's length.

Despite the dramaturgical and temperamental differences among these four plays, one factor unites them—something more common to the decade in which they were written than to any succeeding period. All four heroines have mothers, and all four mothers are presented as *social* problems, not just psychological impediments for young adults champing at the bit for independence in multigenerational homes.[43]

Ruth's mother in *Beyond the Horizon* is a carping invalid, seemingly only valued for the money she slips to Ruth. Mrs. Bett in *Miss Lulu Bett* is derided by her son-in-law, ignored by her married daughter and her elder granddaughter, and a fifth wheel at best. The mother in *Machinal* is unsympathetic, unable to listen to her daughter, unwilling to answer her questions, and uninterested in her own past. Ellen's mother in *Gypsy* is portrayed as sexually voracious and inconsiderate. What does this signify in terms of domestic discontents beyond "I don't want to do things the way my mother did"?

Historians Rayna Rapp and Ellen Ross note the irony in 1920s "lifestyles" liberalism (a putative kind of feminism) dependent on destroying "the old . . . feminism [which] had thrived for several generations."[44] That "older" feminism was one that emerged in communities of women. The "heterosexual revolution" and the drive to find satisfaction in companionate marriage, smaller and more efficient houses, and nuclear families without extended branches under the same roof meant that mothers or other older female family members were no longer fashionable sources of knowledge. Rapp and Ross conclude that there was a striking "contrast between the opening up of lifestyle opportunities for some women and the weakening of feminism as an organized, political movement to transform all of 'woman's condition.'"[45]

Perhaps the differences in the domestic dystopias of these four plays are less significant than their similarities. All posit a break with the past that leaves their young female characters cut adrift, and all show that domesticity, with or without electricity and money, is no track on which to grow old. In 1920s plays, the average modern housewife was being told to sever her ties with the past and warned that there was no future in her situation.

SHOWING OFF

When it opened in 1924, critics called *The Show-Off* "a transcript of life," "realism with startling fidelity," "satire," and "domestic tragedy" (the latter two in the same review).[46] Heywood Broun famously called the play the finest comedy ever written by an American. A 1967 revival prompted one reviewer to hedge bets by labeling it a "realistic comedy-drama" laden with the "sentimental."[47] A reviewer of the Long Wharf Theatre's 1996 revival called it both a "morality tale for our own times" and a "kitchen-sink drama."[48] It can be read as all of these things, because, plot aside, what it stages is the household stress of achieving middle-class domesticity on the shifting sands of the 1920s. Within a single family, the playwright credibly depicts three classes, two generations, and varied approaches to housekeeping, as the extended Fisher family negotiates the journey from oil lamps and icemen to electricity and refrigerators.

The Show-Off is nominally the story of a brash, jazz-age interloper, Aubrey Piper (the show-off), wheedling his way into the respectable working-class family of Amy Fisher, whom he marries between acts 1 and 2. Aubrey's speech is peppered with slang, wisecracks, and idioms that irritate Amy's family. He lives beyond his means, sports a carnation in his buttonhole and a toupee, borrows a car and passes it off as his own, has an automobile accident for which he is fined the equivalent of almost eight months' salary (one thousand dollars at thirty-two dollars per week), shops for houses and life insurance even as he is unable to pay the rent on a modest apartment, and finally wins everyone's respect when he brokers a hundred thousand–dollar business deal for the invention the Fishers' teenage son has concocted in the basement. One by one, the Fisher family members succumb to Aubrey's appeal: The well-to-do brother-in-law and the younger brother give him gifts, the sister respects his genuine love for Amy, and the mother finally accepts the financial security he provides. (Arguably the father succumbs literally to all that Aubrey represents, dying of a stroke in act 2.)

This description alone may be enough to substantiate the observation that no George Kelly play is remembered for its plot. Present-day readers of Kelly's three Broadway successes—*The Torch-Bearers* (1922), *The Show-Off* (1924), and *Craig's Wife* (1925)—may love or hate the colorful characters, but they cannot fail to notice the rampant misogyny that Foster Hirsch cites in the recurrent motif of "the moral 'education' of an errant female" that emerges from the pen of a man whose ideas today are "old-fashioned and undemocratic."[49] The self-absorbed, acquisitive woman who requires her husband's guidance or drives him away through her selfishness is least present in *The Show-Off*, which is also the one play of Kelly's famous trio set in a home not coded as upper class. All three plays, though, are "'a dance of objects,' a fantasia of the minutiae of daily life."[50] These minutiae—everywhere redolent of kitchen sink realisms even as the kitchen remains offstage and rarely mentioned—transform the play into a remarkable study of the contradictions and consumerism that made the 1920s so markedly different from what preceded or what immediately followed.

Cultural historians of the decade unfailingly note the contradictory ideas with which Americans, especially women, lived.[51] Consumerism was meant to answer the very woes that industrialization produced; conformity was the route to individualism. Women attended college in greater numbers than ever before, but graduates in the 1920s, unlike their predecessors, were increasingly interested in fitting in, getting married, and studying home economics. Women of every class were urged by advertising—and forced via common practice—to seek satisfaction in homemaking and to cease work for pay upon marriage. The same products that made housework easier also upped the stakes, creating "new chores and new standards."[52] The 1920s was also a crossroads. Between the end of World War I and the advent of the Depression, hot and cold running water and electricity became the norm in most American homes, women shed their weighty and many-layered costumes for lighter dresses and less restrictive undergarments, automobiles became ordinary features of American homes, and eating in restaurants became a middle-class rather than just an upper-class habit, particularly for the increasing number of white-collar and office workers who labored too far away from their domiciles to go home for lunch.

The Show-Off includes one of three kinds of woman that recur repeatedly in literature of the decade: a stay-at-home matriarch, a nonworking daughter who has married into wealth without love, and a daughter who works in an office, knowing she can earn her own money but hoping she won't have to after marriage.[53] The house in which *The Show-Off* is set is a compendium of the old-fashioned and the newfangled, reflecting a moment when popular women's magazines could feature advertisements for both electric refrigerators and iceboxes in the same issue.[54] The Fisher family has central heating and a gas stove but no telephone and no automobile. The daughter who has married money but still lives in the same neighborhood has a telephone and a Victrola. The Fishers acquire a radio when the scientifically inclined son Joe builds one, but in the first act the matriarch pooh-poohs such a device.

The Show-Off is set at a crossroads—historically, dramaturgically, and spatially. The Fishers' house has lots of things in it that suggest hominess and realism, as references abound to lamps, drawers, closets, clocks, and chairs. But the room in which the action occurs is a kind of no-man's land. The kitchen is offstage, as are the parlor where Amy entertains Aubrey and the basement where Joe does his scientific work. Although the sketch at the back of the Samuel French edition of the script calls for a dining room table dead center, the text indicates that the dining room is someplace to which characters exit—therefore also offstage.[55]

The only person who spends the majority of her waking hours in this house is Mrs. Fisher, as the others all either live elsewhere or go out to work or both. But we never see Mrs. Fisher at home during the day, performing her primary occupations. All the scenes take place at night or immediately after the workday, except for those bringing the family members into the house for an emergency. The main value of the house, it seems, is as real estate, despite the putatively domestic flavor of the play. When Mr. Fisher dies, Amy worries about how her mother will keep the house going on only the brother's paycheck. Aubrey, needing a home for himself and Amy, suggests that *his* salary would help if the couple could move in. Later in the play Clara, the older sister, reveals that her father has left the house to her so that Aubrey and Amy won't wrest it away from their mother. Not once does anyone express love for the house.

Questions of ownership and need reflect a domestic truism easily overlooked if a reader or theatregoer focuses on the standoff between Aubrey and Mrs. Fisher as embodiments of salient features of the two generations or even as two strong personalities. It can be hard to distinguish among middle-, upper-, lower-, and working-class families with regard to domestic realities, because these categories traditionally refer either to the work done or the income earned by the male head of household. Historically, on the home front families are either rich or poor based on two things. One is a commonly shared idea of decency and comfort. The second is the question of whether wives and mothers had to undertake paid employment to maintain that standard. The Fisher family is an odd domestic compendium of rich and poor.[56] The father's salary enables the mother to stay at home until the father dies, at which point his salary is replaced by the brother's salary. If the brother were to marry and move out (prior to his act 3 windfall),

either his wife or his mother would need to find gainful employment because it would not be possible for two households to be "rich" on one salary.

This is Amy and Aubrey's problem. Amy gives up her job when they marry, but Aubrey is unable to live within his means and wants them to move in with Mrs. Fisher. Amy toys with the idea of returning to work, but there are two new twists. First, she reveals that she is pregnant, making her working weeks numbered. Second, it is clear as of act 3 that her salary would have to pay for basics, while at the start of the play she is spending more on a dress than her husband-to-be earns in a week. The Fishers' "rich"/comfortable status, then, depends on the mother serving as unpaid domestic help while the children pursue work or scientific experiments, relieving their father of the need to pay for this part of their lives. They depend on their parents to afford them freedom, flexibility, and pocket money. Were the mother to want the same freedom and flexibility, the entire system would collapse.

The domestic labor on which the family depends is virtually absent from the action depicted by the playwright. Twice Mrs. Fisher refers to boiling potatoes or making a cup of tea. Otherwise, she is reduced by the playwright to knitting and looking at advertisements for sewing patterns. Her daughters discuss the dresses they buy; Mrs. Fisher makes her own clothes and still wears shirtwaists. She also favors plain food and has little or no interest in restaurant dining. In *The Show-Off* Kelly offers his usual misogyny tricked out in an insidious masquerade of domestic detail, revealing a vacuum where the heart of the home should be. He punishes all the female characters, and he does so in the only place they might have any authority—the domestic sphere.

Clara, the eldest Fisher child, eats dinner in town in act 1 and is stood up by her husband right before dinner in act 3, when he says he'll eat out with Aubrey. She is denied even the satisfaction of coordinating meals that her maid would cook, as she telephones the maid to cancel dinner during an extended-family emergency. The one meal Mrs. Fisher is about to cook is aborted when she learns her husband has had a stroke. Amy is too tired to prepare dinner for Aubrey and tells him to get dinner "in town" in act 1, while in act 2 she offers to get him something to eat while dealing with the father's death. Aubrey's refusal keeps the focus on the couple's financial worries and their romance, but Amy is subtly denied any agency, as the play focuses on Aubrey's means of getting money and property, not on any of the women's satisfaction. Clara, who does not need to do her own housework, is revealed to be jealous of her sister's pregnancy and thereby rendered truly redundant in the playwright's scheme of things.

George Kelly almost won the Pulitzer Prize for Drama in 1924 for *The Show-Off*; a special jury of three selected by the Pulitzer committee to offer suggestions about plays that year recommended it. The committee ignored the jury's recommendation, however, and selected Hatcher Hughes's *Hell-Bent fer Heaven*, a down-home play set in a cabin in the South and staging a standoff between wholesome Americanism (in the form of a rural army veteran) and religious hypocrisy, with the soldier getting the girl. The popularity of *The Show-Off* with Broadway audiences is clear from its 571-performance run, its revival in 1932, its 1937 Federal Theatre Project production with an all-black cast, and its 1967 revival by the Phoenix Theatre. It has also been made into a film three times: in 1926, in 1934 with Spencer Tracy as Aubrey, and in 1947, featuring Red Skelton.[57] A 1992 revival on Broadway by the Roundabout Theatre prompted *New York Times* critic Mel Gussow to point out that the set, "filled with period furniture, is especially helpful in preserving authenticity. Watching the play, theatregoers can feel projected back to an earlier, more hopeful time in the theater and in America itself."[58]

Criteria for hopefulness can be debated. If economic possibilities looked limitless to middle-class, white, urban, and suburban theatregoers in the mid-1920s, feminists then and now saw and see the picture differently. The "authenticity" conveyed by the replication of clothing, artifacts, and speech patterns cannot erase the possibilities of seeing another kind of authenticity. Kitchen sink realisms, relegated to the offstage areas never seen by the audience of *The Show-Off*, are dark, empty realities suggesting that "authenticity" in much supposedly realistic drama is just like the sets that supposedly convey it: clever facades dependent on bracing, masking, and flattering lighting.

SELLING MRS. TICKET BUYER

The plays in this section spoke to the tensions of domesticity as a putative career in an era when, despite increased possibilities for middle- and upper-middle-class women to get out of the house, everything from residual tradition and postwar isolationism to the agenda at coeducational universities was pushing them to stay home and accept homemaking as a satisfying combination of science and art.[59] The twinned ideas were to keep their audiences talking about what they had seen but also coming back to the theatre. Accordingly, the idea of ticket buyers as consumers and plays as consumer goods provides a useful lens for their examination.

Christine Frederick's 1929 *Selling Mrs. Consumer* is a four hundred–page portrait of the modern American woman as highly skilled purchaser for the home.[60] Frederick's anticipated audience were manufacturers and advertisers, but her description of the psychology of their target market for goods and services is also useful as a critical tool for thinking about women who attended Broadway plays in the 1920s and plays as commercial products. Most American women in the 1920s chose to marry, although not in equal numbers across the population. Those likely to attend commercial theatre were part of a demographic most likely to resist, avoid, or question marriage as a default and perhaps to have more (or at least more varied) occupational opportunities.[61] Certainly they would be sensitive to questions of leisure, fulfillment, and the pitfalls of both homemaking and the rat race.

Frederick, an authority on homemaking and consumerism, became fascinated with "efficiency" in housekeeping as a young bride in the first decade of the twentieth century and parlayed her interests and skills into a nine-year string of articles for *Ladies' Home Journal*. She also produced two books: *The New Housekeeping: Efficiency Studies in Home Management* (1914) and *Household Engineering: Scientific Management in the Home* (1919), which appeared in seven editions by 1925.[62] Frederick's 1929 "x-ray" (her term, 89) of "Mrs. American Consumer" is remarkable because it acknowledges wide differences in income, age, and education among American women, while still capturing a kind of middlebrow female zeitgeist.

Part of this zeitgeist emerges in paradoxical observations about Mrs. Consumer: She is not gulled by advertising even as she is willing to follow where she is led (334–35, 346–47). She is economical even as she embraces "progressive obsolescence" (240, 263, 246). She loves change and novelty even as she prizes manners, form, and etiquette (45). She is in a "secondary" position to men (15), but she does not like to be a "parasite" (398). Frederick even chastises advertisers for their images of Mrs. Consumer, observing that they derive their ideas about women from showgirls in Manhattan's theatre districts: "No advertising artist seems to have a wife who does her own housework, never had a mother, nor a grandmother" (350); yet the illustration gracing the front of her book "glorifies" the American housewife as a cross between a post–Gibson girl and a young Betty Crocker.

These contradictions yield a complex portrait of a female populace negotiating ideas that education, professionalism, physical fitness, and progressive thinking were their right and obligation, even as they were told by advertisers, educators, and popular magazines (as well as family, church, and boyfriends) that their proper place was in the home cooking, cleaning, and tending to children.[63] It is easy to read Frederick's book as "blatantly patronizing to women" if one applies present-day ideas of egalitarianism and ignores her effort to include working women and the desire for autonomy in her portrait of the housewife as steward of the modern home.[64] Frederick even nodded to what would later be called the double shift: "In an economic age . . . what we are now seeing is the clear determination of women [assumed to be homemakers], ever practical minded, to lift the family standard of living by means of a two-earner system whenever at all feasible" (398).

What characterized this practical-minded modern woman that is of use in thinking about her as a theatregoer? She was possessed of what might now be called multiple intelligences, making her sensitive to the emotional goals of theatre: "[W]omen are not persuaded, as men are, that logic and reason are the only factors with which one should guide oneself. . . . This does not mean of course, that women are using less reason and intelligence. Indeed they are using more. But emotion and instinct bulks extremely large" (44). In Frederick's attempt to characterize Mrs. Consumer holistically, she listed eighteen characteristic "instincts," ranked in order of importance, advising every "seller of family goods" to target at least one thing on the list:

1. Sex Love.
2. Mother Love.
3. Love of Homemaking.
4. Vanity and Love of Personal Adornment.
5. Love of Mutation, Style, Modernity, Prestige, Reputation.
6. Hospitality.
7. Sociability.
8. Curiosity.

9. Rivalry, Envy, Jealousy.

10. Pride, Ostentation and Display.

11. Exclusiveness, Social Ambition, Snobbery.

12. Tenderness, Sympathy and Pity.

13. Cleanliness, Sanitation, Purity.

14. Practicality, Economy, Thrift, Orderliness.

15. Love of Change and Novelty.

16. Delight in Color, Smell, Neatness, Looks and Feel.

17. Delight in Manners, Form, Etiquette.

18. Love of Beauty. (45)

Placing sex love at the top of the list acknowledges that entering into domesticity with a partner is, for most women, inseparable from a desire for erotic gratification. This was still a newish concept in the 1920s, when the idea of companionate marriage became common. Frustration in sex love while pursuing any of the other items on the list was the subject of several popular plays of the 1920s. So was frustration about other items on the list even when sex love was present. Not all of Frederick's listed items need to operate with equal strength or simultaneously in any play or for any individual female spectator. But naming an "instinct" as a hot issue allows it to be put on the table for examination with the probability that it will be taken up, which is, arguably, what numerous playwrights did in the 1920s.

Playwrights invested heavily in the worrisome haven/trap debate; even recuperative endings were preceded by intense struggle and lively discussion. For instance, in the 1921 *Ambush*, although old-fashioned values are prized, three distinct attitudes toward domesticity emerge in two neighboring houses. The main character is a middle-aged suburban man whose nineteen-year-old daughter wants to leave the workforce but also wants all the luxuries money can buy. She believes that a girl who lives at home is perceived as socially superior to one who works. If she could quit her job, she argues, her boss, with whom she may be sleeping and from whom she is accepting expensive gifts, might marry her, presumably enabling her to continue to stay home, albeit a different home. (Hers are clearly Frederick's instincts 4, 9, 10, and 11.)

Her mother, the protagonist's wife, is described as "accustomed to doing her own housework and shows the effects of it."[65] (Instincts 12 and 13 nudge her into her daughter's corner in the developing battle.)

Meanwhile, the next-door neighbor—written as the protagonist's soul mate—is a woman whose fatigue is related to getting and spending but not to housekeeping, as she confides, "Oh, I'm not tired of keeping house and marketing and mending socks—I'm tired of having to be ambitious."[66] (Instincts 4, 5, 9, 10, and 11 are anathema, and she seems to thrive on 14.) Here, finding fulfillment at home is valued, although it "shows its effects" on women who have to do their own housework, unless they can turn their backs on ambition.

Why the daughter should not aspire to escape her mother's lot is not made clear, nor does the play address the impossibility of any average working girl achieving luxury on her own salary, nor the possibility of a woman being ambitious in any way other than in her marriage aspirations or in craving luxury. The choice to stay home was available only to women who did not need to support themselves or their families, women like many in Broadway audiences. Accordingly, however it was framed in theatrical productions, this kind of dilemma spoke to women theatregoers in a way that addressed a particular rather than a "universal" American problem.[67]

One of the most obvious (and recurring) sorts of contestation concerning domesticity, domestic relations, and women's role in the home had to do with being satisfied with homemaking and child rearing. In *The Changelings* (1923) a young Yale professor recognizes that his expectations of ideal wifedom have contributed to his spouse's wanderlust.

> WICKY: Why should *I* have taken it for granted that making a
>   home for me, looking after my comfort, was all you needed
>   from life? . . . You have *brains*, Kay. And God knows light
>   housekeeping isn't a career!
> KAY: Unless . . . unless there are children . . . [ellipses in original]
> WICKY: . . . Ah, but then, of course, it isn't *light*.[68]

In both *Chicken Feed* (Guy Bolton, 1923) and *Saturday's Children* (Maxwell Anderson, 1927), energetic young women rebel and move out of their homes either on the eve of or shortly after their marriages to seemingly simpatico young men. In each case the issue is money—specifically, men thinking they can spend income freely, leaving the women in the lurch when it comes to paying basic bills. *Saturday's Children*'s Bobby (played in the original production by a young Ruth

Gordon) enumerates the necessary items on a $240-a-month house-keeping budget, including $3 for ice (they don't have an electric refrigerator), $35 for groceries, and $10 for insurance (the latest in modern planning). Her parting shot as she walks out to go back to work and manage her own affairs is, "You can wash your own dishes! The hot water's in the right-hand tap!"[69]

Both plays end with reconciliation, promises to share, and—perhaps most important—the assurance that the husbands truly love their wives. Conceivably the "love conquers all" argument defeats the social critique, but the critique goes on long enough that the happy endings can be read much as one reads the marriages at the end of so many Renaissance plots. They offer a way to wrap up the dramatic problems that have been unpacked, but they do not necessarily eliminate future problems or erase the overarching questions that have been raised.

DOMESTIC LABOR IN BLACK AND WHITE

As did African American one-acts of the 1910s, plays for, by, and about blacks in the 1920s folded domestic labor into larger political discussions. Georgia Douglas Johnson's *Blue Blood*, written in 1926, is notable for the way it triangulates three versions of everyday life to posit a reality that would speak across class lines and the decades separating its setting from its emergence.

Blue Blood was Johnson's entry in *Opportunity* magazine's 1926 Literary Contest in the drama category and was one of four plays to receive honorable mention.[70] *Opportunity*, a project of the Urban League, was one of a few magazines targeting African American readers to seek new plays, virtually all one-acts. The NAACP's *Crisis* was another. In 1925, *Survey Graphic*—whose readers were largely involved in social work and which did not specifically target African American readers—expanded the contents of its special issue on Harlem to a book edited by Alain Locke, *The New Negro*.[71]

Montgomery Gregory's essay on drama in that volume articulated the value of the genre for social advancement and also declared that "the Negro . . . alone can truly express the soul of his people," clarifying, "However disagreeable the fact may be in some quarters, the only avenue of genuine achievement in American drama for the Negro lies in the development of the rich veins of folk-tradition of the past and in the portrayal of the authentic life of the Negro masses of to-

day."[72] Johnson's play sits at the intersection of those two realms—
a "traditional," but uneducated past and a mass "authentic" present.
Her play was not directly seeking commercial production. Koritha
Mitchell notes that one-acts about everyday African Americans would
have had limited (if any) commercial appeal and, therefore, "tailoring
one's script for periodical publication . . . meant writing with amateur
performance in mind."[73]

Georgia Douglas Johnson (1877?–1966) was already an established
poet when she turned to playwriting in the 1920s.[74] A native of Atlanta
and an 1893 graduate of Atlanta University's Normal School, she had
briefly been a teacher, later attended the Oberlin Conservatory of
Music, married an Atlanta attorney with whom she moved to Washington, D.C., and was solidly part of that city's black "college-educated
elite society."[75] She was light skinned, attractive by white standards,
and hosted a Saturday night salon that attracted many of the most
visible and important New Negro writers as well as several important
white poets. After her husband's death, Johnson supported herself as
a government clerical worker. *Blue Blood* speaks *from* her own experience, *to* her social cohort, and *about* some transhistorical everyday
phenomena. While, as Sandi Russell observes, "light complexioned
intellectuals, speaking standard English were . . . often alienated from
the majority of the Black populace,"[76] in *Blue Blood* Johnson stages a
cross-class encounter that is credible for the tensions it does not elide
as well as for the subtle ways in which it displays trans-class alliances
forged by exigencies of race and gender—exigencies that had not disappeared in the sixty years between the time the play might have been
set and the time it was written.

Blue Blood is set in Georgia "shortly after the Civil War," on the day
that May Bush is to marry John Temple.[77] The character names suggest the play's efficient dramaturgy, as the lowly Bush family has little
social contact with the haughty, privileged Temple family. The inciting incident is the arrival of Mrs. Temple in the dialect-speaking Mrs.
Bush's kitchen, where Mrs. Temple's class pride prompts Mrs. Bush
to assert the bride-to-be's "aristocratic" heritage, as May is (secretly)
the illegitimate daughter of the biggest (white) banker in town. Mrs.
Temple is stunned and at the crisis point of the play confesses that
the same banker fathered her son—the groom-to-be. The climax occurs when one of May's former suitors enters the kitchen and proposes

again. No one tries to force May's hand, but she elects a loving rescuer and a clean reputation over the appearance of having been jilted. Perhaps the clearest link between past setting and present readership is Mrs. Temple's fear that if she reveals the name of the rapist who also fathered May, an attempt to avenge her will result in a lynching. Neither in the early days of Reconstruction nor in the early twentieth century could a black man assume that protecting a black woman against a white aggressor was safe.

Beyond the broad contours of the play, fascinating elisions and specifics weave a web of credibility in the face of questionable "accuracy." The play is telescoped realism, but its matrix of miscegenation, motherhood, mayonnaise, and marriage pulls viewers into an everyday that is believable even as it is not always quite "right."

In the days "shortly after the Civil War," perhaps 1866, in Georgia, a frame cottage with two stories (the script stipulates a staircase and May going upstairs to change clothes), a backyard, a back door, and a parlor would have been an unlikely dwelling for a working-class black family. As late as 1879 in the sizable city of Atlanta, a contemporary described the working-class black neighborhood of Shermantown as "a random collection of huts." An illustration accompanying this description in *Harper's Weekly* showed "[w]ooden shacks . . . set up in a circle surrounding a well, with a clothesline stretched across the middle."[78] Perhaps even more unlikely than the two-story house is Mrs. Temple's claim that she taught in a country school in Georgia when she was nineteen and engaged to be married. Since she is old enough to have a son about to wed, her teaching days would have occurred in the late 1840s, when teaching slaves was illegal. Had she been a free black living in the South, she would likely not have been in Georgia at all but would have lived where such citizens were concentrated: in the Tidewater area of Virginia and Maryland, the Piedmont region of North Carolina and Virginia, or the seaboard cities of Charleston, Mobile, and New Orleans.[79]

More likely Johnson is invoking the world of her own youth, some time in the 1880s or early 1890s (which would put the play's "present" in the 1910s). The 1880s represented the peak period of post–Civil War black urbanization, with a million migrants arriving in southern cities of all sizes between 1880 and 1915.[80] These cities served as centers of black higher education during Reconstruction, so the fictional Mrs.

Temple might, like the actual Georgia Douglas Johnson, have attended Atlanta University's Normal School and taught locally. Teaching was a special category of work for black women, who by 1910 represented just 1 percent of the South's black working women and who shared a "commitment to social and political activism." These women were social and cultural elites, even though they made no more money than female workers in tobacco plants. Marriage was grounds for being fired.[81]

If the house and Mrs. Temple's status as a teacher suggest a date later than 1866 for absolute "accuracy," few reading the play quickly or for the first time are likely to worry about these niceties, although mention of a car and Mrs. Bush consulting her watch are jarring. Johnson's broad categories of domestic everyday objects suggest a continuum of recognizable quotidians rather than a snapshot of one date-bound moment. Nowhere is this more cleverly handled than with the food and domestic labor that form so much of the activity (distinct from the dramatic action) of the play. When Mrs. Temple pushes her way into the kitchen, underscoring that she and Mrs. Bush move in "somewhat different social circles" but that on this day she feels her place is "back here with you," she foreshadows the recognition of sameness that will force the climax of the play.

Poking around the kitchen, Mrs. Temple asks, "What's this . . . chicken salad?" The place of chicken in African Americans' diet and livelihoods is familiar to the point of caricature and has been historicized by Psyche Williams-Forson, who chronicles the prevalence of the easy-to-care-for birds both during slavery and after; the sale of cooked chicken by post–Civil War black women; and the cruel jokes made at the expense of African Americans for liking to eat chicken, something enjoyed by millions of other Americans.[82] But the three dots preceding chicken *salad* may suggest slight surprise at the relative "gentility," Northern-ness, or "whiteness" of the dish. Chicken salad appears in the first cookbook by an African American, published in 1866. Author Malinda Russell was born to a free mother in Tennessee in the first third of the nineteenth century and worked as a cook, so she might have become acquainted with this dish through a white employer. An introduction to the 2007 facsimile reissue of Russell's book points out that most of her recipes could come from any part of the eastern United States and are not distinctly southern.[83] Her recipe for chicken salad calls for the white meat of three boiled chickens, chopped celery, mustard, black pepper, vinegar, and the mashed yolks of three eggs.[84] It differs little from the four chicken salad recipes in the 1883 *Buckeye Cookbook*, subtitled in its 1975 reissue *Traditional American Recipes*.[85]

The elitist acceptability of chicken salad is nowhere so clear as in an 1896 report in *New England Kitchen Magazine* written by "a visitor to a Georgia exposition" who was horrified by the "typical dinner" her southern hostess served her. "Turnips cooked with pork, *green tops and all*, beef roasted to a cinder, and coffee of Chattahoochian flavor." The only dishes acceptable to her were provided by a Bostonian domestic scientist at the fair's Women's Building, and they included "[b]ouillon in cups, 'tiny crackers,' plates of chicken salad with olives and a single roll, and a green-and-white gelatin dessert."[86] Johnson and her cohort would have been familiar with some New England values, as blacks receiving schooling in the South in the nineteenth century were largely under the tutelage of Abolitionist- and New England–influenced instructors. In any case, as a sophisticated city dweller in the 1920s, Johnson had access to many foods—as did her readers in other large cities.

Perhaps the subtlest domestic touch is the mayonnaise that Mrs. Temple starts making when it is clear that the neighbor who promised to send some has not done so. All the nineteenth-century chicken salad recipes mentioned previously call for dressings including eggs, vinegar, and mustard—basic ingredients of mayonnaise, but not mayonnaise itself. In some of the recipes, such as Russell's, the egg yolks in the dressings are hard cooked and mashed; sometimes the dressing ingredients are cooked and poured over the chicken mixture. Mayonnaise is something different and requires, in addition to eggs and vinegar, oil. Because of the high cost of importing olive oil, mayonnaise did not become popular in the United States until the end of the nineteenth century, facilitated in part by the advent of olive growing and pressing in California.[87] By 1912 it was popular enough for Hellmann's to become a national brand, and anyone with an icebox and no interest in whisking could buy it commercially.[88] The trick to making mayonnaise is adding the requisite oil very slowly (whisking all the while) to a beaten mixture of eggs, vinegar, and spices (mustard is mentioned most frequently) so that the condiment emulsifies properly. A present-day website featuring information about mayonnaise includes one recipe for "Nineteenth Century Mayonnaise" that calls for egg yolks (not whole eggs) and makes clear that this simple difference yields a much thicker mayonnaise. Writes the site's creator, "I do not recommend trying this with a whisk unless you are a trained endurance athlete with the biceps of an Olympian."[89]

Mrs. Temple may strike Mrs. Bush as in line to "git yo'self spoiled doing kitchen work [because] [s]ich folks as you'd better go 'long in the parlor," but the gingham apron Mrs. Temple dons after removing her white gloves says something else (perhaps the hidden endurance of an athlete). For a half page, the women trade roles, and the snob reveals her ease with doing kitchen duty, while the previously aproned cook, "proudly tossing her head," brags of her connection with "that Peachtree Street blue blood" (the address arguing for proximity to Atlanta). The stage directions make clear that Mrs. Temple's emotional state is indexed by her mayonnaise making. She starts out confidently, but when the news begins to unfold, stirs "nervously" and then "suspend[s] the operation of the mayonnaise" as she begins to suspect the worst.[90] When, at the end of the play, Mrs. Temple gives her coat to May so the latter can escape quickly, the sartorial crossings among the women—Mrs. Bush removes her apron; Mrs. Temple is wearing Mrs. Bush's extra apron; May is clad in Mrs. Temple's coat—indicate a cross-class shared reality of secret horrors.

In no way do I imagine that Georgia Douglas Johnson meticulously researched the material culture of the post–Civil War South with an eye to any kind of photorealism. The very carelessness with which she includes the car and the poorer woman's wristwatch in the "shortly after Civil War" setting argues the opposite. But the canny use of domestic objects and tasks to express a transhistorical set of gendered, racial, and class truisms rings comfortably true. Johnson's project, like that of so many other educated "talented tenth" and New Negro writers, was to foster awareness and discussion and to encourage self-respect.[91] The reality that Douglas sought to portray was one of racism, the rape of black women by white men, the silence those women endured to keep their men from risking lynching, and possibly the unspoken necessity of loveless marriage in the face of potential dishonor.[92] Most important here is that this reality infected the domestic sphere, forcing a marriage of public and private that no homemaker could imagine was "individual." In that sense, the play, which today looks structurally a

little formulaic, remains culturally compelling and possessed of a brilliant blend of subtle everydays offering insight into aspects of real life that tell us simultaneously about 1866, 1926, the six decades between setting and readers, and possibly about our own day.

■ ■ ■

Within months of the closing of *Gypsy*, the stock market would crash, and in short order the lives of most Americans would change for the worse. Domestic labor remained prominent in mainstream plays, but its uses shifted. The concerns of white playwrights and those of black playwrights would remain as starkly different as the dress and apron of the formal maid's uniform. This says less, perhaps, about an inability to see that poverty hurt across the color line than about how wide and deep that line was regarding where dollars came from and how inequitably they were distributed across that divide. It also says much about the tropes and problems for which audiences are willing to spend money on theatre tickets.

3   WAITING FOR LEFTOVERS

1930–1939

In his history of the 1930s, *Since Yesterday*, Frederick Lewis Allen compared the conversational buzz at an imaginary New York cocktail party of writers, artists, and people interested in the newest ideas in 1925 with one in 1935. The 1925 guests espoused personal liberties while ridiculing reformers; they scorned Babbittry and boosterism, smirked at the Victorian and Puritan traditions, and extolled the freedoms of living in Europe over the mass-produced or, worse, rural southern lives of unsophisticated Americans. The 1935 artists and intellectuals asserted that the masses were the people who really mattered, that reform was badly needed, and that America was both fascinating and the hope of the free world.[1] The contours of stylishness changed with a new zeitgeist.

In this climate American theatre did not abandon domesticity, but across genres it went underground as a topic of critical discussion, remaining legible nonetheless as both trope and occasional subject of focus. The antidote to anxiety was frequently figured as domestic security, with mom at home and women's employment for wages a nonissue because it was—at least for white characters—understood as suitable only for the young prior to marriage. The foods prepared by stay-at-home wives in plays of this decade also experienced a last hurrah of ethnicity (often Jewish), perhaps because they were created by the last generation of playwrights that included a few who were foreign born and many offspring of first-generation immigrants, as did their audiences. Nonwhite characters in domestic settings were largely shoved into a servant niche, but the final play in this chapter shows the rage and scorn this aroused in some corners of the African American theatre audience.

WEARING LINOLEUM

Broadway endured the Depression providing comic, musical, revival, and dramatic fare that ignored the economic crisis. Nonetheless, there was a distinct edge to depictions of domesticity in plays that either addressed directly or at least acknowledged the Depression. The four examples in this section treat domesticity in multiple classes and locales. While all appeared on Broadway, one originated with the leftish Group Theatre, another was written by a prominent participant in the Federal Theatre Project, and three foreground labor. The widespread phenomenon of workers' theatre and the existence of the Federal Theatre Project—providing employment and drawing audiences around the nation—speak to the importance of theatre even when money was tight and movies were popular.[2]

The middle-class characters in *Her Master's Voice* are skilled in domestic labor and use this to endear themselves to the wealthy aunt and the entrepreneur who facilitate the nutty but happy ending. Clare Kummer's 1933 Broadway comedy opens on Queena Farrar, a young housewife, seated at her piano and wearing a pink rubber apron, trying to resuscitate the operatic skills she was building in Italy when she met and married her husband several years and two children ago. Her high notes result in a crash from the offstage kitchen, where her mother, Mrs. Martin, has dropped a glass. Queena offers to finish the dishes; her mother laments Queena's marriage to a man who can't provide enough and leaves her wearing "linoleum." When the husband, Ned, arrives, we meet a cheery man who has just been fired from an office job at which he admits he was not very good.

As his mother-in-law frets and his wife goes to bed in despair, Ned dons the apron and starts on the dishes. He is wearing the "linoleum" when Queena's wealthy aunt Min arrives and takes him for the houseman. He does not disabuse her, as she is known to dislike Queena's husband on principle, having never met him. He serves her a meal, gets clean sheets and sets her up in an available bedroom, and encounters her the following morning when he is vacuuming the stairs while still in his pajamas. He explains that he stayed overnight to help the family, who wanted things extra clean after learning of her arrival. She is so taken with Ned that she hires him, which is convenient, as she also whisks Queena off for rest, vocal work, and exercise away from her supposedly no-good husband and domestic obligations. With the parents gone, the children are shipped off to neighbors, and Queena's mother is hired as a housekeeper by Ned's former boss.

Improbable though the plot is, it embeds domestic labor in the middle-class home in an endearing, egalitarian way. Queena takes over washing dishes from her mother; Ned takes over from Queena, also appropriating her apron. When the vacuum cleaner needs a part replaced, Ned performs this (stereotypically male) job and also vacuums the house. Queena's mother knows what to cook for her sister's breakfast, just as Ned knew what to offer her for a late dinner. The absent children have had a birthday party where their idea of fun was to give the dog a bath in the tub. Their mother is not worried about the hairs her aunt finds there. Queena's mother has sufficient housekeeping skills that she can work for wealthy Mr. Twilling (who rewards her with marriage). In this solidly middle-class—albeit romanticized—family the housework happens with turn taking, routine griping, and skill sets that are neither fetishized, strictly gendered, nor necessarily taken for granted.

If not for the wealthy aunt and sentimental entrepreneur, the Farrars would be on the verge of joining the "Depression poor"—a term differentiating middle-class people who fell on hard times from the "long-term poor," who were bypassed by most government food programs, remained destitute even after the Depression, and still exemplify the 1930s for many because they appeared in the work of James Agee, Walker Evans, and John Steinbeck.[3] How Depression-poor families coped with losing 25 percent or more of their pre-Depression real income was addressed in 1936 by sociologist Robert Cooley Angell. Angell was interested in cross-class, geographically varied coping mechanisms within families, and he measured these by assessing "family integration" and adaptability. The former considers "common interests, affection, and a sense of economic interdependence," while the latter might be summarized as a collective ability to adjust to change.[4] Families who were highly integrated and highly adaptable weathered the Depression successfully. Unintegrated, unadaptable families did worst. The fictional Farrars are clearly resilient and adaptable.

Reviews in the mainstream press mention the Depression as the cause of the unemployment that launches the action of *Her Master's Voice*.[5] One noted that "being such a prevalent condition probably makes domesticity rank very nearly first among theatrical themes,"

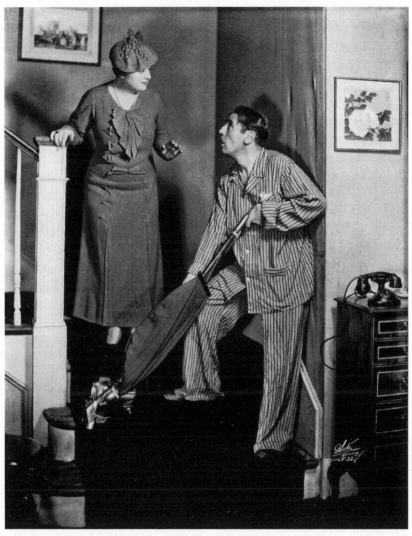

Laura Hope Crews as Aunt Min and Roland Young as Ned Farrar in *Her Master's Voice*, 1933. Photo by White Studio, © Billy Rose Theatre Division, The New York Public Library for the Performing Arts, Astor, Lenox, and Tilden Foundations.

adding that in real life, Roland Young, who played Ned Farrar, was the playwright's son-in-law.[6] Coincidentally, the playwright, whose birth name was Clare Rodman Beecher, was a great-niece of Catherine Beecher, author of the 1841 *Treatise on Domestic Economy*.

The grimmest look at domesticity in 1930s plays occurred in those that featured destitute laborers and farmers. Elmer Rice's *We, the People* has both. The twenty-scene polemic follows two families and leads to a rally on behalf of the young labor activist Allen Davis, who has been wrongly accused of murder and sentenced to death. Allen is a college student and the son of a factory foreman; his mother is a housewife; and his sister, Helen, is a schoolteacher dating Bert Collins, a bank clerk whose family lives on a farm. When the factory closes and farm sales plummet because of government regulation and drought, both households suffer foreclosure. Allen and his father are radicalized. Most labor plays treat women either as union members supporting a strike, housewives striking for better food prices, or family members standing by their men. This one is no exception, although the teacher is not a laborer and Allen's girlfriend is a college student.

We, the People's realistic depiction of domestic life makes it different from the Federal Theatre Project's (FTP) living newspaper *Triple-A Plowed Under* of 1936, though both plays addressed rural poverty (and Rice would work as head of the FTP's New York office). *Triple-A* features very short scenes and characters sporting generic names like Middleman, Farmer, Auctioneer, Worker, and Salesman.[7] In *We, the People*, the Davises and Collinses are shown at home, with wives serving dinners. In the second scene, Mrs. Davis enters from the kitchen to hear Allen's news about his college entrance scores. She exits to start the potatoes, returns to get a dish from the sideboard (and to reveal that she doesn't know what "point seven means," i.e., what a decimal point is), exits, returns with a plate of bread, exits four lines later, appears in the kitchen door to tell the family to sit down, returns to the kitchen, and comes back three lines later with the soup tureen, whereupon the scene ends. She seems neither efficient nor informed, although when her husband is laid off, she takes in a boarder, putting her in the category of working women who were often not counted as such because they labored for money in the home. Her later actions help mark her family as adaptable and integrated in Angell's terms.

The Collins's home is already in trouble at the start of the play. When we meet them in scene 5, Stella, wife of Bert's older brother Larry, is fixing Sunday dinner. She, too, enters from the kitchen to greet her mother-in-law and the visiting minister. Stella returns to the kitchen for several pages and reenters to greet Bert, departing six lines later. She returns a few pages later with biscuits and cider, ignoring Larry, who has turned up drunk after failing to meet his brother at the train station. Larry picks a fight with her and hits her in the mouth. She recovers her composure, goes to the kitchen, and returns with "two large platters of steaming food." The minister says grace, Stella bursts into tears and heads for the kitchen, no one follows her, and Larry pounds the table, saying "(harshly): Well, do we eat or don't we?"[8]

Larry, we learn, fought in World War I and is suffering the effects of gas and shell shock. He is apparently impotent. Rice chooses Stella's words carefully as she tells her abusive husband, "That's not what I got married for, to spend my life in the kitchen, with nothing to listen to, day in and day out, but your crazy talk."[9] It is not the kitchen per se that is driving Stella away. (She has left home for points unknown the next time we see the family.) It is Larry's treatment of her as well as her isolation. The something else to listen to would be a radio, which in 1929 (better times) would have cost $135, 10 percent of a year's earnings for a low-level white-collar worker,[10] and it is entirely possible that the house has no electricity, increasing Stella's burdens. The Rural Electrification Act (1936), which wired houses in remote areas and brought domestic life on many farms into the twentieth century, was still three years away when the play opened.

Rice lets his audience know that in this abusive, dust-punished, impoverished home without radio and without government care for Larry's physical and psychic wounds, life is hard even on a good day. At one point, Larry and Stella's son Donald enters covered with dirt and blood after butchering a hog for the family's dinner. The visual point could not have failed to jolt a Broadway house, where the majority of playgoers likely had limited experience with the steps between meat on the hoof and meat in the butcher's shop or grocery freezer. The scene brings the urgency of rural need and domestic making-do home to an urban audience.

Critics took Rice to task for attributing "all the virtues to the working persons and all the vices to their employers,"[11] but even sympathetic reviewers missed the gendered aspect of what one critic hinted: that the ideal audience might be the "keen-eared Communist."[12] Farm support, Works Progress Administration (WPA) jobs for out-of-work labor, and even eventually, Social Security did little for housewives. One exception was the 1937 Household Service Demonstration Project, which trained seventeen hundred women seeking domestic employment and also employed thirty thousand women on housekeeping-aid projects, enabling homemakers to help families in distress and to earn money from the government. But neither the training nor the jobs provided transferrable skills.[13] Nor would these programs have been immediately relevant to urban and suburban women who could afford theatre tickets in 1937, leaving this economic reality of domestic labor blurry at best for most audiences.

My point is not that women should have been forced into the workplace or that paid work trumps housekeeping as a contribution to family life and self-fulfillment. Repetitive, physically strenuous, intellectually numbing wage work is not a panacea, even if the title of a 1934 article, "In Praise of Domesticity," cloyingly acknowledged that the struggle for equality was uphill and that even women college graduates' priorities were "love, marriage, and creative work, in that order."[14] Plays concluding with a cry for legislation promoting a decent standard of living, farm support, affordable food prices, and the like still leave the economic and legal status of the housewife unquestioned, offering little in the way of court-enforceable rights or a New Deal, absent a husband. In the eyes of the federal government, as in the eyes of playwright Elmer Rice, it is fine for a farm wife to spend her life doing domestic labor, so long as her husband is nice to her. Even the "privileged" wife in this play is too dumb to know what a percentage point is. But domestic labor is "good" for her because her husband is good to her, not because the economy or higher education is.

Legal arguments never carry the weight in the theatre that emotional ones do. As Edith Isaacs, editor of *Theatre Arts Monthly*, noted in a review: "[T]he theatre at its best and freest works not on your reason but on your emotion and imagination. That is why the best social propaganda in the theatre is a good play, well-presented and well-acted, written by an artist with a social consciousness."[15] For many critics and historians, the playwright whose work best packed the emotional punch of the Depression was Clifford Odets, who burst onto the New York stage with two plays in early 1935. The episodic, pro-strike

Waiting for Lefty premiered just weeks ahead of *Awake and Sing*, Odets's Broadway debut, and a traditional play. Both were hits.

Odets has come to be "categorized as the signal playwright of the thirties."[16] *Waiting for Lefty* and *Awake and Sing* are pleas for a world where money would not be the only measure of human worth and where there would be enough resources to provide for the families of blue-collar workers and the modest hopes of young lovers who wish to marry and set up housekeeping. His famous demand that life not be "printed on dollar bills" was coupled with hints of a better world in which men would think and work in fulfilling, communally supportive, and remunerative ways, while women would be relieved of any concerns besides homemaking or escapist consumerism.[17] By describing the two plays this way, I am intentionally overlooking their structural differences and overt politics to foreground the common elements that made them heart wrenching for a spectrum of audiences and critical stances.[18]

Odets himself, despite a brief membership in the Communist Party, struck many drama critics most as a "humanitarian";[19] he positioned himself as interested primarily in "human rights" and answered questions about politics in drama with the assertion that "people attend the theater for relaxation, and if a dramatist has a didactic message to expound he must do so *in addition to entertaining them.*"[20] Director Harold Clurman characterized him as a "headlong romantic."[21] "The Left movement provided Odets with a platform and a loudspeaker; the music that came through was that of a vast population of restive souls, unaware of its own mind, seeking help," asserted Clurman.[22] Within this matrix—the humanitarian, idealistic, entertainer, romantic— Odets's 1935 successes hit home in the domestic sphere. Clurman himself—the original director of the Group Theatre production of *Awake and Sing*—was initially reluctant to stage the play because of what he called its "messy kitchen realism."[23]

For all Odets's leftist discontent with the economic and moral status quo, his conservatism regarding domesticity and women's place in it provided the secure foundation on which to mount his outcries.[24] Both *Lefty* and *Awake and Sing* are rife with the misogyny, utopia imagined via consumerism, and food that Christopher J. Herr identifies as Odets's trademarks of ambivalence.[25] Because the plays traffic in the actual foods, products, nutritional ideas, housecleaning concerns, and sanitary standards of the moment, they convey immediacy. *Awake and Sing* does have much "messy kitchen realism" about it, with its "apples, halvah, duck, pastrami, chocolates, cake, chopped liver, and bread and jam onstage, as well as references to oranges, tangerines, chop suey, pickles, eggs, knishes, tea, coconuts, peaches and cream, raspberry jelly, and champagne, usually as figures of speech referring to economic matters."[26] But the plays are silent on the questions that many radical — or even middlebrow but practical — women were forced to ask about their roles in both the home and the workforce. Odets's 1935 plays fit into a classical Hollywood style then emerging. This style devalued housework as labor and often portrayed it as undermining a good home life, while also using images of it to evoke emotional or symbolic meanings.[27]

The connection with Hollywood is neither speculative nor original. A pamphlet on theatre censorship published in 1935 by the New Theatre League, a national organization of left-wing amateur theatres, stated, "[A]s the film themes are restricted, the taboos of Hollywood become the taboos of Broadway."[28] The advent of talkies led studios to look to the stage for source material. Between 1930 and 1933 the Warner Brothers story department acquired a third of its material from plays and spent close to two-thirds of its acquisition budget on those properties.[29] Although stage plays could be riskier and more ideologically direct than films because of their more limited, specialized audiences, playwrights recognized economic opportunities if their scripts were sold to Hollywood but also realized that theatre censors outside New York might censor their plays to appeal to local tastes. Some pushed the envelope, but they couldn't hope to survive wholly outside it. (*Lefty* was blocked by censors in Boston and New Haven.) Despite Odets's cavalier assertions to not "give a damn what the commercial producer does" and his self-identification as a playwright interested in people who "can't afford to pay $3.30 for a seat," the top Broadway price of the day, he reached precisely those people who could afford it — among others — and was called by one critic "that passionate pink playwright whose youthful works are, not unjustly, the latest rave of white collar Broadway."[30]

Waiting for Lefty was first performed in January 1935 at a benefit for *New Theatre* magazine, house organ of the New Theatre League. Odets had won a playwriting contest sponsored by the magazine. *Lefty* opened on Broadway on March 26, and by May it had played in a dozen other cities from Boston to Hollywood, with productions scheduled in thirty more. The play is set on a bare stage and depicts a union meeting of taxi drivers who want to strike for better pay. The union leader, backed by a gunman, discourages them, and they wait for the arrival of their elected chairman, Lefty Costello, to persuade the union boss that the strike is the right thing. One by one, they tell their individual stories, prompted by the boss's telling them that they "got hot suppers to go to" and one character's furious challenge to "this crap about goin' home to hot suppers? I'm asking to your faces how many's got hot suppers to go home to? Anyone who's sure of his next meal, raise your hand" (6, 7). The hot suppers were to have been cooked by blue-collar wives who might well have been working the proverbial double shift. We then meet one of those wives.

Dozens of reviews differed in their identification of genre, their attitude toward the play's politics and its dramaturgy, and their choice of which scenes to describe, but virtually all mentioned the power of the encounter between Edna and Joe (who had challenged the boss) in the second scene—the first to put a human face on a political idea. Edna, arguably the most memorable character, greets Joe in an empty room, as their furniture has been repossessed. When he pleads that their plight is just "conditions," she retorts, "Tell it to the A&P!" (8). She accuses the boss of putting their kids at risk for rickets because he doesn't pay enough for them to buy nourishing food. She has read in the newspaper that orange juice is good for kids but points out that their kids, who don't get any orange juice, have repeated colds. (Both vitamin C and "protective foods" were popularized by advertisers, home economists, and schools.[31]) Edna has put the two children to bed early so they won't realize they are missing a meal, but a can of salmon has been tucked away for an emergency. Edna is a skillfully limned sketch of Christine Frederick's Mrs. Consumer with a powerful belief in her function but no means to fulfill it. Beginning in the 1920s, housewives were no longer expected to produce their own goods or to possess the skills to do so. They were, as the Depression settled in, expected to care for their families via careful shopping, nutritional food preparation, and full-time emotional support.

Information about vitamins and the healthfulness of canned foods was readily available. A combination of food-processing industries' aggressive marketing, grocery chains' incursions into working-class neighborhoods, and alliances among home economists and food producers made Americans' ways of eating and their concerns about nutrition more homogeneous in the 1930s.[32] The A&P grocery chain used radio to disseminate advice on how to use processed foods in menu planning.[33] Although in her current financial circumstances Edna would not have been able to afford the ten cents per issue that the monthly *Ladies' Home Journal* cost, she might, before the Depression, have read its editorials about the importance of vitamins and learned from its Del Monte and Libby's ads about the nutritional value, versatility, and attractiveness of canned foods.[34] She would also have learned about the importance of sweet breath, soft hands, and eliminating body odor if she wanted to maintain any social status: in 1931 *Ladies' Home Journal* carried more advertisements for cosmetics than for food. Grooming was big business; beauty parlors had gone from being rarities at the turn of the century to being ordinary stops for middle-class women by the mid-1920s, with one industry estimate that 80 percent of American women in 1930 were "investing in good looks."[35] Edna cannot afford such investments, but ultimately she plays on appeal to men as her trump card.

If Edna were truly the communist supporter that Odets's most dismissive (and some of his most supportive) critics thought his most outspoken characters to be, she might have read *Working Woman*, published monthly by the Central Committee of the American Communist Party, and costing only five cents. *Working Woman* published the Joe and Edna scene in July 1935, suggesting that the magazine supported Edna's insistence that Joe back the strike.[36] Support for this stance appeared elsewhere in the magazine. That Edna uses the threat of returning to a wealthy boyfriend she dated before her marriage to motivate Joe is overlooked.

An intertextual reading of *Waiting for Lefty* and *Working Woman* brings into focus precisely the problem that Odets ignored and that even the communist women's monthly could not reconcile. *Working Woman*'s advice to housewives rarely exceeded urging support of strikes or legislation to help their underpaid or unemployed sisters or husbands. The January 1934 issue of the magazine promoted International Woman's Day, dedicated to freeing women from the chains of "class and domestic oppression" and urging working women to join hands lest Fascists around the world "follow Hitler's German effort to force women back into the slavery of 'kitchen, church and children.'"[37] Yet Edna seems content with this arrangement, so long as her husband's paycheck is adequate. *Working Woman* spoke out against the facts that working women were paid less than men and that working women were never supported by New Deal programs the way men were. The magazine also derided *Ladies' Home Journal* and romance magazines for portraying a bourgeois world of spoiled women worried primarily about physical attractiveness and home decorating.[38] But the housewife qua housewife was not challenged to earn money, to get her husband to see the worth of her domestic labor, or to do anything truly communal beyond sharing food with other wives of striking husbands.

The bare stage on which *Lefty*'s scenes are played allows viewers to imagine Joe and Edna's home. Since the play is based on an actual 1934 New York City taxi-drivers' strike and since Joe talks about going "down" to the meeting on 174th Street, the couple likely lives in an apartment in the Bronx, although viewers in other cities could easily imagine local referents. The actual house is less important than the ideal it represents. Edna taunts Joe with his pre-marriage promise of "a cottage by the waterfall" (9).

Dolores Hayden, a scholar of housing patterns, architecture, and urban space, notes that the "dream house is a uniquely American form. For the first time in history, a civilization has created a utopian ideal based on the house rather than the city or the nation."[39] Three models of housing emerged in industrial societies in the last third of the nineteenth century. The "haven strategy" produced individual, detached dwellings (notably suburban houses), each treated as "a primitive, sacred hut." The industrial strategy yielded mass housing devised to be "an efficient machine for collective consumption." The "neighborhood strategy" yielded multifamily housing with a "concern for shared commons, courtyards, arcades, and kitchens."[40] The apartment dwellers in Odets's plays may be multigenerational or take in an occasional boarder, and they may live in apartments created as "efficient machines" regarding deliveries of goods and services and removal of waste, but the ideal to which the young aspire is clearly the sacred hut.

Decades of theories and experiments with cooperative housekeeping had been touted by feminists from Charlotte Perkins Gilman and Melusina Fay Peirce, who thought that all cooking and laundering should be done centrally so that wives would not be enslaved to repetitive tasks more efficiently handled en masse, to Ellen Swallow Richards and her followers, who started public kitchens to provide low-cost, nutritious meals to working women at minimal cost.[41] Even in good times, such as the 1920s, these ideas had not been widely embraced, perhaps because of the threat they posed to manufacturers of household appliances and certainly because of their challenge to the gender status quo. The Depression quashed public sympathy for examining gender inequality "at a time when the family would, it was hoped, fulfill its emotional function as a 'safe port in the storm' when safe ports were in short supply, would perform its social function as the bedrock of social order when order seemed to be dissipating."[42]

Waiting for Lefty is mute on the possibility of a new domestic deal even as it screams for better treatment of labor. Those who cannot imagine a way to have a sacred hut supported by a male breadwinner do not marry. This is spelled out poignantly in the second scene featuring a partially working-class couple. Here, salesgirl (this was considered white-collar work) Florence is ordered by her older brother to break up with her fiancé, Irv, a cabdriver to whom she has been engaged for three years. The brother acknowledges that the problem is not Irv personally; "it's that he ain't got nothing" (17).

Florence is a compendium of a working woman in the Depression. She earns nine dollars a week at a full-time job and is also responsible for cooking supper, caring for her invalid mother, and ironing her brother's shirts. Although the brother works, too, lives in the home, and is unmarried, he imagines having to support two families if Florence and Irv marry, neither wondering who will do the housework if she leaves (i.e., if she and Irv do manage on their own) nor imagining that three could pool more resources than two, especially after the mother's imminent death. When Florence says she wants "everything in life I can get," the list comprises "romance, love, babies" (18). Irv bitterly notes that the "cards is stacked for all of us," with "the money man dealing himself a hot royal flush. Then giving you and me a phony hand like a pair of tens or something. . . . Then he says, what's the matter you can't win—no stuff on the ball" (21). Irv recognizes that the system and not the individual is responsible for economic failures. His family has sacrificed so a younger brother could attend college, but upon graduation that brother joined the navy. Odets's lack of interest (or faith) in a college degree keeps the focus on labor's dilemma, but within this sphere, women imagine a better world in terms of being outside labor, or rather, within domestic labor, unrecognized as actual labor.

Neither popular culture nor the government helped inspire any other view of a better world for women. Professional women suffered the greatest loss of employment during the Depression. Female teachers, for example — already working for less than their male counterparts — were dismissed if they married. Federal legislation between 1932 and 1937 prohibited more than one member of the same family from working in federal civil service. While the idea behind the legislation was to avoid nepotism, the effect was to remove working wives from the labor pool. The National Industrial Recovery Act of 1933 (whose laws were upheld by the later National Recovery Administration [NRA]) legislated discriminatory wage differentials for women. The act's purpose was to improve standards of labor, reduce and relieve unemployment, and increase purchasing power, but when Roosevelt signed the act, his official statement listed the "assurance of a reasonable profit to industry" ahead of "living wages for labor."[43] The discriminatory wage differentials passed despite protests by Eleanor Roosevelt and Secretary of Labor Frances Perkins, and with the admission on the part of the NRA's assistant counsel that "there were no logical grounds for the policies other than custom."[44] (*Working Woman* lambasted Perkins and both Roosevelts for offering too little too late with too much humiliation attached for blue-collar and unemployed women needing immediate relief.)

While it was understandable for people to resent families with two wage earners at a time when many had no wage earner, most women were not taking jobs away from men, as women were concentrated in fields where few men were employed.[45] Blue- and white-collar fields alike had jobs for women only, including stenography and typing in the "clean work" category and candymaking and shoemaking in the more routinized and dirty category. Florence, the salesgirl in *Waiting for Lefty*, was employed in a sector that was largely willing to retain married female employees.[46]

Still, Odets chose the conservative domestic view in depicting her goals and ideals. Sales employees were not covered by the codes devised in the first two years of the NRA,[47] something that a hard-line communist or feminist working within the system might have protested. But rather than object to her own unprotected wage status or take advantage of the fact that marriage would not automatically end her job, Florence and Irv anticipate the findings of a 1936 Gallup poll that asked whether wives should work if their husbands were employed also. When 82 percent said no, Gallup reported that he had "discovered an issue on which voters are about as solidly united as on any subject imaginable—including sin and hay fever."[48]

The public also seemed solidly united in its favorable response to Odets's plays, if not necessarily on his politics. The terms "leftist," "radical," "revolutionary," "Marxist," and "propaganda" appear in reviews of the many 1935 productions of *Lefty* and the Broadway production of *Awake and Sing*, but the critics dwelt most on the emotional punch, sympathy, and realism of Odets's characters and situations. Burns Mantle wrote of the Broadway opening of *Lefty* that it was "vibrating with a realism that is perfect," noting that during the Joe and Edna scene "a woman arose in her place and shouted shrilly: 'That's life; that's life!' Nor would she stop until they had carried her to the exits."[49] The book reviewer for *New Masses* wrote of *Awake and Sing*, "[T]he background and the details of character are unsparingly real."[50]

The *Cincinnati Post*'s review of the New York production called *Awake and Sing* "a startlingly accurate lifesize painting of a lower middle-class Jewish family."[51] A Springfield, Massachusetts, reviewer of the published text of both plays asserted that Odets's concern was "showing these people as they are."[52] A reviewer for the Chicago Group Theatre production of *Lefty* focused on mainstream audience appeal: "I am judging this play by the rules of the theater which I have used for years. As such, it is a masterpiece. The playwright has a story and he tells it in the right way to get the greatest emotional results."[53]

Odets had found a way to reach working-class audiences within their price range. (One review called *Lefty* the "talk of the town below the Macy-Gimbel line," and the double bill of *Lefty* and the anti-Nazi *Till the Day I Die* opened on Broadway with a special price scale of $0.40 to $1.50.[54]) Odets also titillated, engaged, and drew in middle-brow and black-tie theatregoers, the latter depicted in a New York *Herald Tribune* cartoon that showed *Lefty*'s strikers bursting from the stage and emerging from the audience (the play made use of audience plants), while spectators in evening dress fixed makeup, peered through lorgnettes, and cocked quizzical eyebrows from the front rows.[55] Had

Gallup polled theatregoers, Odets might well have achieved an 82 percent consensus on the believability and stageworthiness of his plays.

Like *Lefty*, Odets's *Awake and Sing* portrays the "Depression poor," as the Berger family are struggling but middle class.[56] A 1934 *Ladies' Home Journal* article, "Make the Diet Fit the Pocketbook," shows that the Bergers fall easily within the range of "adequate diet at a moderate cost" and probably can afford the "liberal diet," defined as "the way a sensible family would eat if they didn't have to count pennies and wanted to achieve decidedly better-than-average nutrition."[57] When the fiftyish father, Myron, ominously sees canned tuna as a source of gastrointestinal woes, he marks himself as out of touch with the foods of his era and makes it clear that he prefers and expects home-cooked food provided by the woman of the house.

That woman is Bessie Berger, originally played by Stella Adler and easy enough to read as the stereotypical Jewish Mother. Bessie insists on a spotless house with the window shade at the proper height for a "respectable" appearance, no matter that a family member has raised the shade because he needs more light to see. And since the apartment looks out on an airshaft, the respectability has nothing to do with passersby but is something Bessie seeks to produce within the domestic sphere. She is proud that her children were always the cleanest in the neighborhood and reminds her son that, despite his never having had the shoes or skates or birthday parties he longed for, a twenty-five-dollar-a-visit specialist was brought in when he was sick.

One critic described the character as "Mom Bergner [*sic*], who schemes to wed an indiscreet daughter to a sap who will next year be told he is not the father of her child; who drives her own parent to suicide; who tries to trick her son out of the old man's insurance and makes it impossible for him to marry the girl he loves."[58] Bessie fawns over her wealthy brother, and she derides her father and husband for being, respectively, unable to hold a job because of radical outspokenness and a poor provider who never completed law school. Odets presents this character as a blocking agent and a representative of everything stultifying about overbearing family life. "Marx said it—abolish such families," says Jacob, the grandfather (55). But the only answer Odets offers as a replacement for Bessie's domestic dominance is money—the very thing his young hero says should not define human worth.

Publicity photographs from the original production reveal the kitchen sink realisms that shore up the heroism of Ralph, the son, and Jacob, while dismissing and punishing Bessie and Sam, the hapless son-in-law. The box set of the original production—visible in many of the stills—underscored a particular attitude toward the Berger household's domesticity. On one side of the apartment are Ralph's daybed, the door to Jacob's bedroom, and a stack of books on the table. On the other side are the dining room table and doors leading to the kitchen and other bedrooms. While the kitchen door might open to show part of a working kitchen, the text does not call for this. Conversely, the door to Jacob's bedroom opens to reveal a picture of Sacco and Vanzetti. The world of the apartment is, like the world of the play's ideas, split in two, with idealism stage right along with the only visible windows; "messy kitchen realism" lives stage left.

A singularly telling photograph shows Stella Adler as Bessie cleaning the leaves of a plant, a bit of business stipulated in the script. House-proud Bessie sports a flowered apron, high heels, marcelled hair, and a strand of pearls as she tends to the plant. It is hard to look at the image today without being reminded of another matriarch who takes pride in a potted plant. As *A Raisin in the Sun*'s Lena Younger would say a quarter of a century later, "[T]his plant expresses me." Lena, like Bessie, is trying to do the best she can for a minority family facing an unwanted pregnancy and in disagreement about how best to use a life insurance payment. But unlike Lena, Bessie is neither seen as a nurturer nor as wise. Her refusal to allow Ralph to bring his girlfriend home and her wish that he would ride "up to the door in a big car with a chauffeur and a radio" (66) are presented as cruel and grasping. Yet the characters who facilitate the flight that both her children dream of are those with money. The pregnant Hennie marries unsexy immigrant Sam but runs off with bookmaker Moe Axelrod, who appeals to her weakness for perfume, French soap, lizard-skin shoes, champagne, and the possibility of a cruise to Havana. He can do so because he has a government pension as a result of the leg he lost in World War I. Son Ralph is rescued by the insurance check (although he says that he will give it to his mother) that arrives as a culmination of events that enables him to see his future more clearly.

The photograph with the plant hints at why Bessie, her husband, and her daughter yearn for riches and the power they imagine go with

Stella Adler as Bessie Berger in *Awake and Sing*, 1935. Photo by Vandamm Studio, © Billy Rose Theatre Division, The New York Public Library for the Performing Arts, Astor, Lenox, and Tilden Foundations.

them. On the bottom shelf of the table on which the plant sits is a magazine called the *Romances*. Popular culture in the form of pulp magazines and movies is part of this family's world, and if plays were being written with Hollywood in mind, Hollywood was infiltrating the lives of characters in plays. *Working Woman* called this bourgeois poison, but it was also the only escape into glamour—however vicarious—many people could afford. Even realistic escape routes such as better jobs or formal education required that applicants dress for success and satisfy cultural norms. To know about these required a familiarity with mainstream tastes and fashions, something available in magazines and movies.

Bessie's labor is at best offensive and officious in her family's eyes. Most of the time it is invisible. Bessie is a monster not because she fails to feed her family, mend their clothes, or keep the house and its inhabitants clean. If anything, she is too good at these things. Her wealthy brother, Morty, tells her, "You keep the house like a pin and I like your cooking. Any time Myron fires you, come to me, Bessie" (63). But in a world where household goods, services, and creature comforts can be purchased—Hennie eats both canned tuna and chop suey in restaurants with her friends; Uncle Morty is unmarried, has a Japanese butler, goes to the Turkish bath, and sleeps with showroom models—Bessie is a villain because she fails to provide for her family's *emotional* needs: the thing that cannot be purchased. The "wise" (and socialist) grandfather warns Ralph not to rush into marriage, saying, "Remember, a woman insults a man's soul like no other thing in the whole world" (48). The two characters who appreciate Bessie's cooking do not live with her: her brother and her nebbishy son-in-law. Domestic chores are never handled by any of the sympathetic characters in the play. Even Hennie leaves boiling the nipples for the baby's bottle and some of the dirty-diaper washing to Sam—a rare instance of a man working a double shift but not an unusual example of such a character being coded as weak and sexually unappealing for his potentially feminist and certainly communitarian pains.

Odets would not have pushed the full range of emotional buttons had he not given Bessie a moment to reveal her own private pain. Late in the play she tells Ralph that she worked in a stocking factory for six dollars a week for two years while her husband went to law school. He never finished, and now she knows she is both mother and father in the family. "If I didn't worry about the family, who would? . . . [H]ere, without a dollar you don't look the world in the eye" (95). Ellen Schiff sees in her "a fully dimensional human being" who represented "countless first-generation American Jewish women who, by instinct or from Old World experience, understood 'when one lives in the jungle one must look out for the wild life.'"[59] Ashton Stevens astutely saw all the characters, Bessie included, as trapped by the true villain of the play: money. "Not . . . Capital . . . but just by money, the meager stuff we work for and swap for bread and books and theater tickets."[60] Yet it is precisely the place of women in consumer capitalism that troubles any possibility of happily ever after. The critic for *New Masses* complained that by play's end Ralph doesn't really grow up, Hennie ignores her problems, and while "the details of character are unsparingly real . . . the development is blurred. The solution is sex-mysticism."[61]

Sex mysticism—the stuff of the *Romances*—is the sort of solution a true leftist would refuse to the larger social problems plaguing Odets's beleaguered Americans. *Working Woman* named the problem in a small item about hotel kitchen workers under the thumb of a female boss out to please the guests while letting the staff have whatever may remain as a result of "bad judgment." "We knew it. We've eaten that kind of leftover, too, until we got our sister food workers to strike against the game. You don't have to eat two-day-old hash and wilted salads, girls."[62] Meanwhile, in Odets's play, Bessie, Edna, Florence, and even Hennie remain stuck in a domestic economy over which they have little control—stuck waiting for leftovers.

MAKING A WORLD

In the second half of the 1930s, plays about the fascist threat in Europe shared the American stage with the dramas produced by the Federal Theatre Project about domestic deprivation. After World War II began in Europe in 1939, more plays started to address the possibility and the moral imperative of US involvement. A domestic ideal was proffered both as the reason for fighting the war and as the culmination of women's biological urges.[63] In theatre as in film, "[C]ulture industry narratives and commodity discourses . . . obfuscate[d] the actual labor involved in housekeeping and subsume[d] it within the emotional roles demanded of mothers and wives—roles determined by familiar relations and expressive ties."[64] A major exception to the practice of referring to but not actually depicting onstage domestic labor *as* labor appeared in 1939, overlapping with the earliest Broadway plays to address this specific war. Sidney Kingsley's *The World We Make* is worth discussing because it tried to reinforce conservative, comforting norms while telling a story "about" mental illness.

The World We Make presents a young heroine, post–nervous breakdown, on the lam. She finds inner peace via cooking, cleaning, befriending the neighbors, and nurturing a man. It disappointed some reviewers who recalled the playwright's *Dead End* (1935) and *Men in White* (the Pulitzer winner for 1934). Like Kingsley's earlier plays, *The World We Make* featured meticulously researched settings rendered in detail, including a tenement apartment where the wealthy runaway achieves fulfillment. A number of reviewers wagged their fingers at what they read as a latter-day Belascoism.[65]

The print discussion about *The World We Make* touched on virtually every theoretical and audience reception question raised in this book, ranging from the relation between reality and realism, to the fact that it is not just a script but the entire built and performed realm of production that creates audience response, to the way that different segments of an audience read the real through differing lenses. However, no one seemed troubled by the idea that a wealthy, protected, sensitive young woman could regain mental health and find purpose in life through housework. *The World We Make* looks, in retrospect, tailor-made to address Jennifer Fleissner's assertions that the repetitive performance of domestic tasks in naturalist works serves as a creative attempt at wholeness on the only terms available to the compulsive (woman) in a culture that denies her other outlets.[66]

This particular creative attempt of 1939 is a thematic and stylistic linchpin between two categories of plays. In the 1920s and 1930s labor concerns and multifamily dwellings typified many plays focused on blue-collar workers or the aspiring middle class. The end of the 1930s saw the start of the drive to situate stage wives in ever-earlier marriages in private homes or in apartments where the neighbors are either strangers or irrelevant. *The World We Make* was a last hurrah for one and a foreshadowing of the other, but it stands out from either category by daring to stage domestic labor as *both* labor *and* domestic haven and to do so at a very leisurely pace.

The World We Make tells the story of twenty-something Virginia

McKay, who escapes from a psychiatric hospital, where she has been confined because of her inability to function after the death of her brother in a car crash, for which she blames her cold, distant, wealthy parents. The hospital is the setting for the play's prologue, and the adjustment of the mentally troubled was the theme of *World*'s source, Millen Brand's novel *The Outward Room*. In the first scene proper, Virginia, now calling herself Harriet Hope, applies for work in a steam laundry after three days without food or shelter.[67] After a grueling first day on the job, she goes home with a sympathetic supervisor, and his tenement apartment is the setting for the remainder of the play. There Harriet learns to make spaghetti and soup, bathe in a tub that requires an hour to heat enough water to fill it, share space with cockroaches, and scrub floors. When the supervisor's activist brother dies, she realizes that she can comfort and support her man as he did her and that her future is at his side.

Every daily paper reviewing the play talked about its realism, but the use to which realism was to be put—as well as the ways it was understood—differed among respondents. For an anonymous writer for the *New York Times*, the play "as realism . . . is brilliant, but it throws out of scale a deeply moving study of individual character in search of the normal world."[68] Here the play itself was "real," but its characters somehow were not. John Mason Brown found the laundry "so realistic that . . . it is remarkable only because it is NOT real." He also observed the details of the tenement but complained that "though the dirty linen is dirty in their laundry and the soup steams when it is taken off the stove in their kitchen, my fear is that their genuine contribution (no mater [*sic*] how skillful it may be in its painstaking way) ends just about here."[69] The setting was credible here, but the play as text and performance was uninteresting. Brown also complained about Kingsley's "over-scrupulous naturalism" and "literal" dialogue.

Richard Watts, on the other hand, noted "realistic details of the narrative managed with admirable credibility";[70] Richard Lockridge called Margo's performance as Harriet "completely touching and real";[71] while Sidney Whipple noted but was unmoved by the show's "horrible reality," especially the "sad or revolting realism" in "a cold water flat that seems to have been overlooked by the Sanitation Department."[72] One critic found the credible acting touching, while another found credibility unmoving, despite also saying the play "boils over with authentic characters." *Time* magazine's reviewer, conversely, dismissed the characters as "sure-fire tenement types."[73] Authenticity differs from credibility; good acting is not a substitute for a textual character study; the line between credibility and "sensationalism" (a word used by Brooks Atkinson, who championed the play and the production) is not clear. In short, the reviews were mixed but also mixed up about what comprised realism and what its goals should be.

Responses appearing after the opening revealed how people in show business and "civilians" read realism differently. Owners of small laundries supposedly wrote to Kingsley, "telling him that the scene is true to no laundry that ever existed on land or sea," largely because it combined multiple functions (washing, wringing, sewing) in Harry Horner's single-room setting.[74] Several reviews did not mention the designer at all, attributing every element of the production's realism to the playwright, although it is true that Kingsley served as director and much about the setting is stipulated in the text. The City-Wide Tenants Council sent a letter that reached at least one drama critic, claiming that the tenement flat setting was "far more palatial, more liveable, and spacious than a real one. . . . To have implied that real tenement flats are as attractive . . . is to delude your readers."[75] *Time*'s reviewer put quotation marks around the "realism" often attributed to Kingsley, saying his plays were best described as "picturesque," since he "exploits realism without achieving reality."[76] That reviewer said the psychiatrist's handling of his patients would "make a real psychiatrist raise his eyebrows." Arthur Pollock complained that Kingsley's skill lay in "reproduc[ing]" for the eye," but "the moment his scenery ceases to act for him 'The World We Make' loses headway."[77]

Kingsley himself answered "no" to the question "Is 'The World We Make' realistic?" Calling it "highly stylized," he pointed out that the walls of the tenement were cut away to reveal action in several locations simultaneously. He also noted features of the production that were misremembered by critics, including the opening of a can of tomato paste and using real soap to scrub a floor. The tomato paste never really appeared; it was part of a recipe given verbally, and the soap was "actually a bar of painted wood."[78] Bernard Simon provided the smartest answer to questions in this debate: "Sidney Kingsley does not attempt to be true to life, but only true to the theater," meaning he should offer not "a reproduction of actual life . . . but an exaggeration of real life, an intensification," since "[w]hat the audience really pays its money for is not to see what they can see every day."[79]

Part of what Pollock subsumed under visual accuracy—and which he clearly labeled inferior to "reality with words"—was the crucial scene in which Harriet realized she might "make" a world with a place for herself in it. It was a scene written by Kingsley but one that involves domestic labor in lieu of speech. Three reviewers mentioned it (Watts calling it the best scene in the play), and it is remarkable not just for its detail but for the amount of stage time it gives to domestic labor performed (silently and not as a backdrop to dialogue) by an upper-class heroine. It takes place about a third of the way into the play, immediately following the first night Virginia/Harriet has spent with John at the tenement. He has let her sleep late and departed for work, leaving her a meager breakfast and a note:

HARRIET awakes with a start, looks wildly about her, realizes where she is, springs out of bed, dresses quickly in terror, is about to rush out, sees the note, stops, reads it, uncovers the breakfast, looks at the clock, realizes it is too late for work, sinks into a chair, confused, reads the note again. She calms down, tastes the orange, begins to eat, her self-assurance returning. She pours some coffee, finishes breakfast, sighs, starts to go, looks back at the dirty dishes, returns, takes them into the kitchen and washes them. She starts to replace them on the shelf, but the shelf is so begrimed that it dirties her hand. The filth disgusts her and for a moment she stands there regarding it with revulsion. That feeling passes. She finds a rag and cleans the shelf. Then she stands by the window looking out. She catches glimpses of women at work in their houses. A WOMAN across the alley is shaking bedclothes out of the window, beating them with a cane beater. HARRIET slowly walks into the next room. She slaps the pillow on the bed. Clouds of dust come up. She tears off the bed-clothing, throws it over the windowsill to air. She pauses to catch her breath. She returns to the next room, puts on her coat, slowly leaves the room, shutting the door behind her. In the hallway she pauses, the opposite apartment door is open. She sees MRS. ZUBRISKI on hands and knees scrubbing the floor, watches her fascinated, then starts down the stairs, pauses, returns, re-enters John's apartment.

She touches the floor. It is filthy. She takes off her coat, searches about—finds a pail and a scrubbing brush, puts some water up to boil, finds a broom, rolls up her sleeves, sweeps out the rooms, then pours hot water into the pail, mixes it with cold, gets down on hands and knees, begins to scrub the floor—slowly and clumsily at first, gradually quickening as she learns to put her body behind it. In the tenement windows we catch glimpses of others busy with household activity; a broad general rhythm prevails. The sun has risen above the tenements and pours in thru the window bathing her in a bright flood. For the first time she relaxes and is happy as she scrubs and slowly finds the rhythm. . . . She has become a part of the life around her.[80]

There is no indication of how much playing time was occupied by this scene. Merely reading the description aloud would take about three and a half minutes. The amount of time required to indicate each task (completing them in full would take longer than the whole play) could easily make the scene as long as eight minutes. Eating, washing dishes, stripping the bed, leaving, coming back, locating cleaning tools and products, sweeping, preparing hot water, lathering up a bar of soap, and then scrubbing long enough for the task to become rhythmic and have a somatic effect needed to be shorthanded sufficiently to keep the play moving (an exaggeration of real life, an intensification) yet extended enough to create the *feeling* of "admirable credibility," all the while managing to convey characterological growth via domestic labor.

No one, of course, asked in print how a girl from a very wealthy family knew where to find rags and a bucket and how to use them. (What specific experience or training does it take to know that cold water is not as good as hot for scrubbing floors? What disconnect does it take to write a scene in which the houseworker heats the water for washing the floor but not for washing the dishes?) Neither did anyone point out that it did not strain credulity for a male playwright né Kirshner in 1906 in an unfashionable Manhattan neighborhood to be well versed in how housework gets done. Labor agitation would be a struggle in the play, but settling into shared domesticity was the prize that made the struggle worth it.

Even Eleanor Roosevelt is supposed to have found the play "mov-

Herbert Rudley and Margo in *The World We Make*, 1939. Photo by George Karger. Permission of Charles Starke and the Billy Rose Theatre Division, New York Public Library for the Performing Arts, Astor, Lenox, and Tilden Foundations.

ing," noting "that it held a feeling of hope and was something to take home and remember."[81] One can imagine the split sensibility with which she registered this response. Mrs. Roosevelt had opposed the gendered wage differentials enacted in the 1933 National Industrial Recovery Act; at the same time, she could not have been unaware that most people still saw women's place to be in the home. She managed **107** to be a multifaceted feminist, championing the needs of employed women and recognizing the need to accommodate and support hard-working housewives.[82] She was certainly aware that the girls' equivalent of Civilian Conservation Corps camps offered only domestic training. And she could not have been unaware that domestic labor was not covered by the Social Security Act.[83] The best social security for a domestic worker was marriage to a man with a wage or salary. Congratulating Margo backstage on finding meaning in housework with the clear promise of marriage may have been the best way to walk a fine line. After all, the actress's skilled labor was not in question.

Within a year, star actress Lynn Fontanne would appear in Robert Sherwood's *There Shall Be No Night* as a witty, glamorous, educated woman who could master both carrying out domestic labor and wielding a rifle, if that's what it took to make the world safe for democracy. The decade of domestic labor as valuable in and of itself was about to segue into a period of housework as war work, at least on Broadway.

DOMESTIC LABOR IN BLACK AND WHITE

In 1938 Langston Hughes penned *Limitations of Life*, a two-page play that was one of a handful of his satirical skits presented at his Suitcase Theatre, an amateur company in Harlem whose audiences were 75 percent black.[84] The theatre was intended to create a low-tech, socially conscious stage that would present plays for labor organizations.[85] The International Workers Order, which was linked to the Communist Party, initially provided space on the second floor of its community center on 125th Street.[86] *Limitations of Life* was Hughes's scathing response to the 1934 film *Imitation of Life*, based on the novel of the same name by Fannie Hurst. Directed by John M. Stahl, with a script by Hurst, the movie starred Claudette Colbert as a young white widow trying to support her toddler and Louise Beavers as the black woman who shows up one day looking for work with her own toddler in tow. The two women become a team parted only by death after about sixteen years of living under the same roof.

Beavers, universally praised for her sympathetic portrayal in the film of a mammy character grappling with a mulatto daughter whose overarching desire is to pass as white, spent most of her career playing maids and keeping herself fat enough to continue getting these stereotyped parts.[87] The movie deeply divided African Americans.[88] On the one hand, Beavers's character, Delilah, who enables Colbert's character to earn a fortune marketing Delilah's pancake recipe, thrilled blacks who applauded the arrival of a three-dimensional black female character with a story, a private life, familial tribulations, and a crucial role to play in the rise of a successful business. On the other hand, Beavers's heft, jovial appearance flipping pancakes in a big apron and cook's hat, and the character's naiveté to the point of fearing that the offer of a house for herself and her daughter means that her employer/longtime companion is kicking her out, struck many as somewhere on the spectrum from risible to insulting.

Hughes fell solidly in the latter group.[89] No viewer, white or black, liberal or conservative, could have missed the pancake-flipping Delilah's invocation of Aunt Jemima, a figure Kimberley Wallace-Sanders calls the "mammy within the national household," whose "unifying nostalgia for slaveocracy" contributed to the resolutely white, "budding concept of an American Dream for the American family."[90] Hughes took the notion of an American Dream dependent on the mammy and, essentially, presented its photographic negative. Everything black in the movie became white in his skit. The notion of a photograph is born out both by the brevity of the piece and by its setting: "Harlem . . . Right now."

In the "luxurious living room" with opulent furniture, there are also a stove, griddle, pancake turner, and a "box of pancake flour (only Aunt Jemima's picture is white)." The three characters, whose names are puns on those of two actors and one character from the film, are Mammy Weavers, Audette Aubert, and Ed Starks (the male figurehead whose name in the movie is Ned Sparks). Mammy Weavers speaks elevated British English and returns from the opera. Audette rubs her mistress's feet, tells of her (Audette's) pale daughter's endlessly sitting in the sun in the hope of becoming tanned enough to pass for black, and refuses a day off, claiming she wouldn't know what to do with it.

The stark reversal of stage realisms and the everyday in this short piece intertwine race and domestic labor in ways that divided most white playgoers from most of their black counterparts. Broadway plays of the 1930s featured black maids—sometimes clever and enterprising ones whose strategies facilitate plot outcomes—but these maids were not depicted in their own homes, and their own needs and families never mattered to the main action.[91] By reversing the roles racially,

Hughes was not suggesting that depicting black women as domestics was untrue to real life. Indeed, 90 percent of African American women who worked in the 1930s were either domestics or agricultural workers and, since the setting is "Harlem . . . Right now," it is clear that he was representing a familiar work setup for his urban audience.[92] The everyday for African American domestics, who earned six to ten dollars weekly and might work twelve to fourteen hours a day, possibly every day, might also have included standing outside on a corner in the Bronx known as the "slave market," with the hope that a well-off white woman would drive by and offer short-term employment and lunch.[93]

Rather, Hughes was suggesting that depicting undying devotion to the white family and an absence of any desires beyond servitude was an ideological lie masked by an economic reality. Mainstream advertising, fiction, and films portrayed a world devised by (white) men on Madison Avenue and in Hollywood—one still in the thrall of a fantasy of the South as the land of "moonlight and magnolias."[94] As Wallace-Sanders argues, "Aunt Jemima's popularity directly relates to the belief that slavery cultivated innate qualities in African Americans," including "the notion that African Americans were natural servants."[95]

White audiences were less pleased by *Limitations of Life* than were blacks.[96] The skit darkened them in a way that—even as liberals—they read as unflattering. Here, for blacks and their sympathizers, was Brian Richardson's idea of realism "not as a mirror, and not as a delusion, but as a synecdoche, a model that attempts to reconstruct in an abbreviated but not inaccurate manner the world that we inhabit."[97] Resistant whites in the audience could object to "the politics of the stage," which, in Jeffrey Richards's words, "almost always co-opts and controls the presentation of the political concerns of daily life,"[98] in this case, of course, their *own* daily life, even as those in Hughes's camp could, in turn, read the entire resistant cry is protesting such co-optation on virtually every other stage in New York.

Hughes's strategy in *Limitations of Life* is to use excess and improbability to reveal the fiction on which the presumed real-life referent (both the film and American culture) rests. Black domestics in white houses are, if one knows how to see, carrying on in living color. It is the conventions of mainstream theatre and film that reduce their real—even if drab—everydays to predictable, Manichean hues that are

limitations to the point of being falsifications.

4 WINGLESS VICTORIES
1940–1947

Even before the December 1941 attack on Pearl Harbor, but especially after the United States entered the war, plays appeared depicting aspects of military training, deployment, and the aftermath — psychological and physical — of fighting overseas.[1] Domesticity played a huge role in many of these plays up through the start of the Cold War in 1947. But discussions of domestic labor as dramatic fodder virtually evaporated along with the recognition — which had been present in some Depression-focused plays — that domestic labor is hard, often thankless work. Rather, this work was valuable as a means or a reference to patriotism, an equation not unique to drama in this era.

For instance, the director of the *Detroit News* test kitchen told participants in a 1942 Detroit homemakers' conference that maintaining a clean house "was a patriotic duty because clean fabrics and equipment lasted longer, contributing to the conservation of materials needed for war production." The *Seattle Times* asserted, "Women fight the war with stewpans, knitting needles, alarm clocks that go off at 4 o'clock in the morning, rudely awakened babies, [and] unelastic budgets," stating that "the kitchen and the sewing room are the housewife's battleground."[2] The ideal woman in the wartime American kitchen appeared in an American Gas Association advertisement, looking like a perkily aggressive, wide-eyed chorus girl in a short dress and beribboned pumps, strutting to victory with a pair of bayoneted rifles strapped to her back, a bandolier across her chest, automatic rifle tucked under her elbow, twirling a pistol on her left forefinger in front of a gas stove, and glowing under a headline in which she boasts, "I helped cook 'em in my kitchen." By understanding that gas was not "only a household fuel," this savvy housewife freed up a precious resource for manufacturing weapons. In return for the meals she would make minus full use

Drawing by George Withers. Used by permission of Brian Withers
and the American Gas Association.

of her stove, she was extolled as vital to the war effort. "From the heroic nurses of Bataan . . . to the women at home faced with the problem of preparing nutritious wartime meals for their families . . . we're all playing a vital part in helping to win this war."[3]

As during the 1930s, American theatre of the World War II era depicted domestic labor and domesticity as "naturally" the realm of women. While men did have domestic skills, deployment of these skills in plays spelled comedy, gave warning, reinforced boundaries, or coded dystopia. Men who donned aprons, ironed, prepared food, washed dishes, cared for children, or kept house did so either as a joke, to woo a woman, as a part of military duty, or to provide a dramatic explanation for social disruption. Husbands who contribute to housework or child care are either bound for something better (Ned's singing career in *Her Master's Voice*) or are weak and undesirable (Sam in *Awake and Sing*), regardless of family needs.

Scrubbing floors was taboo for male characters, but men did occasionally iron and cook in 1940s Broadway plays, although always within limits that reinforced gender norms. Joseph Fields and Jerome Chodorov's 1940 comedy *My Sister Eileen*, which ran for 864 performances and was adapted as the musical *Wonderful Town* in 1953, centers on the adventures of two sisters, Ruth and Eileen, who arrive in Greenwich Village from Ohio seeking success in New York. The upstairs neighbors in their low-rent, bohemian apartment building are Helen and her live-in boyfriend, nicknamed "the Wreck." When Helen's mother visits, Helen begs Ruth and Eileen to help her maintain her reputation by letting the Wreck stay in their apartment. "[H]e's awfully handy. He can clean up and he irons well," says Helen, to which the Wreck adds, "But no washing—that's woman's work."[4]

Another ironing man, this one married, prepares to press his own pants in Ruth Gordon's 1944 comedy *Over 21*. Here, the husband is in military training, making it permissible to be responsible for his own knife pleats. Gordon starred in the play as the wife of a man in his late thirties trying to pass the Officers' Candidate School exam and advance from private to second lieutenant. Gordon wanted to show Americans how complicated military training was, to praise the patriotism of her new husband, Garson Kanin, and to showcase herself in the role of a successful writer who could also iron, cook, and play hostess.

More typically, men doing housework in World War II–era plays represent dystopias, either because they are unemployed (read poor providers) or never make it to the top (read poor providers), leading their daughters to lives of promiscuity to acquire luxuries dad could not. Elsa Shelley's 1944 *Pick-Up Girl* and Garson Kanin's 1946 *Born Yesterday* offer dramatic and comic spins on fathers whose performance of housework results in wayward daughters. Men who are good providers don't do housework in 1940s plays, but their housekeeping wives are not prized for being "scientific" or even driven about running a household. In *A Streetcar Named Desire*, the housewife's work is far less important than are her choices of how to negotiate competing emotional demands. Every scene in which Stella appears stages some facet of how housewifedom requires prioritizing, and in 1940s plays the households given priority were those without extended family and with an increasing insistence on the sacred hut at all costs.

"THE HOPE OF TODAY LIES IN THIS . . ."

Nowhere is the equation of domestic labor more clearly or theatrically charted as staunch patriotism than in Robert E. Sherwood's 1940 *There Shall Be No Night*, the Pulitzer Prize winner for 1941. Sherwood was a liberal strongly in favor of US support for the Allies. He spent the latter part of the 1930s reversing his previous pacifist stance, hard won as a soldier wounded in World War I.[5] *There Shall Be No Night* uses a single household to depict the effects of the Soviet invasion of Finland and equates Stalinist communism with fascism. It was coproduced by the Playwrights Company and the Theatre Guild, starring husband-and-wife team Alfred Lunt and Lynn Fontanne, he as a Nobel-winning Finnish scientist and she as his American-born wife. The Lunts were alluring stars and favorites of Sherwood and the Theatre Guild. These actors' presence meant that audiences would read the production as depicting behaviors and images that were admirable and possibly even glamorous and noble.

Miranda, the middle-aged wife, is a gracious helpmate, but when the going gets rough, her husband plans to send her back to the United States. She balks, wishing to stay and assist the resistors. Kaarlo (Lunt) puts it to her bluntly: "Are you trained for anything, but wearing lovely clothes, being a charming hostess?"[6] At the start of the play the answer is no, but when the maid and cook leave, Miranda undertakes a self-

Lynn Fontanne, Montgomery Clift, and Alfred Lunt in *There Shall Be No Night*, 1940.
Photo by Vandamm Studio, © Billy Rose Theatre Division, The New York Public Library
for the Performing Arts, Astor, Lenox, and Tilden Foundations.

directed course in domesticity. She appears in an apron, carrying a dust cloth and proclaims, "From now on all of us will have to eat my cooking. It's three o'clock in the afternoon and I just finished making the beds. They look frightful" (68). When her son announces that he is leaving for the front, she goes to the kitchen to provide him with food for his journey, unsure of what she'll find there. "I—I suppose there's some canned stuff. . . . (*She seems helpless, despairing.*)" (74). By the end of the scene, son departed, she decides that crying will do no good and declares that she is going into the kitchen. When her husband asks what for, she says, "I don't know. I have to start learning how to cook" (82). Ten pages later she has mastered coffee.

By the final scene she has prepared a fine lunch and ordered guests out of the kitchen, where she and her uncle—the only surviving members of the family, as the husband and son have died fighting for free-dom—do the dishes themselves. When she returns from the kitchen for the final five minutes of the play, she *"wears an apron, but her dress is, as always, very feminine and chic"* (170–71). Knowing the enemy is on its way, she replies to a query from a visiting American about whether she is just going to sit and wait, with a firm, "Oh, no. . . . Get out the guns, Uncle Waldemar" (173). She then explains her attack plan, complete with a description of where the ammunition is stored and demonstration of how to handle the gun. And, lest this be mis-interpreted as some kind of Finnish fanaticism, she turns to the 1812 portrait of her Yankee great-grandfather and announces that her fore-bear "thinks it's just fine" (174). Frivolity gives way to domestic labor, and domestic labor is the bedrock of American patriotism. It may have taken all morning to make the beds and weeks to master lunch, but, having accomplished these, guns are easy, and Fontanne embodied the stylish, the domestic, and the gun-toting all in one saleable package.

Stars performing physically demanding domestic labor in the first half of the 1940s were features in plays that combined primers in pre-electric appliance housekeeping with lessons on the proper way to be a wife and mother in times of financial or political stress. Audiences lined up to see the hugely popular Helen Hayes setting up her own cis-tern in the 1943 star vehicle *Harriet* and the elegant Mady Christians washing floors on her hands and knees in the 1944 *I Remember Mama*.

Harriet showcases the need for women to make a political commit-ment to fighting injustice, specifically in the context of World War II. The play, a costume drama based on the life of Harriet Beecher Stowe, ran for 114 performances on Broadway; it then enjoyed an afterlife in other venues, including high schools, until the mid-1950s. Originally directed by Elia Kazan, *Harriet* covers the years from Stowe's mar-riage in 1836 to her 1861 meeting with Abraham Lincoln. Playwright Florence Ryerson, a Radcliffe graduate and screenwriter whose credits include work on the 1939 film *The Wizard of Oz*, cowrote the play with her husband and dedicated it to Eleanor Roosevelt.[7] Stowe's (offstage) visit with Lincoln causes her to rhapsodize upon her return: "The hope of today lies in this: That we, as a people, are no longer willing to ac-cept these tyrants, and the world they make, without question. We are learning that a world which holds happiness for some but misery for others cannot endure" (211). Getting to that climactic moment, however, involved the depiction, the performance, and the discussion of domestic labor.

Ryerson researched Stowe and the Beecher family in some detail. Her depiction of Harriet's many houses and growing family show that merely getting through the day was demanding labor for the nineteenth-century homemaker. The opening scene features a servant lugging a wash boiler filled with iron cooking utensils into the Stowes' unpretentious first home. Harriet anticipates household help, which she does get, but it is limited, as was usual in all but the poorest classes, and would not have exempted her from having to do housework as well. Act 2 opens in the early 1850s with Harriet upholstering a chair made from a barrel. The fabric for the chair is from her trousseau, now enjoying its third incarnation. A neighbor arrives with a hogshead from the cotton factory that will be Harriet's cistern. Despite there being a pump down the street, she prefers water in the house, even though another character points out that some people "hold the 'pinion that water in the house is unhealthy" (78). Ryerson's Harriet is adopting practices that Stowe's sister Catherine espoused in her housekeeping manual.

Catherine's commitment to progressive housekeeping finally drives Harriet's maid away. Mrs. Hobbs, who has patiently labored in the kitchen, bursts in and announces that she's "put up with boys, and babies, and cuttlefish in the sink—but Miss Beecher is the camel's straw!—With her book-writin' and her recipes and her burnt-black puddin's [sic]—(She takes off her apron.) It's past all bearing. I beg to give notice" (135). What is a poor mother of seven to do? Catherine exhorts her sister to take up the Beecher mantle of activism and service, as Harriet demurs, citing the need to keep the household together and make a bit of extra money. Chides Catherine: "You are hiding behind your poverty, your children, anything and everything, to keep from taking a stand on the slavery question" (59). This gauntlet is thrown down early enough in the play that we watch Harriet juggle writing *and* the household before finally committing to public life.

It would be easy to imagine that this feminist plea to get out of the kitchen was either interpreted and accepted (or refused) as just that—an explicitly *feminist* plea—and that whatever individual women (or men) read into the idea of "hiding" behind one's children, this was not a mainstream critical focus. Most critics thought the play was loosely structured and showed "little drive or drama."[8] All praised Hayes's warmth in her role, but her domestic labor was, for most critics, stage labor that rendered the character "compliant and futile (except as a wife and mother)."[9] Only one critic—the sole woman writing for a New York daily—found the "routine" and "usual ringing speeches" of the third act far less engaging than the "homely comedy about a busy wife and mother who somehow or other found time to sit down in the midst of a thousand domestic crises and write a book that rocked a nation and caused a careworn housewife to be greeted by President Lincoln as 'the little woman who made a great war.'"[10] Nonetheless, the play contends that Stowe's exhausting labor cannot substitute for more direct civic engagement beyond the domestic sphere, perhaps exhorting citizens who do not have to provide their own cisterns to consider more political involvement, even as the housework they perform is valorized.

I REMEMBER BLINTZES

Only one other white stage wife of the 1940s performed her domestic labor with the same gusto as Helen Hayes's Harriet Beecher Stowe: the inspirational matriarch of John Van Druten's 1944 *I Remember Mama*.[11] The play ran for 714 performances and was made into a successful film before becoming a television series that ran from 1949 to 1957. It was later reworked as a 1979 musical starring Liv Ullman. *I Remember Mama* is based on Katherine Forbes's unabashedly nostalgic short stories about a Norwegian immigrant family in 1910 San Francisco, *Mama's Bank Account.* The "I" of the title, Katrin, states that she doesn't ever remember seeing her mother idle and that in her memory, her mother is perpetually forty. The mother's domestic labor is front and center throughout the play, but not merely as stage business. It is the very economy by which Mama negotiates the world of commerce, medicine, and finances, and her abilities are folded into her characterological existence.

Mama was played to great success by Mady Christians. Burns Mantle says that, while Van Druten wanted the fifty-two-year-old Christians for the role, the playwright thought she was "too young to be seriously considering character parts,"[12] suggesting a disconnect among images of glamour, biological age, and ideas of how old is old in popular representations of mothers. One unglamorous but warmly inviting publicity photo shows her on her knees scrubbing the floor, a wood stove in the background, her tired eyes trained neither on the task at hand nor on the camera, as if she is lost in thought.

In fact, she is. Mama scrubs the floor, she tells her family, when she needs to think, and in the first half of the play she needs to process having been told she will not be allowed to see her ten-year-old daughter following the child's successful surgery for mastoiditis. Uneasy about the girl waking up in an unfamiliar place among strangers, Mama has a sudden revelation as she scrubs. The very next scene takes place at the hospital. Mama arrives, goes to the broom closet she has noted during her earlier visit, takes out mop and pail, and starts cleaning the floor. She earns the respect of the on-duty nurse (to whom all cleaning women are apparently interchangeable) by scrubbing rather than mopping, and her disguise provides access to her daughter's room, where she reassures both the child and herself.

The rapid changes and multiple locales were facilitated by George Jenkins's set, which had a central area flanked by two smaller ones, any of which could be featured while the others were covered (the central one) or revolved (the two on the sides). The design facilitated, among other things, the representation of several households, providing a way to praise Mama's domesticity by providing visual contrast with other domestic settings.[13]

Mama's cooking ultimately proves the key in launching her daughter as a writer. When a prominent author comes to town and Mama learns of that woman's interest in gastronomy (a word Mama needs to have explained to her by her teenage son, played in the original production by Marlon Brando), she goes to the writer's hotel, where she barters old-country recipes for the celebrity reading Katrin's short stories. Of her offer Mama says, "I am a good cook. Norvegian. I make good Norvegian dishes. Lutefisk. And Kjodboller. That is meat-balls with cream sauce." "Yes, I know," replies the worldly writer. "I've eaten them in Christiania" (76). The exchange is one story for one recipe, and only as the scene closes does Mama suggest, "Maybe if you would read *two* stories, I could write the recipe for Lutefisk as well" (77).

It is not surprising that meatballs would triumph while the lights would go down on lutefisk. Harvey Levenstein observes that in the three decades following the onset of the Depression, food ceased to be a sign of social distinction; where and with whom one ate trumped cuisine in maintaining status. Prohibition dealt a blow to French restau-

Mady Christians in *I Remember Mama*, 1944. Photo by Vandamm Studio,
© Billy Rose Theatre Division, The New York Public Library for the Performing Arts,
Astor, Lenox, and Tilden Foundations.

rants; movies helped propagate a midwestern image of family life and meals; and women's magazines reflected the values of home economists who were products of midwestern land-grant universities and often employees of food-processing companies headquartered in the Midwest. Mainstream plays hewed to a careful food code that could admit no more than mentioning in passing a dish that required soaking salted or dried fish with lye in cold water for ten days to two weeks in three phases, with the water requiring daily changing (except for a two-day period in phase two) to yield a swollen, gelatinous mass with a chemically corrosive quality that requires another several days of soaking before the fish yields its treats when cooked.[14] Pork, cornmeal, beef, grain, and dairy products became the staples of "American" fare (chicken was always on the list), while spicy food and ethnic or regional cuisine were left to local interests.[15] Despite the awareness that New York audiences had of ethnic food based on family origins or availability in some markets or restaurants, Corn Belt tastes defined domestic normalcy in most plays of the 1930s and 1940s.

By the 1940s, the ability to prepare traditional eastern European–inflected Jewish foods was a housewifely kiss of death on Broadway. Rose Franken's 1943 *Outrageous Fortune*, which ran for seventy-seven performances, dealt with Jewish and homosexual self-loathing, mentioned racism against African Americans, and hinted at the possibility of cross-class, interracial lesbianism.[16] Most critics agreed that the play was overloaded with issues and improbable plot manipulation. In the play a glamorous, terminally ill society woman visits a Long Island Jewish family for the weekend. We know she will help the others see themselves, because she is happy to eat the lentil soup and herring that the matriarch prepares and that cause most of the others to cringe (although we witness neither the preparation nor the consumption). The others include the Irish domestics, who object to the seventy-something matriarch being in the kitchen with her "awful smelling fish" and "putting yeast dough to raise. . . . It's foreign ways, that's what it is" (49–50). Ethnic prejudice is coded by challah and herring; the mistress who can cook is punished for cooking the wrong (un-American) things; her critics, ironically, are other second- or third-generation immigrants.

Proper domestic labor inhered in serving chicken dinners made with American recipes, a safe tradition at least since the frustrated wife of William Hurlbut's 1926 *The Bride of the Lamb* fell for a traveling evangelist. Her husband has ignored her labor-intensive chicken fricassee with raisins, so she takes no chances when trying to please the opportunistic preacher, offering him a lavish snack of fried chicken, coleslaw, potato salad, and layer cake, while serving her daughter cold beans, bread and butter, and a piece of fried liver.[17] Food here is clearly code for affection, value, and love.

In Rachel Crothers's 1931 *As Husbands Go*, a restless housewife returns to Dubuque after a trip to Europe, where she has indulged her sophisticated tastes and had a romantic fling. After her taste of foreign fare, she settles back into domesticity, planning the adoption of an orphaned nephew who becomes a surrogate son. With the adoption plans settled, the husband says, "Well, I s'pose it's the same old Sunday dinner—chicken—mashed potatoes and all." The boy adds, "radiantly happy," "We got ice cream—with chocolate sauce."[18] Domestic bliss is coded in the homey menu, although in this play it is a cook who prepares the meal. The same meal concludes Emmet Lavery's 1946 biographical play, *The Magnificent Yankee*, a paean to Supreme Court Justice Oliver Wendell Holmes. Lavery ends the play with Holmes inviting longtime friend and political sparring partner Owen Wister in to dinner, promising chicken and homemade ice cream—patriotism, safety, and nostalgia built on the midwestern, WASP model.

"HE IRONS WELL"

As noted in the discussion of *Over 21*, military service provided an acceptable reason for men to engage in traditionally feminine skills such as ironing. In Robert Sherwood's 1945 drama *The Rugged Path* Spencer Tracy played an idealistic and disaffected newspaperman who enlists in the navy as a cook because he is too old for combat.[19] To remind the audience what he sacrifices to "learn to make coffee the Navy way, so that when you put a spoon in it, it won't sink" (2-7-9), he says he is happy to return from the European front to the small city where he has "a beautiful home" that he loves, "particularly the kitchen with that automatic range, and the oven, and the ice-box that flashes a light when the cubes are congealed. Why should I want to leave this and go back to that tortured continent?" (1-2-14). While women—regardless of their value to their country as paid labor—were being urged to return to their kitchens by 1945, that return was not imagined as a *sac-*

rifice. No proper male character could sing the praises of a kitchen except to signal a dramaturgical crossroads ahead.

Another acceptable reason for male characters to display household skills was to woo women. The soldier on leave in John Van Druten's hugely popular 1943 play *The Voice of the Turtle* (which ran 1,557 performances and was made into a film featuring Ronald Reagan in 1947) thoughtfully tidies up the apartment of his ladylove because she has had a long day at work. He also impresses her by making scrambled eggs for breakfast and by knowing that they come out better in a double boiler than in a frying pan, but when he craves a quiet dinner at home, he has it catered by the French restaurant conveniently located just down the block.

Men who do housework on an ongoing basis in 1940s plays represent dystopias. Elsa Shelley's 1944 play *Pick-Up Girl* is set in a juvenile court and focuses on the problem of teenage girls cruising for military men.[20] The play still has the power to shock, featuring, as it does, a hapless lower-middle-class fifteen-year-old in bed with a man in his forties, questions about getting high at school, a fifteen-year-old boy buying alcohol for adults, an abortion, and an unsuspected case of venereal disease—both the latter visited on the fifteen-year-old girl, who has only the dimmest awareness of what has happened. The girl's father, unemployed from 1929 until shortly before the play starts, has recently moved from New York to California, where he has finally found work. His daughter is ecstatic at his departure. "I was glad you went cuz I was sick of seein' you do the housework, sick of seein' you wear Mom's apron. And I knew you hated it! When you got the job I danced with joy! . . . Cuz then I knew you wouldn't be ashamed any more, before the neighbors and everybody, and Mom's family couldn't throw it up to you any more that Mom was supporting you!" (55).[21] The stay-at-home dad is an embarrassment (despite the fact that, at fifteen and therefore born in 1929, the protagonist would never have known any other domestic arrangement).

The working mother is a problem as well. In this play she is a cook, employed by theatre workers who require her services after their performances, that is, late at night. The judge suggests another line of work. The no-nonsense mother shoots back, "Excuse me, Your Honor, that's easy to say—'couldn't you get some other job.' . . . I'm a cook. No matter what job I'd have I'd be leavin' at seven in the morning and returnin' eight, nine o'clock at night, or even later" (41). Meanwhile, the neighbor who has turned the daughter in is a widow who labors to support her fifteen-year-old son, a talented violinist. She is a seamstress, which makes it possible for her to work at home. The issue is multiply coded. Women may work for money and may do so with domestic skills so long as they don't leave the home. Men can be good fathers only so long as they *do* leave the home. Otherwise their daughters become pick-up girls.[22]

Billie Dawn is also arguably a pick-up girl in Garson Kanin's 1946 hit *Born Yesterday*. Billie, having worked her way up from chorus girl to kept woman, is awash in furs and jewels lavished on her by her loutish tycoon, but she learns about ideas and reading from a reporter hired to tutor her into social acceptability. One way Kanin lets us know Billie can be redeemed is through the story she tells of her father, who took a can of sterno and a frying pan to work every day because he said everyone should have a hot lunch. "I swear I don't know how he did it. There were four of us. Me and my three brothers and he had to do everything. My mother died. I never knew her. He used to feed us and give us a bath and buy our clothes. Everything. That's why all my life I used to think how some day I'd like to pay him back."[23] Here the father who works a double shift is praised, although he is carefully kept offstage. Yet it is arguably Billie's unorthodox upbringing that drives her to a life of high times and being "kept," necessitating a circuitous route to "normalcy."

WINGLESS VICTORY

Americans now often associate women in World War II with the image of Rosie the Riveter, a figure designed to publicize the importance of women's work for pay in wartime industry jobs. Rosie typified very few women, though. Only 10 percent of working women labored in defense plants, and few employers were willing to train women—regarded as short-term employees—for the high-level task of drilling rivets. Most working women were doing what they had done for decades: sex-segregated jobs such as teaching, secretarial work, nursing, social work, or domestic labor. Rosie the Riveter might "have been more appropriately named Wendy the Welder [a lower-skill war-industry job], or more appropriately still Sally the Secretary, or even . . . Molly the Mom."[24] Government-guided advertising aimed at women underscored the connections between factory work and domesticity. For example, one ad clarified the status of women in the workplace in the eyes of government and industry: "There'll come a day . . . when a lot of good new things of peacetime will become important to Rosie the Housewife."[25]

As far as American theatre was concerned, Rosie the Riveter might almost not have existed. Women war workers were virtually absent from Broadway plays of the 1940s, although a few dramas depict wartime nurses overseas, most notably Maxwell Anderson's 1944 *Storm Operation*, which features a nurse stationed in North Africa happily trading her previously touted independence for marriage. She tells a friend, "[I]t's like an incantation, like a magic. It makes you feel entirely different. I'm not joking. Something happens."[26]

Other plays show the occasional young wife taking a salesgirl job to stave off boredom (possibly code for help making ends meet) while her husband is stationed away from home.[27] Otherwise, female characters engaged in wartime or blue-collar work either held no interest for or were considered too risky for mainstream playwrights. Perhaps the reason was that such characters did not speak to an audience made up largely of educated spectators. Perhaps they suggested deprivation in an environment (the commercial theatre) that sought to foster positive feelings even while enmeshed in tough issues.

Plays written during World War II depicted (white) housewifedom as the thing for which the war was being fought. The budding aviators in Moss Hart's *Winged Victory* have or acquire young wives over the course of their journey from small-town friends to various air corps assignments. In the only scene peopled solely by women, three young wives share a hotel room where they wait to say good-bye to their men. As they iron, wash stockings, and sew a collar and cuffs onto a suit (actions stipulated in the text), the longest-married cheers up the newest bride by assuring her, "We'll all have homes, and babies, and good, peaceful lives. That's what this is for."[28]

In Maxwell Anderson's 1942 *The Eve of St. Mark*, a young enlisted man from a rural town becomes engaged while on a short leave. His fiancée lives only two miles away, but they fell in love at Radio City in New York, where he was enjoying a day off and she had won a trip for her culinary skills. "It was some silly business for high school girls in domestic economy classes. She baked the best cake with a certain kind of flour, and that was the prize, the trip to Radio City."²⁹ The business was "silly"; the brand-name is irrelevant to the boy or the audience; and the real prize is the promise of marriage. This play is significant in part because it had a wider audience than just Broadway. It was written for the National Theatre Conference, which represented Little Theatres and college drama groups as well as professionals.³⁰ *The Eve of St. Mark* had had seventy-six separate productions prior to reaching Broadway, including one at the Pasadena Playhouse. Much like the Office of War Information's War Advertising Council and Magazine Bureau, playwrights promoted domesticity as the proper occupation for women during and after the war.

That the fiancée in *St. Mark*'s was a high school girl was neither an accident nor an aberration. Wartime plays also often showed teenage marriages, reflecting the fact that American women were marrying at younger ages than at any other time in the twentieth century. The average marriage age dropped from 26.1 for men and 22.0 for women in 1890 to a 1951 low of 22.6 for men and 20.4 for women. "Before the war," historian Beth Bailey writes, "marriage was thought of as something that would come at the proper time. Marriage was the end of youth; it removed one from youth culture and from the dating system. It was not meant for children nor for young people." By the end of the war, marriage was expressly being touted as "for *youth*."³¹

Certainly a longing for stability contributed to this trend. So did popular myths about women achieving fulfillment *only* through marriage and child rearing, a sort of misogynist pseudoscience that reached new heights with the 1947 publication of Marynia Farnham and Ferdinand Lundberg's *Modern Woman: The Lost Sex*, a tome extolling the inevitability of women exercising creativity through childbearing and fulfilling their inner needs via homemaking and dependency on a man.³² Long before this Freudian-inflected book appeared, magazines and classrooms were preparing teens to be wives. The retreat to domesticity was a patriotic duty. It also fueled a number of Broadway hits.

The hugely popular *Kiss and Tell* of 1943 features the madcap adventures of a young soldier's fifteen-year-old kid sister, Corliss, as she tries to conceal her brother's secret marriage to the seventeen-year-old next door. The wife, who has had to elope because she is underage, finds herself pregnant (after the marriage). Unwilling to inform either set of parents, she needs a lookout when visiting an obstetrician. Corliss keeps watch, and chaos ensues when all suspect that it is she who is pregnant. F. Hugh Herbert's comedy ran 956 performances, making it the tenth longest-running play in Broadway history when it closed in 1945. No one in the play sees adolescence per se as any kind of issue regarding the possibility of Corliss marrying the boy next door (whose main fault is being slightly goofy). The adults cluck over a *fourteen*-year-old who has "had" to get married, but no one suggests that this is a disastrous idea for a child.[33]

Domestic life is not presented as difficult. Corliss's mother sews and knits onstage, but all food service (and presumably any strenuous housework) is handled by the maid, Louise, who has been with the family seventeen years. (Louise is white, but her dramaturgical function was the slot into which black women characters continued to be shoehorned throughout the 1940s.[34]) Wives' gossip about laundresses and cooks make it clear how the domestic heavy lifting gets done in this supposedly ordinary (stage) world. Who might pay for such help in the home of a newlywed fourteen-year-old does not enter the discussion.

One of the topics largely unaddressed in plays discussing teenage marriage was how a young couple would fare by itself. The Servicemen's Readjustment Act of 1944 (popularly known as the GI Bill) and the soon-to-be burgeoning suburbs would make it easier, because of low-interest home loans and inexpensive houses in new developments, for struggling young couples to avoid boarding with parents. Early in the decade, before government and industry stepped in, Sophie Treadwell's 1941 *Hope for a Harvest* resolves the beyond-the-nuclear-family housing question by featuring a farm clan that owns more than one property, enabling whoever marries to move to a home of her "own." The play teems with wartime concerns such as patriotism, sacrifice, hard work, traditional values, and even racial integration—the latter something that many soldiers experienced while in uniform even if their families at home were trying to avoid it. Treadwell had indicted both routinized work and loveless marriage for money in the 1928 *Machinal*, but here she seems to be backpedaling.

In the play, sixteen-year-old Antoinette ("Tonie") smokes cigarettes, does the family cooking (spaghetti, soup, and chow mein from cans), and aspires to be an aviator. She also fully expects to marry, informing her grandmother, "They say if you're an old maid you go daffy or get dopey or something," to which the fiercely independent, thrifty, and industrious grandmother replies: "So that's the latest, eh? Well, when I was a girl it was the married women who were daffy and got dopey. The old maids were up on their feet from dawn till night doing all the work for the rest of them, taking care of the kids and—"[35] Tonie responds that married women no longer have to have children.

Treadwell's text describes a setting for the family home that is a contrast of old and new, featuring a wood stove flanked by a new gas stove and a Hoover cabinet and oilcloth on the table cheek by jowl with a radio and a refrigerator. Tonie becomes engaged at the end of the play when she finds herself pregnant by her immigrant beau. The two families are ultimately united by a kind of patriotism of tolerance, as Tonie's father learns to accept his immigrant in-laws-to-be and they strive to believe that an American girl can properly serve a husband. A sixteen-year-old wife and mother-to-be with the career aspirations knocked out of her becomes the guarantor of a future in which ethnic prejudice can be overcome and family farming resuscitated.

SOLDIERS' WIVES

All the issues discussed in the foregoing sections came together in Rose Franken's 1944 comedy, *Soldier's Wife*.[36] The play, which ran on Broadway for 253 performances, depicts the adjustments a young couple must make when the husband returns from the South Pacific to find a wife who has learned some independence, borne a baby, and is on the cusp of fame as an author. Despite the title, reviewers pointed out that the piece really had nothing to do with the husband's military role.[37] Upon her husband's return the wife repudiates Hollywood offers and a fancier home in favor of a move to a house outside New York City and another baby. It matters not that her husband is a soldier, although unlikely to be redeployed; what matters is that she is a model, proper wife.

Franken's canny strategy was the result of her own personal interests, her grasp of stageworthiness, and her ability to put a finger on the domestic pulse of the moment. A mother who began writing as a young wife, she went on record saying she loved cooking and housekeeping, even as she cranked out successful novels, plays, short stories for women's magazines, and an autobiography, while earning large sums of money and thoroughly enjoying multiple domiciles and shopping.[38] She remains best known for her "Claudia" stories and novels as well as the 1941 play of the same name that ran for 722 performances. Franken, who married on the day she was to start college at Barnard, directed her own plays and was consistently praised for the performances she elicited from her actors. In the case of *Soldier's Wife*, the much-admired young wife was played by stage and screen actress Martha Scott, already known to audiences for her Broadway and Academy Award–nominated role as Emily in *Our Town*.

Soldier's Wife deploys "the domestic humors of cretonne slipcovers, babies dropping gooey zwieback on the floor, and housewives hunting bargains like tobacco humidors with cracks in them."[39] Cleverly, domestic labor happens through props and discussion more than action.[40] Diapers drying on a radiator in act 1 give way to toddler panties drying in the same spot in act 2, but the baby—who seems to require frequent attention—never appears, serving as a marker for maternal feeling and a device for summoning characters offstage so others are free to talk. The single instance of onstage labor occurs as Kate and her older sister, Florence, discuss John's impending return while Kate paints a stool and Florence shells peas.

Both the stool and the lamp that Kate has fixed in John's absence prove dramaturgically important. Kate goes from being able to say that, while on her own, "the emptiness turned into competence, and efficiency. Like widowhood" (149), to having all her competence disappear as she shores up John's manhood upon his return. (He confides to his sister-in-law that the night he came home "was the toughest half-hour of the war.—I guess we're afraid our women can do without us" [68].) The final scene shows the happy couple alone, with Kate mending clothes as John fixes the lamp that, it turns out, she repaired incorrectly. When Kate says she hates to mend, her husband replies, "You do it very badly" (166). Bucking up her husband's ego, loving him, and bearing children trump any other domestic labor this stageworthy wife might undertake, and in case we miss the point, she does all other things domestic badly to boot.

The play's three other characters round out the picture of where and how domesticity is to play out in the postwar world. A savvy editor sends a writer to interview Kate. The editor, named Peter, is a woman, and the blunt-edged symbolism of her name needs no explanation.

Frieda Inescort and Martha Scott in *Soldier's Wife*, 1944. Photo by Vandamm Studio, © Billy Rose Theatre Division, The New York Public Library for the Performing Arts, Astor, Lenox, and Tilden Foundations.

Farnham and Lundberg's *Modern Woman* could do no better with castration, penis envy, and complete, neurotic misguidedness—three of their favorite, repeated tropes for career women. The reporter Peter sends is her ex-husband, Craig, to whom Kate lists the plain recipes at which she excels (corn beef and cabbage and no "desserts that wobble" [78]). She admits to setting out her husband's pajamas at night and opening his eggs in the morning, leading the reporter to find Kate hopelessly uninteresting as magazine material. "Nobody," he proclaims, "loves a housewife—but a house" (87). By the play's end, Craig and Peter have been chastised and sidelined, and it is clear that "everyone" loves a housewife.

Kate's sister, Florence, the final character, is transparently purposebuilt for multiple dramaturgical needs. The mother of two teenage boys, she has lost her husband during war, but to civilian illness rather than military heroism. Florence idealizes him and has no interest in remarrying. She also sees through Craig and Peter. She lives close enough to Kate to pinch hit as a babysitter but far enough away that John can ask casually why Kate didn't move closer to her while he was away. The flip answer is that John would not have had a house key with which to let himself in to a new apartment, but in truth, extended families were not the stuff of which dream houses and idealized domesticity were made. Florence hovers at the edge of the play as if the playwright cannot figure out what to do with her other than use her to make points. In the final act, Florence's older son lies about his age to enlist, providing her with something substantial to worry about but still no way to fit into the main story. The main story, as it would unfold in the first years after the war, took domesticity and domestic labor as givens for women in American plays set in homes. Cooking and cleaning were not discussed, contested, or even praised as work. Rather, a kind of default setting, they served as platforms on which to expose frustrations, sadness, and social ills.

The year after the opening of *Soldier's Wife*, Tennessee Williams began writing a play featuring another military man's wife negotiating the needs of her veteran spouse. That play opened in 1947 as *A Streetcar Named Desire*.[41] Albert Wertheim says that Stella is the fulcrum of *Streetcar*, a play staging "the struggle between the old and the new South" embodied, respectively, by Blanche and Stanley and centering on "which one of them will possess Stella."[42] He might have called it a postwar struggle for the future of the entire nation. This struggle takes place in a domestic setting, with a kitchen in full view, for the body and loyalty of a housewife who is also pregnant. The housewife and her homemaking, though, are a curious mixture of the comforting and the disconcerting. While Stella hews to a selective amalgam of ingredients supposed to make for an ideal housewife, she is a housewife with ideals that give pause for thought.

Structurally, *Streetcar* might be read as the dark doppelganger of *Soldier's Wife*. In both plays, a young wife adapts to the emotional needs of her returning soldier husband, is a mother, has a sister, and is threatened by a working woman from the outside whose values are different from hers and who wants to control the young wife. In *Soldier's Wife*, however, the sister and the outsider—the opportunistic editor—

are two different characters; in *Streetcar*, the stakes are upped by collapsing the two functions—the loving family member and the outsider with her own strong needs—into the single figure of Blanche.

Franken's play acknowledges the postwar ideal of young nuclear families to live in their own "sacred huts," as the sister has her own apartment. Williams forces the issue; Blanche embodies a past that valued old-fashioned ideas in which housing a relative for an unspecified length of time would be taken in stride. Stanley and Stella's small apartment makes this difficult, although the sisters are willing to give it a try.[43] Stanley personifies the desire for more space, "comfort and roominess for family members," and "privacy and freedom of action," which would be among the most common reasons given in the 1950s by people wanting to move out of cramped apartments or shared housing.[44] Accordingly, the housewife's dilemma is presented in *Streetcar* partly in terms of styles in housing.

Most critical writings on *Streetcar* focus on the standoff between Blanche and Stanley, figuring them as culture vs. nature, romanticism vs. realism, poetry vs. animal energy.[45] Few examine Stella in her own right, but those who do point to a housewife's dilemma, a possible metonym for a culture-wide dilemma. Mark Royden Winchell notes that Stella, a generally unremarkable person, has signed up for a world of male dominance, where she lovingly acquiesces to Stanley's demands because the sex is blindingly great. The price is her refusal to believe that her husband is a rapist and her willingness to turn a deaf ear to her sister's (truthful) accusation. Royden asserts that for women, the emotional power of the play may come from identification with Stella, who, to keep her marriage intact, denies Blanche's story. Stella cannot be loyal to her birth family or a woman who threatens hearth and home, but that hearth and home come at the expense of morality and ethics.[46]

Herbert Blau argues that Stella pulls us back to "the illusions understood by Ibsen and O'Neill," suggesting a direct connection (for latter-day readers) between Blanche and Anita Hill, abused by her male interrogators during the 1991 hearings about Clarence Thomas's Supreme Court appointment, which she opposed because she had accused him of sexually harassing her, and also "disbelieved by a majority of women whose own lives, perhaps, depend not so much on the kindness of strangers [Blanche's signature exit line] but on fidelity to the phallic order of things, or investment in the family, with some helpless dependency on the authority of their husbands." This belief is based on subscribing to "readymade desire, on *not* seeing the truth," a truth that is "squalid" yet shores up reality for a majority of people.[47] For Winchell, this "truth" is mythic, as the power of "colored lights" sex fuels "what *Streetcar* is all about. For men, it is a fantasy of complete domination; for women, one of complete submission."[48] This fantasy gains some of its (at)traction in the real world because it is played out by a housewife who not only enjoys fabulous sex but gets away with unwashed dishes, uncooked dinners, unmade beds, and in the original production, unstylish clothing and hair. It offers viewers identificatory rewards with no steep entry requirements. Sexy Stan prefers the slob to the dieter.

Ever since the nineteenth-century "cult of domesticity" carved out a space for housewifedom and motherhood as labor for the public good, women who would later be called stay-at-home moms were in a cultural spotlight. "Domesticity," notes Elaine Tyler May of the American postwar era, "was not so much a retreat from public affairs as an expression of one's citizenship."[49] As Stella goes, one might say, so goes the nation. When she makes her first entrance, at the very start of the play, Stanley hurls a package of meat at her, yelling, "Catch!" (14). Jessamyn Neuhaus observes in her study of 1950s cookbooks that cooking to please men meant cooking meat, and the enjoyment of meat was directly linked to masculinity.[50] Lest we miss the sexual connotation of the meat, Williams has one of the neighbor women, simply called "Colored Woman," ask, "What was that package he th'ew at 'er?" The knowing upstairs neighbor Eunice, a housewife who is also Stella's landlady, says, "You hush, now!" to which the Negro Woman (she is called both within the space of three lines) answers, "Catch *what*!" (14).

Stella is prepared to catch anything Stanley throws her way, and, while she is responsible for meals in their home, her greater means of satisfying him is through sex. It is questionable whether this meat ever gets cooked at all, because Stanley immediately leaves to go bowling, Stella follows to watch him, and Blanche gets sick to her stomach, which make it unlikely that the meat was used that night. The next night Stella prepares a "cold plate" for Stanley, as she and Blanche are having dinner in a restaurant so Stanley can entertain his poker buddies in peace. Continual references to the icebox mean that the apartment may or may not have a refrigerator (although some Americans born in the 1920s, as Stella and Stanley would have been, continued to say icebox in lieu of refrigerator for much of the rest of the century).

Meat that spoils may be a common occurrence in the Kowalski household, as regular housework and careful grooming are not Stella's strong suits. When Eunice lets Blanche into Stella's apartment, she apologizes for it being "sort of messed up right now," adding that "when it's clean it's real sweet" (17). In Blanche and Stella's first encounter Blanche chides her sister for getting heavy, having an unstylish hair-cut, having spilled something on her lace collar, and having only two rooms and no maid. None of this negatively affects either Stella's feel-ings about herself or her marriage or Stanley's feelings about his "baby doll." Not only does she adore Stanley ("When he's away for a week I nearly go wild! . . . And when he comes back I cry on his lap like a baby" [25]), but we later see that she can keep house with little fuss when she needs to. The morning following the infamous poker game, which con-cludes with Stanley throwing the radio out the window, chasing Stella, hitting her, and leaving watermelon rinds on the floor, Blanche returns to find Stella lying in bed with a look of *"narcotized tranquility,"* a comic book in one hand, and the table *"sloppy with remains of break-fast and the debris of the preceding night"* (62).

Stella returned to an amorous Stanley the previous night, and it is clear they have had sex. In the ensuing conversation, Stella says, "Look at the mess in this room!" and picks up a broom. Blanche says she will not have her sister "cleaning up for him," to which Stella's realistic challenge is, "Then who's going to do it? Are you?" At Blanche's indig-nant "I? I!" Stella matter-of-factly says, "No, I didn't think so" (66) and presumably goes about cleaning up as Blanche anxiously tries to plan to get Stella away from the situation in which she is entirely content. We later hear Stella say that she loves waiting on Blanche; she knows exactly how to blot a Coca-Cola spill to keep it from staining; on the night she gives birth she prepares a birthday dinner complete with cake for Blanche and has clean towels right on hand when Blanche re-quests one. (There is no mention of a washing machine in the apart-ment.) And, although she cries when Stanley hurls his plate and cup to the floor in response to her calling him a pig, presumably she would clean that up, too, if she did not exit the scene to give birth.

One of the things that *Streetcar* makes clear is the difference between domestic labor qua necessary work and domestic labor in the realm of housewifedom. If anyone, it is Blanche who has worked her knuckles to the bone doing domestic chores. Stella left the family homestead five years earlier, the summer that the sisters' father died (22), and though she says, "The best I could do was make my own living" (25), we know nothing of her aspirations or earning power. She did not help financially with the family debts; there is no indication that she went to college, no sense of how she might have paid for it, and no suggestion that her earnings ever were part of the budget of her marital home. Blanche, meanwhile, nursed four elderly relatives until their deaths without outside help, which she could not afford on a teacher's salary while supporting five people. But Stella's domestic labor is what counts in this postwar, GI Bill milieu, as it is linked to providing her husband with sexual satisfaction, supposedly filling her time instead of earning money outside the home (she must ask Stanley when she wants money), bearing the future generation, and finally deciding that the only others whose demands matter are those in her nuclear family.

Stella's domestic labor suggests a difference between an ideal housewife and an ideal wife. Domesticity as a praiseworthy goal lost ground during the century preceding *Streetcar*. The very forces (industrialization, consumerism, labor-saving devices in the home) that created the stay-at-home wife dedicated to domestic ideals also conspired against her, as the real motives behind the ideals were profit and control, not better health, education, or welfare for all citizens. "[T]he American home at mid-century," notes Glenna Matthews, "cut loose from social, religious, or political moorings, was sacred only to 'Family Togetherness.' And the housewife who was the chief votary of this cult was supposed to eradicate any vestige of personal ambition or independent thought in order to keep her family happy."[51] Women who got themselves into girdles and makeup to vacuum and who baked cookies for their children's return from school to a spotless house, were "figments of the postwar American imagination . . . expressions of desires and fears in a nation strained by the war and baffled by the unstoppable social changes that shaped the 1950s."[52]

Stella's domestic labor reveals a bored pragmatist, not an incipient Betty Crocker. But as Stanley's wife—not a magazine's or an outsider's *house*wife—she satisfies the essentialist criteria spelled out in *Modern Woman: The Lost Sex*, that women were neurotic because they were seeking satisfaction in the marketplace rather than in motherhood.

"Anatomical differences" define women (223). Farnham and Lundberg claim that the goals of "equal rights . . . belong in the realm of psychopathology" (206) and that "women who live as women . . . [live] as mothers" (360). They maintain that woman "is designed to receive the seed," and those who accept motherhood "rarely experience sexual difficulties" (278). The authors suggest that gratifying such a woman "bespeaks [a man's] true power, and subtly suggests to him that if he can so bemuse the lady of his fancy perhaps he is capable of anything" (277). Farnham and Lundberg label feminists as envious, neurotic, psychotic, misled, deluded manhaters. By these criteria, Stanley and Stella are beacons of success. While *Modern Woman* raised predictable ire among intellectuals, it also made the *New York Times* best-seller list, went through several printings, and sold thirty thousand copies.[53] And it provided a domestic labor loophole for a dramatic character who reads at first blush like a male fantasy.[54]

Thinking about Stella, her understanding of her status as housewife, and her domestic choices involves—and not only in the context of this study—thinking about realism and reality as both referent and performed product. Daniel Mendelsohn offers an insightful suggestion about how slippery the real-world referent is in the fictional world of *Streetcar*:

> [T]his play, like others in the Williams repertoire, never seems to work through a coherent position with respect to the key terms with which it seeks to create its meanings, terms such as "realism" and "beauty" and "lies" and "truth" and "art." Perhaps its greatest sleight of hand is to have convinced so many people that it's about the losing battle between beauty, poetry, and fantasy, on the one hand, and crassness, vulgarity, and brute "realism" on the other— and convinced them to root for the former—without ever quite engaging the provocative question of why "reality" must always be ugly and why "art," in these plays, is always presented as a liar, why it always has such an aversion to the truth, to reality—as of course good art does not. In a way, the play, like Blanche, succeeds only if it doesn't make you wonder about such internal inconsistencies.[55]

Hints of this disconnect are evident in the reviews for the 1947 opening. Critics for the New York dailies saw the Kowalski apartment as

"cramped [and] dingy," "two dreary rooms in a squalid neighborhood," a "hovel," and "shabby," while praising Kim Hunter's Stella as "a genuine person" who is "mellow and philosophical" as well as "patient though troubled."[56] Housewifely ideals give way to a reading that separates who the housewife is from what she does. (Her house is a pigpen, but she's solid, sympathetic, and believable.) None mentioned that Stella was the agent of her sister's removal to a mental asylum, although, if the play is a tragedy, it is arguably Stella's, as she goes in the course of the final scene from telling Eunice, "I couldn't believe her story and go on living with Stanley" (133), to hysterically sobbing, "What have I done to my sister?" (141). Whether one reads this conclusion in terms of symbolism (Stella is merely the agent for resolving the fundamental agon between Blanche and Stanley) or in terms of sex trumping everything else, or in terms of the practicalities of "real life" (Stella is a new mother with no visible means of support, no particular skills, and living in a culture that urges women to stay home), it would take more cleanup skills than Stella has to put this house in order.

DOMESTIC LABOR IN BLACK AND WHITE

Returning soldiers and their wives included African Americans, whose families faced the same problems as others regarding war injuries, nightmares and guilt—what would later be called posttraumatic stress disorder—wartime jobs no longer available to women who still needed the work, and cramped living quarters. Racism, however, was something white soldiers and their wives did not face. It was a topic treated in a handful of wartime and postwar plays, one of which figured it in terms of domesticity, domestic labor, and the home as haven.

Maxine Wood's *On Whitman Avenue* opened in May 1946 under the direction of Margo Jones. The play uses a midwestern suburb to stand in for white America and pulls no punches. A decorated African American soldier named David Bennett, along with his pregnant wife, his mother, grandfather, and kid brother move into the upstairs of a two-family house when the white owners' nineteen-year-old daughter, Toni Tilden, rents it to them during her parents' absence. David shared a foxhole with Toni's boyfriend in the war; his family are articulate, hardworking, skilled, and generous. The white neighbors are largely hypocritical, ignorant, cruel, and backstabbing, with two exceptions. In a foreshadowing of *A Raisin in the Sun* more than a decade later, the neighbors take up a collection to "help" the black family pay for a move to another, more "suitable" home.

Reviews were mixed, with assessments of the text ranging from "awkward and straggling" to the assertion that Wood "has the firm painstaking touch of a [Lillian] Hellman."[57] In the realm of performance, most praise was for Canada Lee in the role of David, but here, too, observations ran the gamut from "flawless," "rounded and resolute," and "simple, normal and sincere" (i.e., "real") to two accusations of "overacting" (not "realistic").[58] As one reviewer pointed out, the playwright "paints her blacks all white, her whites all black and stacks her cards exactly as she wants them."[59]

The playwright makes judicious and subtle use of domestic labor to code both respectability and anxiety. The audience sees and hears about the Bennetts before the Tilden parents meet them. They are model tenants, unlike the previous (white) ones, who had failed to separate papers and tin cans for trash collection. A neighbor who watched the Bennetts for their first three days reports approvingly that they all pitched in and "scrubbed the place from top to bottom."[60] Why they needed to do so is another question, because the Tildens wanted to rent the apartment and it seems unlikely that they would have tried to do so with the rooms requiring floor-to-ceiling scrubbing. A stage direction even makes clear that Kate Tilden is concerned about housekeeping, as she returns from her trip and "rubs her hand over a table and is pleased to find there is no dust. She deftly rearranges a few flowers in a vase" (1-1-3).

We soon learn that Toni is the one who made the house spic and span for her mother's return, as Kate says: "She's always considerate of me when she's done something wrong" (1-1-24). If this is true, the daughter has learned from the mother to displace feelings onto housework, something revealed deep into the second act when the "old maid" neighbor (one of the Bennetts' sympathizers) sees Kate in a dirty smock and knows Kate has been cleaning to assuage a guilty conscience, noting that her own coping mechanism is to shine shoes.

If Kate's and Toni's cleaning are means of allaying guilt, the Bennetts' unseen scrubbing may have its own psychic purpose. The Bennetts spell out what their alternative would have been had the Tilden apartment not been available: sharing a cold-water flat with two other families. They were given notice to leave their previous home—a "dingy" apartment with four rooms, one with no window (recall there are four adults and three generations in the family)—because an airport was being built on the land. The "helpful" suggestion that the Bennetts get an apartment in the nearby Nat Turner housing project is met with the observation that they would be happy to do so but that there are ten thousand families on its waiting list.[61] When they leave at the end of the play, it is to stay temporarily with friends, where two families will be living in three rooms. The scrubbing may be less a sanitary necessity than a kind of ritual of claiming domestic space. Here I am thinking both of Jennifer Fleissner's reading of compulsive cleaning as a means of trying to fit in and also of the importance of African Americans demonstrating their domestic fitness and respectability—at least in plays sympathetic to them—in terms legible to skeptical whites. One accusation in the play is that blacks are "shiftless" and "dirty"—two characteristics that the family's scrubbing (albeit private and offstage) rebuts (1-2-58).

Ironically, no amount of domestic labor can salvage the problems on Whitman Avenue. At the end of the play, Kate Tilden—the fussy housekeeper and hostess—is abandoned by her liberal daughter, with very strong hints that her husband will not return either. The Bennetts' good housekeeping has also failed to preserve the home for which they worked. The playwright dumps the problem in her audience's lap, perhaps anticipating that their sympathetic clucking will be followed by hasty retreat, although clearly hoping for more. Toni is likely the authorial mouthpiece here, explaining the parents' early polite sympathy as only faintly masking panic about racial integration in their own household. They are, she says, "middle-aged liberals running true to form" (1-1-29).

■ ■ ■

Once the questions, worries, and fears linked directly to the war years and their immediate aftermath were "resolved"—with the glaring exception of racism and the less glaring, but festering problem of the isolated, underchallenged, bored housewife—domestic comfort provided fodder for a new dramatic canon during the Cold War era. For the first time, African American domestics would appear on Broadway in their own domestic spaces, as leading characters, and with much more to say and do than facilitate the resolution of problems besetting whites with leisure.[62]

5   DEATH OF A DREAM

1949–1962

"Homeward bound" is Elaine Tyler May's synoptic, double-edged descriptor of American domestic sensibility during the Cold War era.[1] Home—with attendant promises of security, material well-being, togetherness, fun, and mutual emotional support, all within a nuclear unit neither beholden to nor encumbered by any extended family—was where returning soldiers and others who could afford it were headed (bound).[2] At the same time, with traditional gender roles relentlessly marketed as the key to familial, personal, and political stability, both men and women chafed at tasks and typologies by which they were constrained (bound). Men increasingly found jobs in companies where they were expected to conform; they therefore looked to the domestic milieu as a site where they were "unchallenged heads of their households."[3] Educated women gave up plans for careers, although many took jobs for the sake of additional household security, upward mobility, or even to "stay sane" but complained that, despite material comfort, they were burdened by household tasks and got too little help from their husbands.[4]

Burden or not, domesticity was touted as "an expression of one's citizenship." May points to the 1959 "kitchen debate"—the encounter between Vice President Richard Nixon and Soviet premier Nikita Khrushchev at the opening of the American National Exhibition in Moscow—as a prime example of the power of this idea. The centerpiece of Nixon's evidence for the superiority of the American way of life was a model six-room ranch house "filled with labor saving devices."[5] Consumer goods made American life desirable, and enjoying these in private homes far away from the marketplace was where (American) women belonged, according to advertisers, government, schools, and the legal system. Leaving unhappy marriages was problematic, as Cold

War consensus made divorce a source of "social ostracism and character defamation," while capricious and onerous laws meant that divorce
could spell financial disaster for women.[6] The domesticity supposed
to uphold national security and personal happiness was the place to
which discontented people were relegated, since they were to understand that it was they and not the legal and social institutional setups
that were awry.

Entertainment helped purvey these ideas. Many today conjure
images of 1950s domesticity from television programs such as *The
Adventures of Ozzie and Harriet, Leave It to Beaver, The Donna Reed
Show,* and *Father Knows Best*—all series in which white families with
two or three children, a stay-at-home mother, and a father who goes to
work in a suit grapple with music lessons, problems at school, dating,
the importance of telling the truth (or of mastering the socially desirable white lie), and other quotidian nuclear family-focused "issues."
Theatre made different use of domesticity in the Cold War era, which
began in 1947, when the perceived need to "contain" a communist
threat gave rise to the National Security Act, parent of the Central
Intelligence Agency. The fear was that countries in Asia and Eastern
Europe would succumb to communism and quickly overcome the non-
communist democracies. Bruce McConachie argues that containment
was the primary allegorical lens through which American audiences
read popular plays of the Cold War era.[7]

Asserting a single reading strategy does not allow breathing room for
resistant viewers who might have come from the ranks of the domes-
tically discontent.[8] The 1950s was "the decade of popular and avant-
garde music; of abstract and commercial art; of eggheads and dumb
blondes; of gray flannel suits and loafer jackets; of ballet and west-
erns; . . . a site of dualities, tensions and contradictions."[9] Not all cultural products carried a Cold War political subtext.[10] My arguments
about onstage domestic labor and its reception as "real" and meaningful, whether comforting or lethal, assume that at least some people
from all these camps saw plays. Moreover, George Lakoff and Mark
Johnson's theories of cognitive psychology eschew metaphor as means
of making sense of the world and propose instead a philosophy of "embodied realism" in which "mental concepts arise, fundamentally, from
the experience of the body in the world."[11] Surely, the women under
pressure to conform, marry young, stay home, and find contentment in

washing plates and creating meals using ketchup and cornflakes might well have had an embodied experience of repetition, exhaustion, boredom, and their own version of containment that could lead to other readings of mainstream plays.[12]

Live theatre as an institution underwent a significant evolution between 1949 and 1962. Foremost, it was challenged by the rapid advent of free, at-home television. In 1950, nine years after the first day of commercial broadcasting in the United States, 9 percent of American homes had a television; by 1960 the figure was 90 percent.[13] Second, Broadway between 1949 and 1962 featured an array of types of plays, making it very difficult to characterize by genre. Musicals, strong directorial imprints, and technical innovations gave editor Louis Kronenberger pause about how to construe "best" plays. He retreated into literature, asserting in 1955, "Unless the title of these yearbooks is to be changed to *Best Productions*, and *Best Productions* boasts movie cameras for the dance sequences and record players for the tunes, the Ten Best must qualify on a basis of their texts."[14] Even so, three of the Pulitzer Prize winners of the Cold War era were musicals: *South Pacific* in 1950, *Fiorello!* in 1960, and *How to Succeed in Business Without Really Trying* in 1962.[15] The latter is the final production examined in this chapter for its engagement with domesticity in a single—but unforgettable—song.

Third, New York theatre birthed Off-Broadway as the locus of classical revivals or serious plays for which Broadway producers would not provide funding; it rapidly spawned Off-Off-Broadway, which emerged as an alternative to Broadway sensibilities in every way.[16] Finally, and of crucial importance to this study, African American women characters came to occupy central stage time in plays aimed at mainstream white audiences and not necessarily written by blacks. Accordingly, in this chapter, the "Black and White" section moves to the middle.

The plays in this chapter grappled with a myth called the "American Way of Life," which pervaded postwar thinking.[17] With one exception (Albee's *The American Dream*) all opened on Broadway. They were successful in their time, have enjoyed revivals, and are still studied. They spoke to theatregoers because they drew on a promulgated reality that Americans recognized and shared, despite great differences among them. It was a loose coalition of Americans who bought into a shared worldview yet did not entirely constitute a united front—a crucial point in considering theatre featuring domestic labor. Affluent enough to participate in mass consumption, believers in an "American Way of Life" that was basically good, they endorsed a pragmatic politics and the cooperation of business and government. The characteristics often attributed to the culture as a whole reflected dominant values projected onto a wider population that did not necessarily share them.[18]

What is most remarkable about the plays in this chapter is that they are part of a collection of Broadway works set in recognizably middle-class homes where dysfunction and previously taboo (or heavily coded) subjects become the norms. The televised world of *Father Knows Best* was already retro by the standards of much 1950s theatre; it had been the theatrical world of World War II. In Cold War–era plays, the imagined security of the domestic realm is rife with illegal, immoral, and dystopian activities. These include recreational drug use (*The Member of the Wedding*); serious drug addiction (*A Hatful of Rain*); teenage girls cutting themselves (*The Rose Tattoo* and *The Climate of Eden*); spousal domestic violence with a lethal weapon (*Come Back, Little Sheba*); parental violence against children (*The Climate of Eden*); incestuous desire (*A View from the Bridge*); and eating disorders (*The Dark at the Top of the Stairs*).

Other topics that in earlier plays had appeared in institutional or rarefied settings now hit home. These include alcoholism (*Come Back, Little Sheba*) and homosexuality (*Cat on a Hot Tin Roof*). Even murderous children returned to roost in the realm of roller skates and peanut butter sandwiches (*The Bad Seed*). Faked orgasms in an unhappy marriage made a veiled but recognizable appearance (*A Clearing in the Woods*). The domestic realm as depicted on the Cold War stage was haunted, as were most of those who labored in it.

The 1962 end point signals less a particular event than the last year characterized by political and theatrical values about to undergo steady erosion. Politically, the Cuban missile crisis of 1962 and the assassination of President John F. Kennedy in 1963 marked the climax and then the end of an epoch. In the theatre, New York's Café LaMaMa presented its first full-fledged play (*One Arm*, based on a story by Tennessee Williams) in 1962; the experimental, Off-Off Judson Poets Theatre won an Obie in 1962; Edward Albee's critique of American complacency moved from the Off-Broadway world of the 1961 *American Dream* to Broadway with the 1962 *Who's Afraid of Virginia Woolf?*

That year was the end of a period of shared commonplaces regarding domesticity and dining norms as well, as the following year would see the publication of Betty Friedan's *The Feminine Mystique* and the television premiere of Julia Child in *The French Chef.* Both stay-at-home momdom and the regime of recipes built on canned cream of mushroom soup began to topple; concomitantly, a certain kind of theatrical kitchen sink realism became recognizably dated.

CLOSE(D) QUARTERS

The orderly postwar house was a private dwelling for a nuclear family, sans in-laws or unmarried siblings—a house sheltering families in pursuit of "opportunity, success, and financial gain," crucial components of the Cold War American Dream.[19] Within this house, much dramatic dystopia can be located by paying attention to the "food axis, " Elizabeth C. Cromley's term for "the accepted relationship of kitchen, food storage, and dining space."[20] In her study of American houses from the 1840s through the 1990s, Cromley traces how architecture encoded ideas about the necessity of separating—or merging—food-related household functions based on ideas of propriety and sanitation. In middle-class nineteenth-century homes cooking belonged in a *service* "zone," for household work and servants, while eating meals occurred in dining rooms, which were part of a *social* zone, used for guests and family sociability.[21] Over the first half of the twentieth century, kitchens became smaller and more sociable; household electricity and appliances made it easier for the housewife to do her own domestic labor; and "the careful division of servant from served was no longer pressing."[22]

By the mid-twentieth century, open-plan houses rendered formerly hidden work visible, with kitchen labor "reframed as social activity" and the stylish norm the "housewife in full view of her husband, children, and guests, available to do their bidding."[23] The food axis might also be expanded and used metaphorically to provide an emotional grid for assessing how food and its attendant domestic labor are deployed in plays. If the architectural plan prescribes physical routes for food to travel and a setting for social interaction, the emotional axis might propose an ideal route from enthusiastic and efficient preparation to appreciative consumption to satisfied savoring to stress-free cleanup. In the plays discussed here, the best-laid food plans of housewives are disrupted by psychological crises and needs that refuse to be gridded onto normative food axes.

Few houses in theatrical productions spoke so well to the unmentioned problems embedded in the private-home-as-haven-with-nouveau-food-axis desideratum as the one in the 1949 *Death of a Salesman*. Jo Mielziner's set design, intertwined with Arthur Miller's text, communicated the fragility of a domestic ideal divorced from larger social awareness, as the design made manifest not merely interior, decor, properties, ambience, cramped or generous spaces, or the like but the very situatedness of the sacred hut in the larger world—the locus of private domestic labor within a public sphere. Miller describes the house this way: *"An air of the dream clings to the place, a dream rising out of reality. The kitchen at center seems actual enough, for there is a kitchen table with three chairs, and a refrigerator."*[24] Dream and kitchen are locked in close embrace.

Ironically, the reality behind the dreamlike, fragile home makes the dream impossible to fulfill.[25] Mielziner's setting concretized a social dialectic legible through domestic architecture, conveying the vulnerability of the single-family house imagined as birthright and fortress as well as the hubris and even indifference of the Lomans to their fellow city dwellers. In 1949, suburban sprawl was a growing gleam in its collective fathers' eyes, and the housebound housewife, Linda, surrounded by appliances that keep needing repairs, is a hint of things to come. The Lomans' house is not part of a new suburbia, but it can and could be read as a site of both old-fashioned values and future communities, to the extent that it houses a nuclear family imagining itself worthy of material success and shelter from the needs of others, including the needs of nonwhites for access to decent, affordable housing. Because the house has been the Lomans' for a quarter century and was purchased at a time when the postwar values in which the play is enmeshed were yet to come, the stage family became a present-day stand-in that conveniently conveyed both a past about which viewers might be nostalgic and a present to which they might aspire. Here, stage characters can do what actual people cannot: be in two historic and psychological places at once.

Mielziner believed that "the most important visual symbol in the play—the real background of the story—was the Salesman's house."[26] The designer's goal was to make clear the changes between the past, **145** when the house was surrounded by open country, and the present, with the house hemmed in by apartment buildings.[27] The skeletal house with invisible walls enabled characters to move freely to other times and places in a cinematic way via Mielziner's "effective abstraction, [which gave] the spectator the opportunity to 'fill in.'"[28] Arnold Aronson highlights how situating the Lomans' house on an island on the stage "has the effect of saying that the location we see on the stage is a mere fragment of the character's total world." He quotes Mielziner's observation that "the surroundings have cut off [Willy's] freedom and his hopes. . . . [C]heap apartment houses hem him in on all sides."[29] The housewife's world, however, does *not* extend beyond the house; she has no larger universe. She lives in her own scripted part of the scenic world, which might as well be of a different order.[30] The Mielziner set as a whole links to a world within which the portion that housewife Linda occupies represses any connections. The set is considered praiseworthy for what it shows about Willy's entrapment while naturalizing or ignoring Linda's proscribed realm.

Spectators are offered in this built environment a Linda Loman who can be read simultaneously as Willy's "foundation and support" and as a "two-dimensional pseudomasochist . . . some kind of gendered service station."[31] Whether Miller's scripted Linda has imprisoned herself or has acquiesced to a situation she has ceased to control, her situatedness within Mielziner's set and the specific tasks actress Mildred Dunnock performed in accordance with Miller's text added up to the repetitive stuckness of the naturalist heroine whose housekeeping is an attempt at wholeness on the only terms available to her.[32] The inaugural performance of *Salesman* underscored that domesticity is what Barbara Penner defines as a set of attitudes and values centered on the home, formed publicly, and learned and enacted in a range of places.[33]

The house in the stage setting was and is obviously a symbol, but it must seem, as in Miller's description, to be "actual enough." Linda's labor, likewise, is symbolic, even as Dunnock's performance in real time was "actual enough." Linda's domesticity exemplifies public ideas and attitudes about women's work in the home, but, while she learned these once, she is largely unable to evolve. Interestingly, her one moment of angrily standing up for herself involves refusing to do housework, as she tells her son Happy, when he tries to placate her with a bouquet of flowers to compensate for his having abandoned Willy in a restaurant bathroom, "I'm not your maid any more" (124). Linda's domestic labor along with Mielziner's outlined, no-walls house, are facets of this play one can see through.

Mielziner's set displayed a small number of household accoutrements, foremost the refrigerator, which we learn has required repairs almost since it was new. Indeed, virtually everything with which Linda engages either requires repair or repetitive maintenance. She finds the hose with which Willy contemplates killing himself when she makes a trip to the cellar fuse box because "the lights blew out" (59). She asks Willy if he can do anything about the shower, because "it drips" (66). She sews the lining in Willy's coat, and she mends her own stockings, much to his consternation. She enters several times with a basket of laundry, usually ready to hang on the line to dry. The one thing we do not see her do—something that might be construed as creative or nurturing—is cook. Willy refuses her offer to make eggs for breakfast, and the late-night snack she proffers is a whipped-cheese sandwich, the cheese being a new product she has purchased. The emotional food axis in this household is not only awry—it is close to being erased. The single meal that is a focal point in the play, the abortive dinner at the restaurant, is one to which Linda is not invited. She is the only character in the play who never leaves her house (here including the yard) until the very final scene at the cemetery. The house, ostensibly a female space, for Linda is largely a place where she waits for her husband.[34] Set designs featuring houses impose nothing permanent, but they offer ways to experience and try on new ideas about houses and housing.

We will likely never know who in the audience for the 1949 production of *Salesman* might have read Linda's domestic labor as tragic in its own right. Certainly Miller claimed indirectly that such a reading would have been fine: "I've never written about issues. I've written about what happens to people under certain circumstances. . . . People are going to make completely different things out of it. And if the work itself has a certain human vitality, that will happen more than less."[35] By the early 1960s, with the dawn of second-wave feminism, some who might have been in that audience understood that hanging laundry, fretting about refrigerator fan belts, replacing fuses, mending stockings, and waxing the floor until "she keels over" (41) made Linda Loman the sort of person to whom attention must be paid.

EATING AND DISORDER

Cromley's food axis offers a valuable tool for considering the domestic dystopia and anxiety in William Inge's now-iconic play *Come Back, Little Sheba* (1950), where the route from food preparation to food consumption proves fraught.[36] Offers of food are refused; meals are set out and diners fail to appear; food purchases are mishandled, misunderstood, or just missed; cleanup fails to take place; and the wrong person is forced to pick up the slack in the kitchen when the housewife neglects to play her proper role.

The play takes place in a house whose architectural food axis has been rerouted for financial reasons. Doc and Lola Delaney, a middle-aged, midwestern chiropractor and his wife, have turned their dining room into a bedroom to take in a boarder. They need the rent money because Doc is rebuilding a practice that fell apart during the years he was a violent drunk. He drank because he was disappointed; he was disappointed because he was forced nineteen years earlier to give up medical school to marry Lola; he married Lola because she was pregnant. Doc, like Lola's father, thought Lola was "fast" in high school, and, while he has stood by her, it is questionable whether he values her, much less respects her. Lola, who lost the baby and now cannot have children, wanted to work, but Doc forbade it. She sleeps late, avoids cleaning the house and cooking breakfast, relieves her loneliness and boredom by chattering to service and delivery people stopping at the house, and gets vicarious pleasure from the romantic liaisons of the boarder, a college student named Marie. Doc, meanwhile, may be in love with Marie; he certainly disapproves of her doing life drawings for her art class. Doc also disapproves of Marie's dating a jock, Turk, while she has a clean-cut boyfriend with money back in Cincinnati. The arrival of the boyfriend after Marie has spent the night with Turk precipitates the climax of the play, which involves a carefully prepared dinner. The denouement is also coded through a much-anticipated breakfast.

At the top of *Come Back, Little Sheba* we see a kitchen doing double duty as both service and social area. It is a mess, the table covered with dirty dishes from the previous evening's meal. As Cromley notes, food preparation and its attendant waste disposal constitute dirty business—business that has no business in the realm of sociable dining. The Delaneys' house collapses "two extremes of 'dirt' and 'not dirt',' defining "dirt" in the way identified by anthropologist Mary Douglas as 'matter out of place.'"[37] First thing in the morning, the previous night's waste is definitely out of place. So, we are meant to understand, is a working man about to take up domestic chores with a towel tucked into his vest pockets as an apron, which is what we see as Doc faces the mess and clears it away.

Inge uses food and food-related activities throughout the scene to signal the characters' disordered desire and frustration. Doc prepares juice, coffee, and a sweet roll for Marie, who notes how unusual it is for a married man to get his own breakfast. He offers to prepare an egg for Lola, who declines. Lola later asks if Marie would like an extra sweet roll, saying she does not want hers. Food is of little interest to Lola, although Doc berates her later in the play for being fat. She does, however, pay a great deal of attention to food intended to provide a special treat or care for others.

Cookbooks and women's magazines in the 1950s relentlessly held out cooking as the proverbial "way to a man's heart."[38] This function of housewifedom "was presented . . . as one element of their nurturing function within the family, not as work that could be shared."[39] Part of this nurturing through food was about satisfying the tastes of all family members, something Lola undertakes with attention to the differing needs of Doc and Marie, who can be read as a kind of surrogate daughter. She tells Lola, "You've been like a father and mother to me" (12), while Lola ruminates to Doc that if their daughter had lived, "she could be going to college—like Marie" (33). Inge portrays Lola's forays into stocking the larder and getting meals in terms of nurturing, never in terms of mere routine or simple, take-it-in-stride nourishment.

For instance, as Doc leaves for work, Lola tells him to come home if he gets hungry. When the postman arrives, Lola proffers a toy that came in a "box of breakfast food" (18), which she will not need, as she has no children. The absence of brand-names or even the word "cereal" may be a hint that Lola has problems as a food shopper, something that becomes evident when the milkman shows up. She invites him in and asks if he has cottage cheese, to which he replies that he always has cottage cheese and she need only check what she wants on her order slip. "I always mean to do that," she says, "but you're always here before I think of it" (19). She asks for coffee cream and buttermilk, explaining how her husband just can't get enough to eat now that he has stopped drinking.

Joan Lorring and Sidney Blackmer in *Come Back, Little Sheba*, 1950. Photo by Vandamm Studio, © Billy Rose Theatre Division, The New York Public Library for the Performing Arts, Astor, Lenox, and Tilden Foundations.

Consumerism, a key feature of 1950s housewifedom, is barely on Lola's radar.[40] However, by the end of the first act, having learned that Marie's Cincinnati beau is arriving the next day, Lola vows to cook "the best meal you ever sat down to" for the young couple (26). In question is less Lola's skill set than her motivation to embrace domestic labor. Stage directions in the first scene specify that Lola, facing her dirty kitchen, "clearly . . . is bored to death" (16). The rest of the play, however, confirms that she knows how to clean.

By the start of the second scene, the house has been transformed. Lola has scrubbed and polished everything and is washing the dinner dishes. Inge spells out the link between housework and the need for love as Lola responds to Doc's praise of the orderly house with a question: "I can be a good housekeeper when I want to be, can't I, Doc?" (28). She apologizes for not making much of a dinner and asks Doc if he'd like more beans. For once, he is not hungry. As they relax after dinner, their conversation provides not only backstory but more indications of the couple's lack of shared interests. Lola likes to dance and wishes Doc would take her out more, but he demurs, saying clubs are not a good idea since he stopped drinking. "Some night," he says, he'll take her out to dinner (34). Food becomes a signifier of festivity and community, but its pleasurable consumption is deferred indefinitely.

The dinner Lola prepares for Marie and her fiancé, Bruce, is described in loving detail in the next act. Lola reminds Doc to get home early and tells him what he can look forward to that evening. Her menu comprises "stuffed pork chops, twice-baked potatoes and asparagus, and for dessert a big chocolate cake and maybe ice cream" (44). She asks Marie to help her move a dining table into the living room—the only place big enough and suitable for the dinner—observing that it would "be nice now if we had a dining room, wouldn't it? But if we had a dining room, I guess we wouldn't have you, Marie. It was my idea to turn the dining room into a bedroom and rent it" (47). Lola has traded a normative food axis for a (surrogate) daughter, and now, for a brief moment, she looks forward to having some version of both at a single, special meal. That these two quotidian pleasures cannot coexist in this seemingly ordinary midwestern household is the pain that Inge is tracing—via food and housework—in a play that prompted reviewers for the original production to use such phrases as "lives of quiet desperation," "a Missouri 'Cherry Orchard,'"[41] and "the awful internal bleeding of mismated lives."[42]

When dinnertime arrives, Lola offers cocktails to Marie and Bruce, but Doc has absconded with the single bottle in the house, and, as Lola realizes he has gone on a bender, she shifts gears and claims there is no time for cocktails. She tells the couple that Doc was held up at the office. "I'm going to be the butler and serve the dinner to you two young love-birds" (52). The switch from hostess / fellow diner to servant re-orients the food axis, disconcerting Bruce and Marie, who ask Lola to eat with them. She declines, retreating to the kitchen to search fran-tically for the missing bottle, her panicked first step in dealing with Doc's falling off the wagon, an event precipitated by Doc's seeing Turk sneaking out of Marie's room that morning. Doc's illusions are shat-tered, and as becomes clear when he returns to the house, Marie and Lola both are sluts in his mind.

Lola's menu may read to present-day audiences as heavy and old-fashioned or even lowbrow. Twice-baked potatoes are, like the pork chops, stuffed (the condition to which Lola seems determined to make her guests), and recipes involve baking the potatoes, scooping out the insides, and then mixing the cooked potato with shredded cheddar cheese, milk, butter, and other seasonings or sautéed vegetables if desired, then restuffing the skins, and rebaking. Recipes for stuffed pork chops often include apples, but the obligatory ingredient is bread crumbs. Canned cream of mushroom soup—one of the stereotypical staples of 1950s cooking—still shows up in online recipes.[43] The des-sert is redolent of a child's birthday party.

What would New York audiences have thought in 1950? Probably they would have seen normalcy and nurturing. That Lola is preparing everything from scratch makes a point about both her underused but clearly existent skills and her devotion. American tastes in cuisine in the 1940s and 1950s were remarkably similar across class lines, and these tastes were not particularly sophisticated.[44] When *Better Homes and Gardens* issued in 1953 a revised version of their 1930s cookbook, the section on menu planning still called for dinners anchored by meat accompanied by a starch and salad, although the latter usually meant something "jellied or otherwise sweetened."[45] Of interest with regard to the Broadway audience for Inge's play is a 1961 survey of Manhat-tanites, which revealed little difference in diet preference from the rest of the nation, with New Yorkers typically favoring steak or chops at dinner, accompanied by a green or yellow vegetable, salad, and gelatin or canned or fresh fruit for dessert. Lola's inclusion of asparagus puts her ahead of the jellied-salad crowd in eating greens, while the choco-late cake makes her a little less calorie and vitamin conscious than the fruit-eating Manhattanites.[46]

152 One exception to the Manhattan norm was the small, elite clientele

for gourmet dining in expensive restaurants, deriving their status "in part, at least, from the sophistication of their consumption habits."[47] Economically, these would have been people who could afford to be among the 9 percent of Americans owning television sets in 1950 and also able to pay for Broadway tickets, in the last decade when Broadway still figured as a key player in elite culture.[48] They would as well have been plausible readers of the *New Yorker*, committed in this era to distinguishing between elite and mass culture.[49] Accordingly, it is hard to posit a single audience response to the Delaneys' diet. Lola is at once unsophisticated, normal, skilled, artisanal, completely non-kosher (both pork *and* dairy with meat), not like New Yorkers (the sophisticates) and exactly like New Yorkers (the Manhattanites in the survey). The ache of her loneliness, her husband's failure to care about any of her interests, her mother telling her on the telephone that she may not come home during her husband's binge because the father will not have her in the house, and her awareness of aging cut across class and culinary lines even as the individual foods and the menu hold possibilities for multiple readings.[50]

The play's climax occurs in the kitchen, the morning after the failed dinner. In an instance of a food service area turned toxic, the kitchen becomes the site of a brutal attack by Doc. He calls Lola a slut whom he "had" to marry and attacks her food preparation and housekeeping. The dinner, he says, was for *Bruce*, although Lola says it was for Doc, too. "What are you good for?" Doc taunts. "You can't even get up in the morning and cook my breakfast. . . . You won't even sweep the floors, till some bozo comes along to make love to Marie, and then you fix things up like . . . a Chinese whorehouse with perfume on the lamp-bulbs, and flowers, and the gold-trimmed china *my mother* gave us. We're not going to use these any more. My mother didn't buy those dishes for whores to eat off of. (*He jerks the cloth off the table, sending the dishes rattling to the floor*)" (56).

In a Stanley Kowalski moment, Doc, only able to see women as Madonna/housekeeper or whore/non-housekeeper, draws domestic boundaries that Lola cannot honor because they are inconsistent. In a rage, Doc grabs a hatchet from the back porch and goes after Lola, who has evidently had enough experience to know how to clutch him in such a way that the arm with the axe is disabled. Doc passes out; two AA buddies arrive; Doc is sent to dry out at the hospital (although not before the AA duo suggest some hot food). Doc, unsurprisingly, refuses, as Inge uses acceptance of food as an indicator of accepting the person who prepares it. A neighbor who has assisted Lola leaves to make breakfast for her children. Lola is greeted by a now-engaged Bruce and Marie, who announce that they are going to have breakfast downtown at the hotel. In one fell swoop, Lola's real and her surrogate family have walked out the door, ironically on the heels of her cleaning up her domestic act.

The final scene, occurring a week later, stages a reconciliation in terms of reorienting a disordered food axis. Lola, hoping Doc will arrive that day, greets the milkman, who praises her for using the checklist for her purchases. She has ordered "a lot of extras" pending Doc's return. Doc arrives. Once he apologizes and each acknowledges fear of being left by the other, matters turn to food. Doc says he declined a hospital breakfast and figured on making his own, but Lola jumps right in, offering scrambled eggs, fruit juice, toast, marmalade, and bacon, which she notes is expensive—another hint that she has only recently reentered the world of knowledgeable grocery shopping. Husband and wife agree that they need to move forward and forget the past—the past being a realm of sexuality, dancing, and hope. Lola's final line, both comforting and almost an absurd double entendre, might be read—with cautious optimism—as renewed hope for a revived sex life for the couple or—with the unblinking eyes of a cold realist—as an ominous statement that they will remain in a conjugal stalemate forever. Lola embraces Doc, goes to the stove, and announces, "I'll fix your eggs" (69).

DOMESTIC LABOR IN BLACK AND WHITE

To appreciate the shift that occurred in the 1950s in stage representations of black domestics and domesticity, one could hardly do better than to consider two unexpected hits bookending the decade on Broadway: Carson McCullers's *The Member of the Wedding* (1950) and Lorraine Hansberry's *A Raisin in the Sun* (1959). Each places an African American domestic worker at the center of its story. Together, *Member* and *Raisin* moved the black maid forever out of the margins in which she had been confined in mainstream commercial theatre for the previous three decades.[51]

Looking back on these two dramas, a careless cultural analyst may conflate *Member*'s Berenice Sadie Brown and *Raisin*'s Lena Younger.[52] Both are roles for black women in their late forties, fifties, or early sixties. Both characters are maternal but strong-willed. Neither is figured in relation to a white mistress. But these two main characters, their two stories, and their two kitchens point in opposite directions, one backward to a pre–mass commodity/post-Reconstruction, pre–civil rights Jim Crow South, and the other forward from the (unequally shared) prosperity of the Cold War to upward mobility.[53] Ironically, *upward* mobility may necessitate paying a price in the loss of community or neighborhood freedom of movement, something else revealed by a close look at how these two capable domestic captains maintain stewardship in the homes they are tasked with piloting through rough social waters.

Member's Berenice anchors the kitchen of the white family for whom she works, her own home unmentioned in the 1949 drama, although the 1946 novel on which *Member* is based has an extended scene there.[54] Berenice is no stranger to marijuana, unemployment, cross-dressing, homosexuality, teenage widowhood, and, by the end of the play, a death reported as a suicide but likely a lynching. The onstage kitchen she inhabits is heated by a coal stove, and she cooks on a cast-iron woodstove. There are electric lights and a refrigerator, although Berenice continues to call it an icebox. When her white employers move out of the house at the end of the play, Berenice neither goes with them nor has any sense of where she will seek work.

Nine years later, *Raisin*'s Lena is a city dweller seen in her own (rented) apartment juggling the needs of her family with regard to higher education, investing money, the anticipated integration of a neighborhood, and the purchase of real estate. She ends the play on the cusp of relocating to her own (owned) home, where she will perform domestic labor to the extent she is able or chooses for her own family—a form of liberation purchased for the price put by an insurance company on her late husband's very life. From woodstove to vacuum cleaner, the black domestic has moved from exotic other to what might be called exotic same, or perhaps tamed other. Racism remains unresolved, but mass culture will henceforward be the realm inhabited by blacks and whites.

The mass-produced, mass-mediated kitchen—including myriad housewares, grocery store comestibles, the proverbial kitchen sink, and the stove over which maid and mother both "slave"—will cross color lines with capitalist indifference, fueled by the gas, electricity, and water grids comprising a colorblind network of linked consumers and, by the end of the 1950s, will connect almost everyone.[55] During the postwar years producers of mass-market household goods began to advertise in publications aimed at African Americans. The first to attract "mainstream" advertising, *Ebony*, debuted in 1945.[56]

My purpose is *not* to suggest that following *A Raisin in the Sun* there was no appreciable difference between the struggles of black women and the struggles of white women represented in domestic dramas nodding to housework (much less in real life). Rather, it is to suggest that the materiality of the domestic realm on which fictional black lives were predicated changed. To miss this is to miss the cultural and demographic actualities on which characters and conflicts are erected. It is also to consign a particular type of character—the black domestic—to an ahistorical realm impervious to the sorts of nuances and specifics that make integration, frank discussion of sexuality, and physical contact between races ordinary and rich in the older play and somewhere on the spectrum from impossible to irrelevant to painfully fraught in the later one. My project here is to unpack the workings of character and culture in these two plays precisely in terms of domestic labor and the kitchen.

The Member of the Wedding is short on plot while long and deep on character.[57] It portrays a brief, crucial period in the lives of its three principals: twelve-year-old Frankie, a restless and imaginative tomboy shunned by the girls in the neighborhood; her seven-year-old cousin, John Henry, a sweet-tempered boy who loves dolls, baking cookies, following Frankie, and hanging around the kitchen; and Berenice, the African American woman who cares for the children and is cook, caregiver, confidant, and locus of stability. She works for Frankie's father, a widower since the day of Frankie's birth.

Frankie yearns to belong somewhere, and she becomes obsessed with the idea that her brother and soon-to-be sister-in-law will take her with them on their honeymoon and into their future lives. She is, of course, disappointed in this. The desire for the bride and groom to become the "'we' of me"[58] leads to her having to be dragged from the couple's car as they are about to depart for their honeymoon, but by the end of the play—a denouement occurring three months following the central wedding weekend—Frankie's despair over feeling like a freak is displaced by a close friendship with a new neighborhood girl and some definite interest in a neighborhood boy. Frankie moves into what appears to have the makings of normal adolescence. Little John Henry dies offstage of meningitis, after giving only a hint of not feeling well.[59] Berenice is able to help both children but is herself left "alone and motionless" in the play's final moment.[60] Her foster brother has hanged himself in jail; the younger of her two charges is dead; Frankie and her father are moving to a suburb, and Berenice has given notice, as the new household will include an aunt for whom Berenice "could never get used to" working.[61]

Berenice's relation to the kitchen is more than one of character to setting or environment, although it is certainly that. The kitchen in this play is almost a character itself; it is also a kind of metaphor and doppelganger for Berenice. As goes the kitchen, so goes Berenice. While the source novel features scenes in several other parts of the small city where it is set and places the wedding at the bride's home in another town, the play stages virtually all its action in the kitchen, with a few encounters and one scene occurring in the adjacent, visible backyard. Lester Polakov, the set designer for the first production, relates that the play originally had a scene at a downtown bar, but this was scrapped in tryouts.[62]

Accordingly, the kitchen in the play as produced and published is telescoped into an almost oppressive centrality exceeding that of the novel, although there it is also plenty stifling and self-contained. Polakov's sketch of the kitchen shows it to be spare, dominated by the two non-electric stoves, but as a definite *extension* of the main house. The suburban ideal would figure the kitchen as one of the *central* gathering areas of the house, often featuring an open arrangement contiguous with den or living room. *Member*'s kitchen is its own world.

To understand the kitchen as a character, it helps to refer to the novel, although this intertext is not requisite for understanding its connections with Berenice. Some of the novel's ideas about kitchen and domestic are repeated in the necessarily shorter script; others were generated via casting, design, and staging in the production. The novel calls the kitchen a "sad and ugly room," stating John Henry had "covered the walls with queer, child drawings . . . [that] gave the kitchen a crazy look."[63]

Sadness clings to Berenice, who mourns her first (of four) husbands, whose death thirteen years before the start of the play created an emptiness that has never disappeared. Berenice herself is described as having a "flat" face and a glass eye that "stared out fixed and wild," creating strangeness—like the "craziness,"[64] a facet of perception rather than objective diagnosis—in part because it is blue. The drawings, flat face, and blue glass eye also appear on the first page of the published script; the drawings and drab but serviceable kitchen appear in production photos. Later in the novel McCullers calls the kitchen "too flat and too square," on top of it being gray, and "a stale gray" at that.[65] Analogously, Berenice is described as "broad shouldered and short,"[66] bodily dimensions that jibe with "square." Actress Ethel Waters, at the time she originated the role of Berenice, was tall, but she had become fat enough to fit adjectives like "bulky" or "boxy."[67]

Proportional dimensions and physical appearance, although offering fruitful points of comparison, are not the only ways in which the kitchen speaks as character or as analogue for a generationally bound domesticity. Time itself is figured in terms of the kitchen, as, for example, the time Frankie spends at home between going out in the morning to wander her town and going out at night to find a soldier with whom she has made a date is called "the long kitchen afternoon."[68] The kitchen of the play's conclusion is largely empty save for a chair and the coal stove. Sitting anchored in place in this scene—a scene about moving, about leaving the past behind, and about both emptiness and hope—is Berenice, in both novel and play. She is beset by memories of John Henry and the foster brother as well as of her first and truly beloved husband, as she sits wearing the fox fur wrap he gave her years earlier. Haunted, motionless, no longer working, abandoned, stripped of everything important: the description fits both Berenice and the kitchen. In an unsubtle authorial move, McCullers has Frankie observe that the kitchen clock has stopped just a few pages before the curtain falls on the "motionless" Berenice.

Perhaps the most potent way in which domestic worker and kitchen are conflated emerges in how other characters treat the two virtually as one, simultaneously drawn to and resentful of both. In the opening scene, John Henry's mother, Aunt Pet, suggests more than once that Berenice has some powers over her little boy that might be suspect, asking "what on earth" Berenice *does* to him to make him "stick . . .

Ethel Waters in *The Member of the Wedding*, 1950. Photo by Alfredo Valente. Used by permission of Richard Valente and the Billy Rose Theatre Division, New York Public Library for the Performing Arts, Astor, Lenox, and Tilden Foundations.

over here in your kitchen morning, noon and night."[69] That it is the kitchen on which she focuses and that she reads the kitchen as belonging to Berenice are more than throwaways. Trudier Harris, in her study of domestics in black American literature, states that the kitchen in a white home with a black domestic "becomes the black town, the nigger room, of the white house," adding that it is both the place to which **159** the domestic retreats to await bidding to other parts of the house and "the one room in the house where the white woman can give up spatial ownership without compromising herself. Kitchens have connotations of hard work and meniality—sweat, grime, broken fingernails, and other things from which the mistress wishes to dissociate herself."[70]

Berenice, like the kitchen, offers haven as well as sustenance. She listens to Frankie's troubles; plays cards with the two youngsters; alters the dress Frankie buys to wear to the wedding; cooks and serves meals; makes the wedding cake, cookies, and sandwiches; watches the children; and washes dishes. Frankie relies on Berenice for comfort but also derides her as incapable of understanding anything, attacking Berenice for perceived insults and constraints. In one particularly confrontational moment, Frankie threatens Berenice with a carving knife. When the latter says, "Just throw it! You just!" Frankie does, aiming it carefully at a door leading out of the kitchen. Her emotional target is Berenice; the physical target is the kitchen door. When Frankie bids farewell and imagines she is leaving for good with the bride and groom, her short line of dialogue begins with "Goodbye, Berenice" and ends with "Farewell, old ugly kitchen."[71] The number of times McCullers includes "kitchen" in the stage directions, even when it is redundant, is telling.[72]

Berenice's kitchen, like Berenice herself, is also most emphatically not suburban or the sort of kitchen in which young housewife Aunt Pet would likely see a desirable future for herself. Immediately following World War II, the US government promoted suburbanization through a nexus of initiatives that included demolishing inner-city housing, constructing highways, introducing tax shelters for developers, and providing tax breaks for homeowners. William Levitt "used kitchen appliances as an advertising tool to seduce prospective working-class couples" to his Levittowns.[73] In the penultimate paragraph of the novel Frankie notes that the new house has a basement and a laundry room, an observation she slips between fantasies about European travel and crushes on art and new friends. This does not entice Berenice; it does not embody Berenice. When the play's Frankie fantasizes in her penultimate line about going to Luxembourg one day, Berenice responds that the place-name reminds her of soapy water, referencing laundry flakes and the first mass-marketed complexion soap: Lux.[74] On the surface, it would seem she cannot envision a larger world than the one circumscribed by her domestic environs, skills, and chores.

To acquiesce to this assessment, however, would be to miss the rich life that Berenice has outside the kitchen until the play's foreclosing string of disasters. It is this life that would be snuffed out in the new, suburban kitchen, which, if that stands for creature comfort in terms of appliances, spells confinement in terms of independence and cultural identity. One wonders if Berenice would be asked to wear a uniform. She would certainly no longer be able to walk to work. Frankie hints at Berenice's rich world at one point: "When Berenice says 'we' she means her lodge and church and colored people. . . . All people belong to a 'we' except me."[75]

Berenice reveals a great deal about her world, as she describes stepping out to the movies and regales the children with the story of her four marriages. She stops short at going into detail about not liking to sleep alone, deciding the discussion is too frank for John Henry's ears. She does not cavil about telling Frankie about a young man who fell in love with another young man, took to cross-dressing, and "changed his nature and his sex and turned into a girl."[76] Berenice's social world also permeates the kitchen, as an elderly vegetable peddler, Sis Laura, stops by to sell her wares. Astute observers of the original set might have noticed that the few packaged foods on the set are on a shelf too high to reach easily. Tellingly, the vegetable peddler also dies during the course of the play.

If one reads Aunt Pet as a proto June Cleaver of the white suburbs depicted in *Leave It to Beaver*, one can see how Berenice's world is irrelevant in the commodified realm of a suburban ideal.[77] Audiences could see that Berenice's story was, despite the size of the maid's role, secondary to Frankie's, to the extent that the latter's is dramatized and catapults the girl into a future. It is important to remember Pam Morris's observation that "what is seen as 'reality' depends on the social position of the perceiver" and to consider the social position of the original audiences for the play—largely, although not exclusively, white, middle- and upper-middle class residents of the metropolitan New York area.[78]

But audiences of the original production also read Berenice through a lens not available to a present-day reader of the text: the person, per-

Portion of the stage set for *The Member of the Wedding*, designed by Lester Polakov, 1950. Featured: Julie Harris, Ethel Waters, and Brandon DeWilde. Photo by Alfredo Valente. Used by permission of Richard Valente and the Billy Rose Theatre Division, New York Public Library for the Performing Arts, Astor, Lenox, and Tilden Foundations.

sonality, and career of actress Ethel Waters.[79] She was the only star in the production and had been a headliner in New York for more than a quarter century when *Member* opened. Reviews reveal that it was difficult for many to read the play's realism any other way than via Waters, yet a Waters—and a Berenice—understood in terms of typology, show business, and a certain amount of timelessness rather than via cultural materiality.

Ethel Waters had made two memorable appearances on Broadway in the 1930s, both in performances that brought to light abuses familiar to all southern (and many northern and midwestern) American blacks. In the 1933 Moss Hart/Irving Berlin revue *As Thousands Cheer*, Waters sang three numbers. "Heat Wave" and "Harlem on My Mind" fit the usual upbeat, feel-good nature of a musical revue, but Waters's third song, "Supper Time," was a dramatic piece she performed wearing an apron and a bandana on her head, appearing before a plain brick wall on which was displayed the silhouette of a man hanging from a tree with a rope around his neck. The song is an interior monologue in which the woman is dutifully putting dinner on the table for her children, wondering how she will tell them why their father is not coming home.

Years later, actress Carol Channing stated in an interview that Waters's entrance and the number were shocking. "We didn't know in those days about lynchings in the South."[80] Channing does not define "we," leaving open possibilities such as northerners, northern whites, theatregoers, people in show business, or the politically uninformed.[81] Waters would write in her autobiography that the song told "the whole tragic history of a race" and that "[i]n singing it I was telling my comfortable, well-fed well-dressed listeners about my people."[82] In the 1939 play *Mamba's Daughters*, Waters played a woman who murders a man for cavalierly seducing her daughter. The actress received seventeen curtain calls on opening night.[83] She wrote later that in the play she had burned to tell her own mother's story, one she herself would encode in her autobiography, where she reports her mother giving birth (to Ethel) after being raped at age twelve.[84] Both song and play show women taking domestic labor in stride while wrestling with familial abuse, much as in the antilynching plays discussed in chapters 1 and 2.

If audiences or critics remembered these earlier performances, they exercised a kind of adulatory amnesia in praising Waters in 1950. A few were careful to observe that Berenice as played by Waters was no simple "mammy,"[85] but many reviews opted for a vision of Waters-as-Berenice in timeless, ahistorical terms such as "Christlike," "earthy," and "Old Testament Agelessness," extolling the "mystic heritage of her race."[86] One reviewer called her "the symbol of the . . . nobility we all have, at some time or other, taken carelessly for granted," while Brooks Atkinson of the *New York Times* summed her up as "natively-wise" and possessing "through instinct . . . a strong hold on the fundamentals of life and belong[ing] to the human race body and soul."[87] Positive though these statements are, they relegate both character and actress to a kind of sentimental, pious, vaguely Christian-humanist essentialism.

Waters's autobiography, published just a year after *Member* opened, revealed many of the ways in which Berenice's life was precisely like the actress's own, up to the point that Waters achieved success as a singer, which was in her teens. The similarities included segregated slum housing with no toilet, a first marriage (of several) at age thirteen, drug-addicted community members, same-sex relationships, and domestic service or other housekeeping work.[88] In other words, praising Berenice out of deference to Waters's status and personality (she had "overcome" her past and had been one of the highest-paid black performers on Broadway) actually ignored the reasons why the history she brought to the role might be of interest for its timely resonance and specificity rather than for any comforting, distancing iconicity.

The Waters of *Member of the Wedding* portrayed a real way of life defined by poverty and racism, but not by stupidity, ignorance, or an absence of interior life, critical insight, skills, and community. This way of life, was, however, too lacking in bourgeois, consumer ideals to be worthy of a positive ending, at least one penned by a youthful white writer memorializing her own aspirations. Frankie yearns to leave her hometown, and at the end of the play her trajectory is foreshadowed as she leaves the house with the oppressive kitchen, unabashedly labeled "stripped [and] ugly" by one reviewer.[89] For at least three decades following the opening of *Member of the Wedding*, the suburban ideal would contribute to urban decay, inner-city black slums, and "white flight." From a present-day perspective, Berenice's sexuality, easy ac-

ceptance of homosexuality, recognition of drugs as a problem, independence, and willingness to work to pay her own way—all the while
manifesting domestic skills that sustain but do not define her—look
curiously ahead of their time, coal stove or no.

The relation between Lena Younger, the matriarch in the 1959
A Raisin in the Sun, and her kitchen and domestic labor, is something
altogether different, and the play itself was unlike anything else previously seen on Broadway. It was the first play in that arena to be written by a black woman, to be directed by a black director, and to offer a
contemporary look at black life in a form that was not musical comedy
or even comedy. This look was immediately recognized and embraced.
The word appearing most frequently in the 1959 reviews is "honesty"
(or "honest");[90] the play's enduring status coupled with the continued
belief in its honesty has earned it more recent praise for its relevance
and resonance.[91] The original production ran 530 performances and
won the New York Drama Critics' Circle Award for Best Play of 1959.

Raisin depicts the working-class, multigenerational, African American Younger family living in a cramped Chicago apartment with no
private bathroom, many cockroaches, the threat of rats, and dreams of
a better life. The grandfather/patriarch has recently died, and on the
day the play opens the family is awaiting a ten thousand–dollar check
from the life insurance company. The play's action concerns their decision about using the money, a decision about what kind of family,
what kinds of blacks, and what kinds of Americans they will be, as well
as what kind of domesticity they prize. The matriarch (Lena) wants to
make a down payment on a freestanding, single-family house with a
yard; her adult son (Walter) wants to go into business as the co-owner
of a liquor store; his wife (Ruth), the daughter-in-law in the family,
is eager for the new house, as her young son (Travis) currently sleeps
in the living room and is beginning to be influenced by street life;
the college-student daughter (Beneatha), aspiring to medical school,
hopes for tuition money.

Lena makes the down payment on the best affordable house she can
find, but this is in an all-white neighborhood, and her son is outraged,
both over the loss of the full amount of the check and because he is not
interested in living among whites. One of Walter's business partners
absconds with two-thirds of the money, leading Walter to despair. He
also decides to accept the offer of the white neighborhood's represen-

tative to buy back the house at a profit to the Youngers. The family's mutual caring, moral fiber, and willingness to integrate a neighborhood in the name of justice and their right as working Americans to a cleaner, crime-free home emerge as the son reverses his decision, something facilitated dramaturgically by his mother insisting that his own young son be present when he accepts the white man's offer. The realization that the family's six generations of hard work in the United States are more important than the short-term profit had audiences sobbing and cheering.

Raisin presents Lena ("Mama") in her own kitchen, which is really just a kitchenette on the edge of the living room. Virtually everything in the Youngers' domestic setting does double duty. The living room also serves as dining room; the sofa is the grandchild's bed; the one-time breakfast room is now a bedroom; and, as the playwright notes of the living room in which all the action is set, "weariness has . . . won in this room."[92] Lena may seem to resemble her domestic environment, but she wants something better. Despite her white hair, age, "careless" speech (39), and playing multiple roles in the household— doting grandmother, stern parent, adulatory widow, sometime wage earner, disappointed victim of racist economics—Lena ends *A Raisin in the Sun* standing, and her final action is to leave for good the environment that she refuses to allow to destroy her family or, more specifically, their dreams.

Her relation to domestic labor is both bifurcated and pragmatic. In her own home, Saturdays are devoted to housecleaning, with all three women hard at work. On the day of the move, Lena demands to carry the box containing her skillets herself, as she plans to cook a big meal the minute the family gets to their new house. While she and her daughter-in-law work or have worked as domestics, they express no sense of affection for their white employers and are even dismissive of their employers' ignorance and selfishness. Ruth works through an agency instead of having a long-standing situation with any one family, giving her a perspective based on multiple households. Lena recognizes that white mistresses regard black domestics with suspicion, distrust, and sheer ignorance, advising the pregnant Ruth, who is too weak to go in to work on the day the play starts, to say she has the flu: "They know 'bout the flu. Otherwise they think you been cut up or something when you tell 'em you sick" (43). Domestic work at home is a labor of life and source of pride; domestic labor for others is an oppressive necessity.

Domestic labor is, however, a crucial locus of cracks in the family's solidarity, particularly with regard to its future. Foremost, despite the unity they seem to espouse when they finally decide to purchase the house—Ruth notes that with four adults in the house, all can work to help make the mortgage payments if need be—only some of that work, work for pay, is envisioned as an equal opportunity venture. All domestic labor falls to the women. At the start of the Saturday housecleaning scene, ten-year-old Travis claims he has finished his chores and is excused from further work, although the scrubbing and spraying for vermin are far from finished. We don't know what those chores were, but his grandmother has demonstrated at the start of the play that she thinks it is all right for him to leave for school without making up his daybed, a minimal and "clean" task at worst. At the start of the play, Ruth gets up before her son and her husband so she can awaken both and make separate breakfasts for them, on a day when she has ironing to finish (possibly for a client) and work as a domestic in someone else's home ahead of her. In other words, the women in this household are expected and expect to be responsible for a double shift.

Hansberry was no fan of embourgeoisement for its own sake. In an article published shortly after the opening of *A Raisin in the Sun*, she discussed the quest for dignity, not material betterment, as the important one in any worthy American Dream. "It is easier," she wrote, "to dream of personal wealth than of a communal state wherein universal dignity is supposed to be a corollary."[93] Whatever is supposed to be communal in the Younger home does not apply to the labor it takes to fight the dirt and dinginess that are high on the list of reasons to want to move.

In a scene that was cut from the original production but restored in revivals, Mama tells a visiting neighbor that her husband "always said being any kind of a servant wasn't a fit thing for a man to have to be. He always said a man's hands was made to make things, or turn the earth with—not to drive nobody's car for 'em—or—*(She looks at her own hands)* carry they slop jars. And my boy is just like him—he wasn't meant to wait on nobody" (103). The look at her own hands may indicate that she has endured servitude (or it may refer to her love of gardening); the failure to mention Ruth's work suggests that either gender or blood determines what work "fits" whom. Either way, Ruth falls outside the catchment.

Ruth is repeatedly depicted in the script as ironing, and Walter once asks her in frustration why she is always trying to give him something to eat, to which she replies, "What else can I give you?" (88). Whatever the family imagines the future holds for them in their new house— "betterment," a yard, and a bedroom for Travis, self-respect for Walter, a comfortable retirement for Mama, medical school for Beneatha— Ruth can anticipate only more domestic labor.

Perhaps the most intriguing character regarding domestic labor is Beneatha. Her student status and wish to be a doctor suggest that she will eventually be able to hire her own domestic labor if she wishes, although she pitches in during the Saturday-morning scene. Nonetheless, she may also pose a threat to the communal schema Hansberry posits. Steven Carter, in his reading of *Raisin*, points out Hansberry's "one serious artistic misstep" is her depiction of Beneatha as willing to purchase a fifty-five-dollar riding habit about which we learn shortly after seeing Ruth deny her son fifty cents for a project at school.[94] Beneatha, arguably a typical college girl, has been part of a theatre group, signed up for horseback riding, brought home photography equipment, and is about to start guitar lessons. She rails at an upstairs neighbor whose daily vacuuming is a nuisance ("How much cleaning can a house need?" [46]), all suggesting that she is self-absorbed but also that housecleaning is for her a source of neither comfort nor identity, as it clearly is for both her mother and her sister-in-law, and possibly for the woman upstairs. Louis Kronenberger, editor of the *Best Plays* series in 1959 and full of praise for the play, called Beneatha "arty [and] callow."[95]

Her self-absorption and what her mother calls her tendency to flit from one thing to another may be the most realistic—at least according to statistics—thing about her. A late Cold War–era *Mademoiselle* magazine survey revealed that young women "wanted to be well-rounded rather than to excel."[96] A 1961 Purdue University poll showed that about 35 percent of American teenagers intended to be professionals, "three and a half times the 10 percent of American workers who actually were professionals that year."[97] Beneatha, whose studiousness is never portrayed in *Raisin* and who seems no more interested in biology than in subjects in the liberal arts, may well be on the road to privileged housewifedom—the ultimate realm in which her brother can imagine Ruth, and a realm in which, at last, someone else will do the housework.

Recent scholarship on *A Raisin in the Sun* has focused on the politics and behaviors of "home" that the play explores.[98] Kristin L. Matthews argues that the house purchased by the Youngers embodies the desire for psychic as well as physical space in which to achieve both their individual dreams and their shared goal of equality and citizenship. This nexus of aspirations depends on the expectation that at least the older two women will continue to perform domestic labor for the whole family. Matthews connects Ruth's persistence in keeping the apartment orderly and her push for the move as suggesting "literally and symbolically . . . a resigned acceptance of her position of disempowerment with both the socio-economic system and the structure of her family."[99]

Soyica Diggs Colbert cannily points to Lena's maintenance of gender inequality via the act of giving the insurance money to her son, who is defrauded of what he thinks is an investment in a business venture. This "mistake" suggests "the extra steps women must take in order to enhance the functionality of the economy of repeated actions, which through their repetition reconfigure the symbolic order."[100] These repeated actions include the domestic labor that shows up over and over again in the play in Ruth's ironing and meal preparation, Beneatha's Saturday cleaning, and Lena's care for her plant. Travis will grow up, Beneatha will graduate from college, Lena will plant her garden, and Walter will perhaps find another job, but breakfast time will recur each and every morning and Saturday will come, no matter what, once a week, guaranteeing Ruth's stuckness, and possibly Beneatha's.

As Diggs notes, the setting of the play—the cramped apartment— "serves as a reflection of each character's limitations, working to constitute who they are and believe themselves to be."[101] Playwrights who reimagined *A Raisin in the Sun* a half century after its original appearance see alcoholism for Travis and the evolution of Clybourne Park (the white neighborhood in which the Youngers' new house is located) into a black slum.[102] Both projections include a breakdown of care for the household.

It is foolish to expect any play to "solve" the problems it presents, and in the case of *A Raisin in the Sun*, bearing, as it does, so much cultural weight on its shoulders, such an expectation would only diminish the possibilities it opens up. Critical work on the play has examined, most obviously, racism, but also citizenship, pan-Africanism, civil rights, socialism, and the limitations of thinking in terms of universalism. Domestic labor—especially in the context of any American Dream—belongs on the list.

THE AMERICAN DREAM, AGAIN

Early in 1961, with *A Raisin in the Sun* still on the boards, Edward Albee's one-act *The American Dream* opened at the York Playhouse in New York City under the direction of Alan Schneider.[103] This dark satire marked both the end of one era of playwriting and the dawn of another, both with implications for representations of domestic labor. Albee had already garnered attention with the violent, anti-bourgeois two-hander *The Zoo Story* (1960), and his producer, Richard Barr, who would also produce (with Clinton Wilder) *The American Dream* and later *Who's Afraid of Virginia Woolf?*, "carefully marketed" Albee's career by linking him in publicity materials to the European absurdists.[104] *The American Dream* got mixed reviews in the New York dailies, but the importance of the thirty-two-year-old playwright to both Off- and Off-Off-Broadway was unmistakable.[105] Indeed, in 1967, British theatre writer Brian Way would say, "*The American Dream* and *The Zoo Story* are the most exciting productions of the American theatre in the last fifteen years."[106]

The American Dream depicts a vapid, upper-middle-class couple, Mommy and Daddy, in their comfortable but sterile home. They are unable to love physically, as Mommy is repelled by sex and Daddy is out of commission due to an unspecified surgery. They are also unable to love emotionally—the effects of dismembering the child they adopted more than twenty years earlier because of the boy's refusal to look at Mommy in the manner she desired and his touching his genitals. The couple also ridicules Grandma, whose emerging dotage is largely an annoyance. In the playwright's attack on American consumerist complacency, much of the anger is directed toward the American family.[107] In this family, domestic labor codes a dystopia whose failures are strictly gendered; particular wrath is reserved for the mother/housekeeper manquée. Not for nothing is the female protagonist called Mommy rather than (for example) Woman or Wife.

Albee's script calls for two armchairs set on opposite sides of the stage, a sofa, an archway, and a door. Reviews of the original production indicate that William Ritman's set also featured empty picture frames. The suggestion of there being nothing to depict, or nothing worth looking at, is not subtle, nor is the playwright's indication that this is an apartment in which nothing works (shades of *Death of a Salesman*) and where no one is able to fix things or aggressive about finding good service people. We learn in the first minute of dialogue that the doorbell, the refrigerator, and the toilet are all broken. A few pages later we learn that Mommy grew up poor but married the mon-eyed Daddy, who also supports Grandma. Grandma performs domestic labor, although Mommy "can't stand" watching her parent do the cook-ing, housework, polishing silver, and moving furniture. She threatens to send Grandma to a nursing home, but she "can't bring herself to give up the free maid service."[108]

Mommy represents the worst of all possible femininities. She mar-ried for money, does not want to have sex, has rejected her child, would like to put her parent in a nursing home, and does not want to clean her own house. Even the energetic, indomitable Grandma is not exempt from female-targeted criticism. Her domestic labor is marked by an at-tempt to put one over on a clueless America, as she secretly entered a baking contest and won twenty-five thousand dollars with her recipe, which comprises a store-bought cake left to get stale for twenty-four hours (136–37). Domestic labor is no better than a store-bought cake, as no one can tell the difference; it is no guarantee of love, evident in Mommy's freely threatening to move Grandma to the nursing home; and it still requires outside specialists when things break down. Those who perform domestic labor—women—are put out to pasture when they get old. Those who don't perform it—other women—are selfish connivers. There is no way Mommy can win in this realm. Her do-mestic labor, even if were to exist, is replaceable. Her parenting was grotesque. And her gender is under attack, even via internalized self-loathing. One of the major insults she hurls at Daddy is, "You're turn-ing into jelly; you're indecisive; you're a woman" (111).

The equation "woman = housewife who performs domestic labor," in conjunction with the equation "woman = inferior and useless" is neither tenuous nor speculative. Feminists who would in the early 1970s embrace Marxism in their critique of wives' position under capitalism defined women as "that group of people who are responsible for the production of simple-use-values in those activities associated with the home and family."[109] Mariarosa Dalla Costa stated unequivocally in 1973 that "the role of the working class housewife . . . is *the* determinant for the position of all other women."[110] That women as a category were weak and less than men had been the thesis of the widely known *Modern Woman: The Lost Sex* of 1947, in which lack of interest in children, housework, mothering, and satisfying a man were linked to women's own unhappiness, neurotic children, impotent husbands, and disorder in the world. In this schema a proper woman is inherently weak and dependent upon man.[111] Perhaps Mommy had read the book; she knows that womanliness—good or bad—is defined by weakness.

Critics for the original production of *The American Dream* reserved particular vitriol for Mommy—vitriol invited but not necessarily required by the text. Mommy was seen as "aggressive," "rapacious," and "domineering," while Daddy was read as "mummified," or "acquiescent, puttering."[112] Both Albee's character construction (which, in my reading, does not mandate a "rapacious" performance by the actor playing Mommy and leaves plenty of room for a conniving, indifferent, and passive-aggressive Daddy) and attitudes in the ambient culture support these misogynist readings of Mommy as "the controller and castrator of a defenseless and emasculated Daddy."[113] That Mommy/housewife has been "effeminated" cannot enter the critical consciousness, in part, perhaps, because no such word exists.

The "predatory housewife" is a dramatic character at least as old as George Kelly's 1925 Harriet Craig (see discussion of *Craig's Wife* in chapter 2), but the vitriol undergirding such a housewife's depiction as not just grasping and needy but dangerous, stupid, controlling, damaging to her sons, and politically risible, got a shot in the arm from the 1955 publication of Philip Wylie's "bestselling diatribe, *A Generation of Vipers*," which accused middle-aged women of "jibber[ing]," being "nosy neuter[s]," and having "beady eyes behind their beady brains," as they deform their sons in the wake of their idleness, stupidity, and self-absorption.[114] While later critics have nodded to the autobiographical underpinnings in the play (Albee's adoptive parents spent little "quality time" with him; his mother was domineering; he loved his grandmother), in 1961, a critique of bourgeois complacency that figured housewife as viper and husband as henpecked putterer did not arouse (male critics') ire.

As if on cue, a wholly opposite picture of domesticity and domestic labor hit Broadway with full force in the latter part of 1961. *How to Succeed in Business Without Really Trying* garnered seven Tony Awards at the end of the season in 1962, including Best Musical, as well as the Pulitzer Prize for Drama. *How to Succeed*, which ran for 1,417 performances in its initial incarnation and was revived on Broadway in 1995 and again in 2011, is a satire of corporate ladder climbing, but while it skewers conformity, the yes-man mentality, and the distance between self-important executives and their irrelevant output, it does little to interrogate a gendered status quo. The women in the musical are effective workers, but they can look forward to only limited options: high pay and unmarried battle-axdom; low professional status with the hope of marriage as rescue; or glamour and money for those of the hour-glass figure and sex-for-money persuasion.

For feminists, *How to Succeed*'s signature poison kiss is the lyrically sappy song "Happy to Keep His Dinner Warm," in which the ingénue, a secretary, rhapsodizes about her desire to marry, retreat to suburbia, and watch her adored hubby "go onward and upward." She fully expects to be ignored and awaits the day that she can announce she's pregnant.[115] Betty Friedan's *New York Times* obituary quoted the song verbatim to limn the woman whose chains Friedan sought to break as "happy to keep his dinner warm till he came wearily home from downtown."[116] Domestic labor in Westchester represents Cinderella's dream come true; presumably it also suited Prince Charming.

Asking which was the outcome of a fraught Cold War period of consumer comfort, conformity, early marriages, and a baby boom—housewifedom as the realm of dead souls or domesticity as a girl's fondest dream—poses the wrong question. American culture, two larger-than-life feminist icons, and a cascade of new legislation would in short order keep both stances in full view. More important, perhaps, for most women the two stances were less polar opposites than they were partners in a complicated dance of identity. That American theatre itself was also in the throes of a changing profile signaled fascinating performance times ahead.

6   PRISONERS OF TOTAL BLAME

1963–1993

By any account, 1963 was a game changer for the United States. Labeled by historian William E. Leuchtenburg as "a year when everything began to come apart," 1963 is easily pegged even by nonspecialists for President John F. Kennedy's assassination and Rev. Martin Luther King Jr.'s "I Have a Dream" speech delivered during a march on Washington by two hundred thousand people showing their support of civil rights for blacks.[1] It was the year that the United States, the Soviet Union, and the United Kingdom signed the Nuclear Test Ban Treaty, signaling a thaw in the Cold War. But 1963 was also the year that domestic labor entered American consciousness as a political, financial, and lifestyle issue, and it did so simultaneously from stage left and from stage right.

The publication of Betty Friedan's *The Feminine Mystique* and the first airing of Julia Child's television cooking show, *The French Chef* (her book *Mastering the Art of French Cooking* had been published two years earlier), within months of each other threw down two gauntlets. Friedan's diagnosis of what she called "the problem that has no name" exposed what she saw as the mind-numbing repetitiveness, isolation, and stifling irrelevance of the cookie-baking, diaper-laundering, hostessing lives of housewives without paid work or any place in the public sphere. Child, arguably presenting a diametrically opposite mind-set, celebrated the creative pleasures of cooking in one's own kitchen via her witty, casual but passionate, hands-on combination of instruction and entertainment in the realm of homemade gourmet cuisine.

Friedan's book is almost universally credited with launching the so-called second wave of feminism in the United States.[2] Her head-on assault on social norms and then-legal practices that trapped a broad

swath of women in the dead-end roles of homebound, financially dependent housewife and mommy extolled cultivating the self. Ironically,
at least one of Child's scholarly champions sees that as her mission.
Dana Polan observes: "Child believed fundamentally . . . that the best
means to a person's self-realization in any domain, culinary or otherwise, was through energetic engagement in vital activity, not through
avoidance of it. . . . To shortcut the culinary process would be to shortcut the cultivation of self."[3] If Betty Friedan and Julia Child were ten-
nis players, one might ask whether it makes more sense to pit them
against each other or to team them up in a doubles match. For three
decades, American theatre would be one forum in which an ideological
version of that question was bandied about.

To say that this argument extended over thirty years is not to say
that no major shifts occurred to define those decades politically or culturally. The 1960s fostered the rise of youth culture; the use of recreational drugs as part of a resistance to the proprieties of the earlier
postwar years; and vociferous objections to the Vietnam War, all perhaps subsumable under the (too) broad rubric "the counterculture."
The Civil Rights Act of 1964 banned discrimination based on race and
wage discrimination based on gender in its Title VII. (It did not ban
gender preference in hiring.) By 1968, a conservative counterpoint
made its power clear when the nation elected Republican Richard
Nixon president.

During the 1970s many of the developments of the 1960s entered
widespread public consciousness, leading to the tag "the me decade"
because of popular focus across the political spectrum on private fulfillment. Title IX of the 1972 Education Act, prohibiting sex discrimination in any educational program receiving federal aid, signaled the
arrival of the women's movement. If domestic labor had not been left
behind by American women, it had moved over to make room for
higher education and work outside the home for pay as ordinary expectations—and ordinary overload—for many. Perhaps most significantly,
the 1970s was a decade of personal growth and a distrust of government. The latter came into focus during the 1973–74 oil crisis and was
solidified when Nixon resigned in 1974 in the wake of the Watergate
scandal. Conservatism wedded to consumerism set up national housekeeping in the 1980s as "Reaganomics" delivered lower taxes, smaller
government, and deregulation. The latter led to the sort of mergers

and Wall Street greed that benefited the glamorous few, created life-style envy among more, and wrought safety-net havoc for the many on the bottom (such as the housecleaners in Joan Holden's *Nickel and Dimed*, discussed in chapter 7).[4]

Nonetheless, the three decades that began in 1963 share two phenomena—one regarding labor and the other theatre—that make it reasonable to consider the period as an era. Foremost, these decades fall under the rubric of "second-wave feminism," and it is through this lens that many debates about domestic labor were read in these years. The "home-work dilemma" defined second-wave feminism in the popular imagination and has functioned as almost an axiomatic historiographic paradigm.[5] Yet housewives' struggles for acknowledgment of their labor *as* labor, for parity in the workplace, and for help with domestic labor from husbands and children neither eliminated the need to perform domestic labor nor erased the possibility of doing some facets of it with creativity and pleasure, thus problematizing any clear-cut feminist vs. housewife standoff.

These questions are taken up in my examination of Neil Simon's *Prisoner of Second Avenue*, Israel Horovitz's *Park Your Car in Harvard Yard*, and Sam Shepard's *True West*. Martha Rosler's *Semiotics of the Kitchen* is a key site for examining this issue via performance. Marsha Norman's *'night, Mother* shows it in microscopic action. Neither *Semiotics of the Kitchen* nor *'night, Mother* depicts the housewife as spouse.[6] Accordingly, disentangling domestic labor from housewifedom continues to challenge our readings of the era in which both the stultifying nature of the work and its conflation with the worker were exposed.

The second cultural umbrella uniting these three decades is the collection of changes in theatre that altered the performance landscape in which domestic labor could and would be examined theatrically. This era saw both the entrenchment of Off-Off-Broadway and the burgeoning of the regional theatre movement.[7] Starting in the 1960s, not-for-profit would overtake for-profit as the normative business model, enabling the development of niche theatre movements to target particular interest groups.[8] Three specific developments in the 1960s retooled the American theatre landscape overall. First, the creation of the National Endowment for the Arts (NEA) in 1965 would provide support for non-mainstream theatre and performance work that pushed boundaries,[9] and in the first five years of NEA grants, more money went to theatre than to any other branch of the arts.[10]

Second, theatre gained serious traction during the 1960s in higher education. Between 1960 and 1967 the number of undergraduate theatre majors tripled, from about fifty-five hundred to eighteen thousand, and twenty schools added graduate programs. By 1967 there were 168 institutions offering master's degrees and 38 offering the doctorate in theatre studies.[11] The training ground for mainstream theatre professionals would shift to the newly accredited halls of the academy, encouraging the notion that social intervention and pushing the envelope were proper functions of theatre, since research and experimentation were provinces of the university.

Third, "performance art," a slippery term denoting embodied work that fits a basic definition of theatre (planned, performed in real time, aesthetically motivated, featuring an audience and a performer in a designated place) entered the arts lexicon. In 1990, the famous case of the NEA Four put a damper on some of the angriest, most free-form performances that spoke about and against the straitjacket of domesticity. Karen Finley, whose *Theory of Total Blame* is the penultimate piece discussed in this chapter, was one of the four artists whose 1990 NEA grants were recommended in the peer-review process but denied by the agency in the name of "decency." The four filed suit against the NEA, charging that their grants were denied for political reasons. They settled out of court in 1993, receiving the grants denied three years earlier.[12] Performance artists—whose work was by then solidly ensconced in theatre studies—saw clearly the hostile and reactionary way in which the government was claiming to be synoptic in its granting procedures while acquiescing to conservative backlash. If their activism did not cease, some methods would be recalibrated.

That reactionary pushback was parsed at the end of the period covered here by Susan Faludi, who won the 1991 National Book Critics Circle award for her *Backlash: The Undeclared War against American Women*. This landmark study makes clear the distance between the reality of women's lives and the cultural fantasies that continued to link women with domesticity. Faludi's study shows how, during the 1980s, news outlets, mainstream movies, television series, government, and the New Right collectively shared a powerful, if unofficial, directive agenda packaged as essential to women's well-being. "The message be-hind all this 'advice'? Go home."[13] Pop culture gurus and limited, mis-handled surveys delivered the idea that "cocooning" (hunkering down with family for "comfort food" at home), the "mommy track," and a "man shortage" should be American women's greatest concerns, al-though, as Faludi tartly notes, "cocooning . . . had yet to make a blip on the U.S. Bureau of Labor Statistics charts. Women steadily increased their representation in the work force in the '80s—from 51 to 57 per-cent for all women. . . . And the increase in working mothers was the steepest."[14]

When women themselves were queried, for example, in the 1990 Virginia Slims poll, their greatest complaint was lack of money, fol-lowed by the refusal of male partners to do their share of child care and housework.[15] The latter—men expecting women to do the lion's share of domestic labor even when both partners were employed—was the unrelenting point of Arlie Russell Hochschild's 1989 book, *The Sec-ond Shift*. One other facet of domestic labor remained largely stuck in place even as women became fixtures of the paid workforce: the gulf between domestics and employers, which continued to be raced as well as classed, something addressed with mordant humor in this chapter's final case study, Douglas Turner Ward's *Happy Ending*.

The productions in this chapter were offered on and off Broadway, one in an alternative theatre in San Francisco, in art galleries, in clubs, and on video. Most of the traditional plays had healthy lives in re-gional theatres and in colleges and universities. If the 1963 appearance of Friedan and Child in the national field of vision was a declaration of "game on," their fans and foes were still buying tickets to the match thirty years later.

PRISONERS IN PUBLIC

Neil Simon's *The Prisoner of Second Avenue* opened on Broad-way in 1971, garnering a Tony nomination for Best Play and running for 798 performances. It quickly arrived in major theatres in Chicago, Boston, Rome, and later London, enjoyed summer stock revivals, and was made into a film in 1975. Simon is often dismissed as a writer whose background in television made him an expert in the one-liner at the expense of any depth, but *Prisoner*, written the same year that the feminist monthly magazine *Ms.* first appeared,[16] is a good site for examining the intersection of audience and production with regard to what is read as real and by whom and for considering the shifting ground on which domestic labor and women's worth in the paid workforce are valued. That it took an economic downturn and attendant anxieties to reveal in a comic context some of the ways in which the housewife's personal is political is telling.

Prisoner is set in a newish high-rise apartment building on New York's expensive Upper East Side, where upper-middle-class, soon-to-turn-forty-seven Mel Edison is suffering from angst and paranoia. The air conditioner cannot be properly adjusted, the toilet leaks, the walls are too thin, it is too noisy, and the smell of garbage is everywhere. This breakdown of consumer appliances and a perceived invasion of privacy are familiar dramaturgical markers of personal crisis. If Arthur Miller's Willy summoned for audiences the plight of their outer-borough fathers or uncles, while Albee's Mommy and Daddy were a distanced "filthy rich," Simon's ad executive Mel and his wife, Edna, were readily seen as "us," according to numerous reviews. When Mel loses his job and the apartment is burglarized, Edna goes to work as a secretary, gamely going home each day to make Mel a hot lunch and buck him up.[17] Only when Edna's company goes bankrupt and she, too, is unemployed does her composure crack, as failing utilities at home prove the last straw.

Set against the backdrop of a real recession (one review was headlined "An Upbeat View of [then New York Mayor] Lindsay's Inferno"),[18] *Prisoner* centers on Mel's emotional state.[19] The situation is resolved by a deus ex machina: twenty-five thousand dollars from Mel's brother, which will allow Mel and Edna either to purchase a summer camp as a new business or to pay for Mel's anticipated psychiatrist bill. Systemic problems are resolved for individual characters unable to see the systems qua systems, with narrative closure deflecting wider analysis.[20] One of these systems was the assumption of women's home-centeredness, with "social order . . . conceived of as wedded to the home," embedded in an era when economic changes had created a new normal in which "even an intact family with a fully employed male head-of-household could hardly maintain expected consumption patterns without two wage earners."[21] Mel and Edna may be intended as "typical," but they are only just catching up with the widespread economic realities of ordinary American housewifedom.

The assertion that "realism is always presenting a particular theory of what will count as a picture of reality" leaps to life in reading critical responses to *Prisoner*.[22] Richard Coe, reviewing the pre-Broadway tryout in Washington, D.C., states it "so accurately reflects what many of us are thinking that for quite a time I thought Simon's play was all about me."[23] The theatre critic for Greater New York Radio asserted that "we realize we're watching . . . our own lives; . . . we are all prisoners of Second Avenue."[24] A *New York Morning Telegraph* reviewer found the play "startlingly close to the actuality and to the experiences many of us have gone through ourselves."[25] Richard Sylbert's setting was singled out as "wonderfully real" and "ready to move into."[26]

Writers targeting more leftish, working-class, or nonwhite readers challenged its unproblematized "accuracy" or "realism." The *Village Voice* critic derided an audience member for commenting at intermission that Simon "writes so realistically," sarcastically noting that "of course, 'The Prisoner of Second Avenue' was not written for me," adding that, to the audience Simon addresses, his plays "are nothing if not, you should excuse the expression, 'relevant'; he speaks directly to an eager and receptive congregation about their own immediate concerns."[27] Elsewhere an unimpressed reviewer dismissed Simon for work that "distills for the expense-account crowd the comfortable trivia of their lives, their vexing non-problems, their placid tempests."[28]

The arts editor of Harlem's *Amsterdam News* wrote in a piece published by the *New York Times* that he was one of just three observably black people in the audience the night after opening, commenting about the racism in Simon's line about leaving the city "to them" and winding up with a zinger on Mel's financial bailout: "A bundle of 25 big ones because he's up against it. Welfare, anybody?"[29] The problems presented in the play are meant to spring from the public sphere, but Simon's sense of public is determined by what theatre producers mean by that term, which is the pool of potential ticket buyers, or what Herbert Blau sees as those who can afford to support an outrageously narrow "aesthetic economy . . . [that] still determines the public."[30]

Domestic labor has a clear place in the world of upper-bourgeois anomie. Edna is limned as either irrelevant, invisible, or incompetent in four key areas of twentieth-century domestic labor—parenting, housecleaning, cooking, and consumerism—yet she serves a key dramaturgical function as a helpmeet, patiently listening to Mel's rants, offering him clean clothes or food, saying she is ready to quit her job to please him, and finally giving him cause to rouse himself and micromanage the domestic realm when she begins to fall apart. As a parent she is a cipher, since Simon has written the Edisons' offspring illogically out of the script. (The play opens in July, when we learn simply that the couples' two daughters are "in college."[31] They never appear, either during summer vacation or as their father is suffering a nervous breakdown.)

We know Mel and Edna employ a woman to clean their apartment two days a week and that Edna, who wants to straighten up a bit in the wake of the robbery to compose herself, is the butt of a one-liner in which her concern that people are coming over is greeted by Mel with the observation that those people are the police. "You're worried they're going to put it down in their books, 'bad housekeeper?'" (27). Simon has already treated us to a joke about Edna as a decorator when Mel throws an "ugly" pillow on the floor, because it renders the eight hundred–dollar chair it adorns too uncomfortable to sit on (5–6). As a consumer, Edna is savvy (the chair and pillow are fashionable; she knows which grocery stores deliver) but also unorganized and careless. On the day of the robbery she has gone out for groceries because there was "nothing in the house to eat" (26), leaving the door unlocked because she has lost her key.

Cooking is the area in which Simon shows how the housewife's world is legible to him, and presumably important to his audiences, only to the extent that it depends on taking its clues from the husband's needs. In the opening scene, insomniac Mel waxes nostalgic for food. "I haven't eaten food since I was thirteen years old. . . . I haven't had a real piece of bread in thirty years. . . . If I knew what was going to happen, I would have saved some rolls when I was a kid" (10). Edna patiently offers to make him food, noting that she "remember[s] how they made it" (10).

In a sort of throwback to the out-of-step father in *Awake and Sing*, Mel seems to have missed the fact that canned goods, precooked foods, and bakery bread had been staples for decades. He may, of course, simply be criticizing his wife's lousy cooking, although her saying that she remembers—tellingly, how "*they*" did it—suggests that she, like *Come Back, Little Sheba*'s Lola Delaney, is too bored, depressed, or demoralized to muster the energy for home cooking (or cleaning, or remembering to shop or where she put her key). It may also indicate that Mel married her for all the glamour that the kitchen-bound mothers, aunts, and grandmothers of home-cooking fame failed to display. In an interview with Lee Grant, the actress who originated the role of Edna on Broadway, journalist Richard Natale described Edna as "a victim of a certain middle-class lifestyle."[32]

Victim or no, Edna sees the preparation of hot noonday meals for her housebound mate as her wifely obligation even after she becomes a fulltime breadwinner. At the start of act 2, she enters with a cheese soufflé she has purchased at Schrafft's, an upper-middlebrow chain known for its appeal to women and its comfort foods, explaining that she doesn't have "time to fix anything today," as her office is busy and she has only eighty-five minutes (!) for her lunch break (40). Here Simon's disconnectedness from the very material he is writing comes into full focus. The stage directions call the soufflé a "casserole" and stipulate that Edna "gets out some pots" as she asks Mel to keep her company while she is "cooking."

Casseroles, which involve the slow cooking of multiple ingredients in a single pot, can accommodate leftovers or inexpensive cuts of meat in their recipes; they require minimum effort, represent unsophisticated cooking, and can be left unattended.[33] But the soufflé "is considered the prima donna of the culinary world,"[34] as it requires stiff egg whites to give it lightness and can easily collapse if not treated properly. Whichever the purchased item is, it is hard to understand why Edna needs "some pots" if she has no time to cook. Arguably a shallow baking pan would be ideal for heating the already-prepared soufflé in the oven, but a pan is not a pot, and by 1971 an upper-middle-class home with a consumer wife might well have had a microwave oven, for which a metal pot would be the ultimate no-no. Mel protests that he is embarrassed by Edna's making him lunch, saying he can either make his own, of which there is no evidence, as he has started the scene looking for something to eat in the kitchen, or go out, which would defeat the point of economizing during his period of unemployment, although Edna's returning home in a taxi goes unremarked as an expense.

While the play is supposedly "universal" because of its portrayal of anxiety in the face of deprivations beyond the control of the individual, this anxiety is gendered and professionalized. For one reviewer, the working wife and "husband-at-home situation humiliates the male spouse to the point of mental depression." Another refers to Mel's unemployment as a form of "emasculation."[35] Mel tells Edna that he sensed he was going to be fired because secretaries earning $85 a week were bringing him coffee and Danish and not charging him for it (28). This is quite possibly the amount that Edna might be earning when she goes to work as a secretary. Oddly, this salary would add up, at $4,250 a year (assuming two weeks of unpaid vacation), to $25,500 over a six-year period—a little more than the $23,000 Mel says he has paid his psychiatrist in exactly that amount of time and just slightly more than the $25,000 that his family estimates will bail him out this time. His wife's work, in other words, could never replace the salary he is accustomed to spending on himself alone, never mind the household. Her double shift is not even an afterthought.

Lee Grant, the original Edna, also played Sophie Portnoy, a stereotypical overbearing Jewish mother, in the film of *Portnoy's Complaint*, which opened during *Prisoner*'s Broadway run. While actors usually look for sympathetic angles on the characters they play, Grant called Sophie "a dog from the very start. . . . She is determined to solve everything by food. The sum total of her communication with her family is getting the food in one end and making sure it comes out right from the other."[36] Since Simon's characters are, despite their generically American names, nearly always recognizable as Jewish, there are some domestic labor dots that can be connected here. Edna is a desirable wife because she is not like Sophie Portnoy, but it is Sophie's kind of food that Mel cannot forget. Edna is willing to work for wages but is unable to earn enough to support the family because she has spent much of her married life as a housewife, whose labor her husband feels free to demean because his culture allows him to do so. No wonder Grant saw the play as a tragedy.

Women in 1971 earned on the average less than sixty cents for every dollar men earned,[37] even as they continued to feel that the proverbial hot lunch was their responsibility. The political was doubly personal for the income-seeking wives of unemployed men. Nonetheless, Simon offered a tiny hint of the changes that might be brewing. As Edna rattles on about her sore feet, fatigue, and the fact that she hasn't had time to eat or even sit down all day, she is also exhilarated. "I don't know where I'm getting the energy, I must have been saving it up for the past twenty-two years" (41)—the length of time she has been a wife. A changing public sphere would make it unlikely that the Edisons' daughters would ever be able to replay their mother's homebound housewifedom.

This impossibility—domesticity without much domestic labor for a middle-aged woman—was thrust in the faces of Broadway audiences twenty years later in Israel Horovitz's *Park Your Car in Harvard Yard*.[38] The play features a crusty, retired octogenarian with a Harvard pedigree and the working-class fortyish woman he hires as his housekeeper and companion. He, pointedly named Brackish, was the high school teacher whose stringent grading caused the housekeeper's husband to drop out of school and whose marks cost her a college scholarship. She, Kathleen O'Hara Hogan ("K.O.'d at birth" by her initials, as she notes [101]), is there to watch Brackish die, arriving as the widow of the short-order cook who left her nothing. Unsurprisingly, Kathleen teaches Brackish compassion, and he gives her self-respect.

While many critics found the story "contrived[,] . . . psychologically questionable," "jerrybuilt," and "fundamentally uninteresting," some saw a "poignant portrait" and "a play of small but pertinent details."[39] Despite *Park Your Car*'s old-fashioned, skeletons-in-the-closet dramaturgy and sentimentality, it offers a rare use of domestic labor that does more than illustrate a woman's hard lot or devotion; does more than index a household's economic or emotional rise or fall; and links public and private in particularly American ways. The play uses ironing and laundry, cooking, and home care for the elderly to interrogate capitalism, market competition, and the expectation that family values, albeit touted as a national desideratum, generally fall to women, who are expected to uphold them out of love and duty, the dollar be damned. Arguably, *Park Your Car*'s realism as dramatic genre was at odds with the naturalism of ongoing, repetitive domestic labor—both aesthetic vestiges of other eras but alive and kicking in the way people tell their own stories and the way they live day to day.

The play takes place over the course of a year, with each season assigned a different facet of domestic labor to convey both daily routine and situational revelation. The first winter features laundry; spring deploys cooking with some nursing; late summer/early fall pairs the same duo, although less of both; and the final winter intertwines cleaning with palliative care. In each instance, action is accompanied by verbalized self-awareness, and the intersection of domestic labor and the public sphere is omnipresent if one knows how to look.

In the first act, Kathleen undertakes to iron all of Brackish's white shirts. She starts working in the kitchen, but he invites her to the living room, where it is warmer. The shirts soon festoon the whole stage. The housebound employer hardly needs so many, but the new arrival needs to prove her mettle. The faulty iron keeps bubbling over; Kathleen declines to drain off some water, since she is nearing the end of the task; finally the water is rusty and it stains a shirt. By the end of the long scene, Kathleen has dropped the whole armload of shirts into a puddle of rusty water in a move that might not be accidental. Meanwhile, in the course of the scene we have learned that Brackish has utterly forgotten that Kathleen's husband saved him from drowning more than twenty years earlier, although he remembers the incident itself.

As the act continues, Kathleen bleaches the shirts, burns a pot, scrubs it out, and sits down to work on a quilt. Brackish begins to act like the music appreciation teacher he once was, utilizing the repeated motifs in the Bach "Chaconne" to ponder the frightening specter of realizing, in contemplating accumulated memories, that one has "heard all this before" (80). Kathleen responds that she, too, is frightened by repetition, realizing she has "done all this before . . . over and over again. . . . The bed getting made and unmade . . . the food shopped, cooked, eaten, shopped, cooked, eaten" (80). In the final act of the play, Brackish, who has learned compassion and some humility from Kathleen, is throwing out old papers from his deathbed. The stage is again littered with an excess of white personal objects, staging a kind of chiasmus in the mise-en-scène.

If the trajectory of the two characters' drama is less than fully credible in terms of everyday life—she wants, at the play's crisis, a make-up exam in music appreciation at age forty-one; he had an ongoing affair with her mother; neither character has children; his feigned deafness allows her to rail about him—the financial and social intersections of domesticity and the public sphere are entirely grounded in social actualities. Brackish taught in the local public high school, routinely failing students from working-class families. Without the grades for a college scholarship Kathleen—the daughter of a lumper (stevedore) and a blue-collar housewife—is stuck in a world where any outside paid work will leave her part of an underclass. Her choice of domestic labor in the context of revenge is dramaturgically expedient; it is also rife with American capitalist realities.

As Nancy Folbre argues, the exclusion of nonmarket work from what she cleverly puts in quotation marks as "the economy" devalues both the work itself and the women who are expected to do it as a "moral responsibility."[40] Such work includes cleaning and cooking, but Folbre focuses on the caring (for children and those who are ill, disabled, or elderly) aspects of domestic labor, observing that as women moved into the paid labor force in increased numbers starting in the 1970s, little was done to compensate for what used to be their free labor. The paid workers who replace that labor—nannies, visiting nurses, cleaning women, babysitters, day-care workers, and housekeepers—are almost universally female, engaged for low pay regardless of experience and not recognized as serving any public—versus individual—need. Quips Folbre, "As one old economist's joke puts it, if you marry your housekeeper, you lower GDP [gross domestic product]. If you put your mother in a nursing home, you increase GDP."[41] She summarizes the complexity of her case bluntly: "Care is not just another commodity."[42]

In *Park Your Car in Harvard Yard*, the retired public schoolteacher who has staked all his values on his Ivy League education and his autonomy lives in a house built nearly a century earlier by a lumper, and he now requires the care of the daughter of another lumper, likely because his pension will allow little more and because he refuses to go to a (probably publicly funded) nursing home. His housekeeper has been kept from advancing in the public sphere by a heritage of poverty and an indifferent (public) school system. Kathleen is part of the so-called working poor, while her more privileged employer benefits from the fact that caring labor is far cheaper than Kathleen's professional, workforce labor would have been had she earned that college degree. Their mutual need for each other's skills, staged on the turf of domesticity and refusing to push domestic labor out of the ongoing picture, may not be progressive in literary terms. But its economic critique, if one cares to read it, is just that.

ENTRAPMENT A-Z

In 1975 Martha Rosler gave not just one name, but twenty-six to the problem of confining women to kitchen duties. Her *Semiotics of the Kitchen* is a six-minute video shot in her own compact kitchen and featuring Rosler in the role of a television cooking host. It mimics the form of the television cooking program to challenge the idea that women "belong" in the kitchen and that there is anything natural about linking the two. In the piece, the "protagonist," a woman in her early thirties, displays and names in alphabetical order, items found in ordinary kitchens. "Apron. Bowl. Chopper. Dish. Eggbeater. Fork. . . . Hamburger press. Ice pick. . . . Knife. . . . Ladle. . . . Pan. . . . Quart bottle. . . . Spoon. . . . Tenderizer. . . ." She performs a simple action with each, some of these either frivolously wasteful/empty (stirring an empty bowl; tossing away the imaginary contents of a ladle) or alarmingly violent (slashing the air with a knife; pounding the table with the meat tenderizer). Beginning with the letter "u," she abandons the connection of alphabet to items and shapes the letters with her arms like a kind of cheerleader. She concludes by tracing "z" in the air with a knife, putting her knife down, and shrugging.

Rosler has described the work as "[a] woman in a bare-bones kitchen demonstrating some hand tools and replacing their domesticated 'meaning' with a lexicon of rage and frustration . . . [an] antipodean Julia Child."[43] It is easy to see thinly suppressed rage in the stabbing actions with the fork and ice pick; the slashing with the knife; and the pounding with the chopper and tenderizer. The monotone and expressionless face bespeak numbness, an easy interpretation of a recognizable response to a setup of separate spheres or the second shift. Here are Friedan the rebel and Child the expert in one body, signaling through the flames, as it were.

Rosler wanted both her feminist and antiwar performative work to be "accessible, to avoid sliding into recherché theorizing that general audiences won't get."[44] Her goal was "to think about real, historically grounded social relations and the ways in which they inform the personal," noting that she "start[s] not with the self and its reflection in social interaction, but from the outside."[45] However constructed, imagined, reified, or symbolic the "real world" outside the kitchen may be, it has colonized the thinking of the culture that would relegate this woman ("anywoman") to her kitchen. While Rosler invoked the "real" to name the social relations she sought to depict, she eschewed naturalism as that which locks narrative into an almost inevitably uncritical relation to culture. Rather, I am aiming for the distancing effect that breaks the emotional identification with character and situation that naturalism implies, substituting for it, when it is effective, an emotional recognition coupled with a critical, intellectual understanding of the *systematic meaning* of the work, its meaning in relation to common issues.[46]

Little surprise, then, that Helen Molesworth's reading of Rosler's performance in *Semiotics of the Kitchen* is that it comprises what would logically occur "if the stage directions were written by Bertolt Brecht; . . . Should we giggle or shudder at the trapped quality of Rosler's slightly maniacal home cook?"[47]

Can a work be both realistic and Brechtian? Brecht's insistence that "realism" was the right term for his own work makes it possible to think about the multiplicities in Rosler's work as riffs on "kitchen sink realism." Brecht asserts, "Realism is not a mere question of form" but the genre par excellence for "discovering the causal complexes of society / unmasking the prevailing view of things as the view of those who are in power."[48] Rosler argued in 1981 that "[m]eaning may be produced by the subject, but on the basis of a relation to real conditions," including the effects of language and, in *Semiotics of the Kitchen*, "the transformation of the woman herself into a sign in a system of signs that represents a system of food production, a system of harnessed subjectivity. . . . [T]his woman is implicated in a system of extreme reduction with respect to herself as a self." The shrug at the end, in Rosler's own interpretation, suggests stuckness, but not a permanent, hopeless condition—indicating that activism was a goal.[49]

This work draws on the recognizable but eschews naturalism or closure, achieving what Molesworth reads as a "combined . . . aesthetic of identification (traditionally associated with second-wave feminism) with one of distanciation (usually affiliated with poststructuralist feminism)" to show the imbrication of public and private under capitalism.[50] Along the way, it allows viewers to see whimsy (the shrug); multiple and simultaneous responses to a single situation (boredom, anger, indifference, the suggestion that the hands can function efficiently while the mind is somewhere else); and perhaps even confidence (she knows exactly what to do with all those implements and can get the job done in a very small, very clean place). It doesn't offer answers, but it does stage questions and provocations.

Accordingly, *Semiotics of the Kitchen* fits its contemporary feminist project: wages for housework. This movement, articulated in a range of texts published between 1972 and 1976, sought to expose the financial worth of the unwaged domestic labor necessary to keep the paid workplace going. The wages for housework movement wanted to show that the putatively nonproductive (or, in Marxist terms, "reproductive") realm of the household is not separate from the putatively productive realm of the (paid) workplace but is "an economic unit with complex linkages to the waged-labor economy—a structural component of, rather than a haven from, the world of work."[51]

Kathi Weeks highlights the "cognitive dissonance" that results from an insistence that "a woman receive payment for what is supposed to be a spontaneous desire rooted in women's nature."[52] Of course, for those espousing the argument (or stabbing tables with ice picks in videos), this was cognition without the dissonance, reality without the recuperative insistence of drama's generic "realism." The problems with wages for housework included the fact that paying a housewife for her labor would not get her out of that labor, leaving a gendered, separate-spheres structure intact in the quest for "an expansion of the wage relation rather than a transformation of its terms."[53] The idea that a man might be the stay-at-home spouse was not in the forefront under much second-wave liberal feminism. Rather, the uneasy equation of woman with domesticity left room for backlash, which started as early as the first feminist cri de coeur.

Backlash is one way to read Sam Shepard's 1980 *True West*, a play that could give Martha Rosler a run for her money on the letter "t" because of its explosive, over-the-top use of an everyday kitchen appliance: the toaster. (The headline for a short article announcing a 2000 revival was "Toasters at Risk Once Again."[54]) One of Shepard's so-called family plays of the mid-1970s to early 1980s, *True West* was a departure from the sort of elliptical, poetic, nonlinear short pieces that characterized his earliest work in New York's East Village in the 1960s.[55] Stephen J. Bottoms warns readers at the outset of his comprehensive study of Shepard's work that the playwright tended to focus very narrowly on "the problems of straight white male Americans," something to remember in assessing the realism attributed to *True West*.[56]

Shepard's evolving interest in character, family, and past manifested starting in 1980 in work that Bottoms puts under the rubric "dirty realism." This term encompasses the work of fiction writers grouped together for, among other things, "trivial and mundane details . . . and often rather grubby incidents in the lives of ordinary Americans."[57] *True West* is set in a kitchen, which Shepard stipulates, "should be constructed realistically."[58] In this context, Shepard stages an encounter between two brothers that virtually every scholar as well as every newspaper and magazine critic has called "mythic." Brian Richardson labels *True West* "superrealism," noting the irony of the title "where the most impoverished and cliché-ridden notions of this imaginary space jostle incongruously with the frustrating experiences of life in suburban Los Angeles."[59] Daily critic Clive Barnes hedged his bets on the mythic encounter in the recognizable kitchen with the label "symbolic— realistic."[60] Shepard, as if setting us up to appreciate the full irony and the possibilities in the good brother/bad brother mashup staged on shopworn scenographic terrain, has the slobby brother, within the first seven terse lines of the play, ask the neat brother, who is house-sitting for their mother, if the neatnik is "keepin' the sink clean" (5). Whether dirty, symbolic, super, kitchen sink, or something else, realism is in *True West*'s DNA.

True West's brothers are the forty-something Lee, an unwashed, unemployed petty thief just back from a long stay in the desert, and the thirty-something Austin, a college-educated screenwriter with a wife and children in the suburbs of northern California. The men are sometimes read as two halves of one self.[61] Austin is at Mom's house to work on his screenplay treatment without distraction; Lee is there solely to distract his brother. Over the course of the action the brothers incorporate each other's identities. Lee co-opts his sibling's chances with a film producer, persuading the minor mogul that he, Lee, can deliver an "authentic" western tale better than his brother. Austin, increasingly jealous and rambunctious, begins to adopt Lee's ways, including drinking to excess and attempting cat burglary. Where Lee has previously stolen a television to hock or sell for pocket money, Austin returns with a cache of toasters, leading one critic to exult, "Is there a

Bruce Lyons and Dan Butler in *True West*, Cherry Lane Theatre, New York, 1983.
Photo by Martha Swope, © Billy Rose Theatre Division, The New York Public Library
for the Performing Arts, Astor, Lenox, and Tilden Foundations.

more wacko scene anywhere than when the lights go up on about 15 shiny toasters that meek Austin has stolen to prove some insane point? 'There's going to be a general lack of toasters in the neighborhood this morning,'" crows Austin, who proceeds to put bread in all of them.[62] If Shepard is critiquing a precession of simulacra, he scripts his dismay via a procession of same.

As the bread is browning, Lee goes in search of a pencil, emptying every drawer in the kitchen and leaving an array of utensils all over the floor. Austin, while buttering his dozens of pieces of toast, reveals that he wants to go to the desert with Lee, to which Lee snorts that Austin could never survive there. When Austin points to his newly proven ability to steal, Lee retorts, "A toaster's got nothing to do with the desert" (48). Austin pleads that he can cook, to which the reply is,

"So what! You can cook. Toast" (48). When Lee finally knocks a proffered plate of toast out of Austin's hand, Austin drops to his knees, gathers up the toast, agrees to a deal in which Lee will take him to the desert in exchange for his typing up Lee's script and granting Lee full writing credit. Lee seals the deal with a bite of toast.[63] This is the play's penultimate scene, concluding with utensils, toast, butter, beer cans, and dead plants where an orderly kitchen used to be—the product of the antithesis of domestic labor.

In the final scene, Mom comes back. The reason for her absence was announced in the first line of the play: she "took off for Alaska" (5). She explains her unexpected return as the response to missing her plants, but upon surveying the mess and seeing the plants dead, she says it's "one less thing to take care of, I guess" (54). She asks the brothers not to shout in her house, to go outside if they are going to fight, and why Lee has to heist her china and silverware when plastic plates and flatware would surely serve him as well in the desert. The house remains a mess, the men fight, and Mom heads for a motel, announcing that she "can't stand this anymore" (58). Austin begs her not to go, promises to clean up for her, and tells her that this is where she lives, but she says she doesn't recognize it. It is, she says, "worse than being homeless" (58).

A mere handful of reviews and even fewer chapters of scholarship note that it is Mom who has lit out for the last American frontier.[64] Many reviews don't mention Mom at all; some mention the character but not the actress; the smallest number mention character, actress, and performance. Reviews quoted here are from multiple productions, although critics focused on the script and the kitchen more in the 1980 New York reviews than anywhere else.[65] Mom, keeper of the home fires to which her adult offspring return, is punished by critics for her taste in housing, her stoicism in the face of disaster, and perhaps most of all for her resilience. She is not living vicariously through her offspring and is not going to clean up after them. Mom is capable of efficient domesticity but minus the need to be defined by it. She is also without any further interest in performing it in the name of some kind of "responsibility" for others who only trample on it.

Journalists read her otherwise. "Why is she so damned dissociated when she returns?"[66] She "would rather live in a dream world than face the emptiness of her life and the repulsiveness of her brood."[67]

One actress is "inexplicably affectless."[68] Scholars, with one major exception, have little to add. Mom is "a patently plastic version of the values that Austin had once endorsed as genuine."[69] "Shepard's mother character surrenders to a fatalism. . . . The mother's role is a passive one; she is the handmaiden to the man's need, desires, and dreams."[70] Mom is "an archetype and a parody . . . threatening and life-denying."[71] Her well-kept home, meanwhile, is at best a suburban tract house (the most frequent description), at worst "ticky-tacky suburban."[72] One might recall that urban row houses, now an ownership goal of sophisticates who can afford them, were the tract houses of their day — complementary but basically similar domiciles built cheek by jowl on a single chunk of land.

Reading Mom's relation to her domesticity and domestic labor as passive or parodic says less about the unspoken maybes in the play than it does about hewing to an imagined party line. Shepard stated in a 1980 interview that he "thinks men are more interesting" than women, that "[t]he real mystery in American life lies between men, not between men and women."[73] One critic observed, "In mythic America characters go east, west, and occasionally south—but seldom north. When a mother splits and leaves the kids unguarded and alone to work things out for themselves—this is True North, the deep freeze of Oedipal despair."[74] That the kids are middle-aged and that Sophocles's Jocasta rejects in the most violent way possible any continued coupling with her son seem like two excellent reasons to see this mother's trip as a move of independence or quest rather than one of abandonment. Her years of buttering her sons' toast and cleaning their messes are in the past. That Shepard's Mom character might eschew domestic labor in the face of ingratitude yet not see the marketplace as her only alternative seems to have eluded most critics—as though only the quest for a career or penance for the sins of tackiness would do.

The sole scholar to shine a positive light on Mom's role in *True West* is Sheila Rabillard, who points out that Mom's end-of-the-play interest in Picasso (she invites the sons to a local exhibit) inserts a wedge into the play's investigation of the romantic myth of the artist as individual genius.[75] For Rabillard, *True West* makes audiences keenly aware of "the dramatist as consumer of culture's signs. . . . Neither spectator nor playwright is figured as source of origin; both are participants, instead, in an ongoing cultural system."[76] Mom, then, is a player among many, but one unwilling to be pinned down by the stereotypical, mythic parameters of housewife/mother as nurturer/ housekeeper/cook/decorator. She may be our key to an *evolving* cultural system. She has kept house for a husband who abandoned the family and sons who trash her kitchen. Domestic labor here is neither trap nor haven. It does not provide fulfillment or identity. It is maintenance work not fetishized by the one who performs it. While the brothers remain deadlocked in a stranglehold as the lights go down, Mom has shown that she is able to leave, come back, and leave again, as if in some kind of existentially realist *fort da* maneuver. She may or may not grow new plants, but the one she will leave to tend to itself is the family tree, whose branches will have to figure out by themselves on which side their bread is buttered.

GUNS AND RUSES

Few plays can match Marsha Norman's 1983 Pulitzer Prize winner, *'night, Mother*, for its relentless evocation of realism and its focus on domestic labor. Virtually all criticism of the play, either journalistic or scholarly, uses the words "real," "realism," or "realistic" either to praise or to condemn it, with one daily reviewer, inevitably, noting the set's "kitchen portion . . . complete with running water in the sink."[77] And no description fails to nod to the fact that the main, ongoing activity in the play—whose dramatic action is the preparation for the suicide of one of its two characters—is domestic labor. Because the performance of the domestic labor as stage activity is not the same as the textual dialogue about many other things (albeit including housekeeping), I want to put pressure on how this omnipresent but nonverbal physicalization is what makes the play hard to categorize singly and what contributes to its ability to provoke such powerful, yet widely differing responses.

The characters, a mother and daughter, are scripted to be ordinary but "very specific real people who happen to live in a particular part of the country," and the playwright discourages as "wrong" any "heavy accents which would further distance the audience" from the characters.[78] Most critics for the original production read them as middle- or lower-middle-class denizens of the New South, possessed of little taste, one of whom has answered "to be or not to be" before the curtain rises.[79] Gender and class prevent some readers and spectators from reading these characters as "universal."[80] Nonetheless, a number of critics, including Robert Brustein, then artistic director of the American Repertory Theatre, which gave the play its first professional production, did read it as universal and even classical in construction.[81] These critics, however, downplayed the stage activity, as if it were secondary and not germane to the discussion of what might not so facetiously be called the meaning of life.

Those who did focus on the domestic labor frequently used it as a reason either to pity the characters whose lives are circumscribed by this meaningless activity or to deride the play as dealing with the trivial. Stéphanie Genz observes, "[W]e could start by abolishing the image of the self-sacrificing housewife who likes nothing better than baking pies and polishing floors. For most, housewifery will never have any utopian or dream-like quality but simply be a routine part of our lives,"[82] but the routine is not synonymous with the meaningless. I want to consider this play in performance as a rare instance of domestic labor standing for necessity, with all that implies: the irreducibly requisite and the unavoidable. If one is to discuss the fullness or emptiness of a life and the capacity to act—arguably the main issues in the play—then cordoning off one of its obligatory, skill-dependent facets in the name of triviality suggests an already stacked critical deck. Because the domestic labor is performed much more than it is discussed, its presence as ongoing track during the live experience of the play is crucial to an understanding of how the play does its work.

If one were to watch a video of 'night, Mother with the sound turned off, she might be forgiven for mistaking it for Martha Rosler's Semiotics of the Kitchen minus the irony. Such a viewing of a videotape of the original Broadway production, directed by Tom Moore, is possible, and it shows a combination of ongoing, routinized housework and occasional outbursts involving household utensils being hurled to the floor.[83] The long-sad, about-to-shoot-herself Jessie elects to spend most of her final evening with her mother, Thelma, filling candy jars, cleaning out the refrigerator, taking out the garbage, and giving instructions about the location of items such as light bulbs, fuses, and matches. Thelma ("Mama") makes cocoa, but she also throws pots, pans, a tray, and silverware on the floor in two different moments of protesting her daughter's decision. Jesse cleans up both messes.

Daily critics noted this, but they were most interested in the realism or lack thereof in the construction of the characters, the suicide plan, the mother-daughter relationship, or the set itself. Critical concerns included whether or not Jessie was truly a tragic figure,[84] her epilepsy and unhappiness as reasons for her suicide,[85] and her relationship with a mother variously described as "bird-brained," "limited," and "a mixture of flutter and wry pain."[86] One critic found it "hard to accept that an incipient suicide could carry on so reasonable a discourse right before blowing out her brains," while another found it "the most understandable, cogent explanation of a suicidal mind I've seen."[87] Some found the kitchen/living room as designed "tacky" and "a modern shrine of alienation," but others saw a home that was "cozy" and "could qualify for a Good Housekeeping Seal of Approval."[88] *Variety*'s critic called it "Polaroid accurate."[89]

Overall, these critics seemed concerned with displaying mastery in their judgments of what is real, what is tasteful, and what is meaningful, one even offering rather an acceptable list of theories on which a realist reading of the themes and relationships in *'night, Mother* could be erected. "Believers and atheists, Freudians and anti-Freudians, rationalists and idealists, Marxists and capitalists, parents and children—everyone will have his or her interpretation," wrote John Simon. Only one writer for a magazine offered thoughts about the ongoing domestic labor in the "real" world of the play that went beyond observing its banality or crushing lack of challenge. For Gerald Weales, the "details of keeping house, ordering groceries, retaining the comfort . . . [constitute an] activity [that] is, in part, a dramatic strategy of Norman's, a way of using such practicality to emphasize that Jessie's planned suicide is not an act of madness or revenge."[90] The emphasis on activity is the only hint that domestic labor means something performatively as well as dramaturgically.

Scholarly criticism has made good on Simon's list of available interpretive frames. In 1987, Jenny Spencer used psychoanalysis to parse *'night, Mother* as a "psycho-drama of female identity," proposing that the performance of domestic labor is both a form of nurturing, as Jessie uses it to help her mother prepare for a solo future, but also "methodically planned torture . . . a symbolic murder," as Jessie extends her refusal to become like her mother via drawn-out activities that are doubled for the audience by virtue of being both enacted and explained.[91] Jill Dolan's 1988 materialist feminist concern was the power of mainstream media to co-opt and to construct ideas of universality and what constitutes feminist work. Readings of *'night, Mother* that praised its "universality," she argues, flattened its female specificity,[92] although her own nod to the play's focus on "domesticity" does little with domestic labor as a locus of female identity, resistance, or (materialist) reality.

Linda Kintz's 1992 essay on *'night, Mother* draws on theories differentiating the public from the private spheres to trouble the theatrical status of lower- and lower-middle-class women who work in the home and whose presence in a play may signal a lack of importance or inspire feelings of contempt. Kintz sees the failures of both psychoanalysis and Marxism, pointing out the difference between these theories' abstract, idealized wife/mother and the actual, disparaged housewife/domestic worker who is none other than "Thelma busily counting the supply of cupcakes and Jessie spending her last minutes explaining to Thelma that she should not forget to empty the lint filter on the dryer."[93]

Domestic labor here makes a thematic rather than a performative appearance. A year after Kintz's critique appeared, William S. Demastes suggested that reading *'night, Mother* as classical realism is a category mistake, proposing instead that the play is "anti-realist realism" and arguing for a reading grounded in "the domain of epistemology rather than sociology,"[94] with Jessie embracing an existential understanding of reality and Thelma wanting positivist explanations, thereby staging both a generational and an ideological standoff. Our failure as audiences is not, Demastes believes, a result of the play but of our "*choosing* to be naturalists" stuck in seeing a (realist) play in ways that do not mesh with how "we must perceive *reality*."[95] In this reading, domestic labor must be inferred, even though it might be seen as the glue holding the existential and the positivist everyday in fragile communion.

Varun Begley, in his 2012 study of the play, does use domestic labor as a critical lens. Calling *'night, Mother* an instance of "critical realism" as well as of "conflicted realism," Begley argues that "[d]ramatic realism effects its manipulations, in part, through a particular organization and display of objects."[96] Resisting the idea that everyday objects and products are simple "metonyms for the status quo," he asserts that theatre's "inherent materialism . . . might be deployed against the status quo and its realist vernacular."[97] He zeroes in on food and crafts to note that the former is a locus of resistance in this play. Jessie never liked eating; her mother never liked cooking. On this night of reckoning, Thelma declares, as she sweeps all her pots off the counter, "I'm not going to cook. I never liked it anyway. I like candy. Wrapped in plastic or coming in sacks. And tuna. I like tuna. I'll eat tuna, thank you."[98] Food preparation is something the denizens of this household reject as a creative endeavor. Crafts *are* creative expressions, and Begley points both to Thelma's needlework (which we see all over the stage, both according to Norman's directions and in the video of the original production) and Jessie's lists, which "commemorate the kind of domestic labor that patriarchy renders invisible."[99]

These valuable interventions invite a focus on objects and their uses, not merely on discussion, relationships, and the psyche. Nonetheless, domestic labor as ongoing performative activity does work whose resistance may reside not only in the way scripted characters are using or talking about objects (that is, doubling the dialogue) but in the way the playwright and director are using stage time. Not just the named activities—cleaning out the refrigerator, filling the candy dishes, bagging up the garbage—but the unnamed ones such as wiping off any surfaces with possible smudges, something Kathy Bates as Jessie did several times in the original production and the sort of activity available for improvisation or embellishment by future actresses in the role—point to the inescapability, repetition, and second nature of domestic labor. One may pay for it, one may do it sloppily, one may avoid aspects of it, but unless food and shelter are attended to in some way, the organism succumbs. The performance embodies Jennifer Fleissner's naturalism, offering "neither the steep arc of decline nor that of triumph, but rather . . . an ongoing, nonlinear, repetitive motion . . . that has the distinctive effect of seeming also like a stuckness in place."[100]

Fleissner is specifically discussing naturalist *plots*, and *'night, Mother*'s plot does move relentlessly to a climax. The play's *activity*, on the other hand, is neither moving toward a climax nor defining a singular household or mind-set. The two complementary strands—the textual and the performed—are cut from two different kinds of cloth. The realism of the text—that which so occupied the daily critics, no matter how they defined it—is paired with but not the same as the realism of the housework. To find an instance in which the two strands are more comfortably wedded, one might look to the 1975 film *Jeanne*

Dielman, 23, Quai du Commerce, 1080 Bruxelles. Filmmaker Chantal Akerman deliberately set out to make a feminist work in which most of the film's 201 minutes depict the minutiae of domestic labor. *Jeanne Dielman* ends abruptly with the housewife committing an unanticipated murder. Akerman scholar Ivone Margulies says the picture is a filmic paradigm for uniting feminism and anti-illusionism.[101]

'night, Mother, almost universally regarded as illusionist, pursues two kinds of realisms, one aspiring to literary canonicity (this one arguably containing both Demastes's epistemological and sociological reals) and the other a kind of experimental, underground feminist tool. The stuff of naturalism (women wedded to housework) is anything but a "natural" alliance, hence the anti-illusionism and irony. In 1983 this left male critics looking for authority in terms of recognizable standards, which sometimes meant struggling with cognitive dissonance, as they observed audiences weeping while they themselves were shrugging.[102] In the final moments of the play, Thelma asks Jessie for help regarding how to explain this last evening to those who will inevitably ask about it. "[T]ell them what we did," replies Jessie. "I filled up the candy jars. I cleaned out the refrigerator. We made some hot chocolate and put the cover back on the sofa."[103] What the actresses playing these characters *do* in performance is as crucial as what the script has them say. One strand cannot do without the other, together conveying what Ben Highmore, in his study of everyday life and cultural theory, calls the "heterogeneous and ambivalent landscape of everyday modernity," an everyday that is "also the home of the bizarre and mysterious."[104]

"Bizarre" is arguably a fair description of Karen Finley's 1988 *The Theory of Total Blame*, although the work is hardly mysterious. Lynda Hart calls it "an unconventionally conventional play," comparing its familial representations to those of Sam Shepard or to Albee's *American Dream*.[105] Michael Feingold, identifying the play's "cubist version of a family," calls *Blame* a "feast of normality."[106] The author's note at the start of the play states it "is always to be presented in a realistic setting. It . . . shall never be deconstructed or placed in a black hole, no-props set. The physical setting of a Home is important to all of our memories and is integral to the play" (224). Finley claimed she wanted to write "a 1990s version of 'Long Day's Journey Into Night,'" Eugene O'Neill's alcohol- and guilt-fueled close-up of a dysfunctional

American family of adults unable to overcome their personal hurts or their collective need to keep the matriarch trapped in a mythic but toxic position.[107] Here, as in the solo performance work that earned Finley the label "the chocolate-smeared woman,"[108] her theme is the violence enacted in the name of normalcy against women, minorities, outcasts, or "black sheep"; her métier is the use of unfiltered language and behavior to assault the slick, materialistic selfishness of a realm she once described as "[t]his white clean pureMrCleanGlenCovepopu-luxeMicrowavereadytoservereadytowearlife."[109]

The Theory of Total Blame takes place at a family holiday gathering and features Finley's signature foulmouthed woman and messy use of food to focus on entrapment resulting from prescribed and proscribed domestic and familial roles. Irene, the "alcoholic matriarch whose pussy smells," was played by Finley in the original productions of 1988–89. She started the play seated at an old kitchen table (one review described the set as "provided by the Salvation Army"), "outfitted in a housedress, her legs wide open to expose all, shaping a large slab of ground beef into a meatloaf."[110] Hart elaborates on the activities of this "masochistic mother who never stops working," to note her

> constantly trudging back and forth from the refrigerator to
> the table where she is preparing food. She randomly grabs
> items from the refrigerator, and mixes them up into disgusting,
> unconsumable, virtually unrecognizable, messes. . . . Her meatloaf
> ends up all over her body, bits of raw beef hang from her nose,
> stick to her hair, litter the floor. Ketchup runs down her arms and
> legs. She shoves uncooked beef into one son's face. Irene has no
> recipes and she refuses to feed her children.[111]

Here the mirror held up to the everyday is minus the distorting lens of good manners or theatrical propriety. The adult children in *Blame* are daughter Jan, raped and impregnated at age eleven, endlessly seeking approval from her mother, and failing to get this, succumbing to asthma attacks her mother calls psychological; Buzz, who, after leaving behind a pregnant girlfriend, has spent ten years traveling in search of spiritual fulfillment and who is more upset about the death of the family dog than about his father's suicide; Ernie, obsessed with the military, although he has never served, rarely leaves the house, and is only capable of sex with strangers; and Tim, who remains comatose on the sofa throughout the play, sometimes doubling as the dead father. Son-in-law Jack identifies the gathering as "a roomful of emotional derelicts" (225).

Irene's dialogue careens from resentment to insecurity to sarcastic irony to touting the value of putting one foot in front of the other to raw explosion of pain to humane insight, all linked to her domestic role. She tells her children that she's always intended to make their lives as miserable as possible; conversely she tells them that waiting on them is her raison d'être, since a "mother stops being a mother once she stops being needed" (228). She rewards herself with alcohol, because "no one else rewards me for going to work every day. No one else goes to work like I do. I clean this damn house. I had five kids, three miscarriages, and one abortion. I've been a mother, a whore, and a slave. I've been needed, rejected, and desired but never valued by any of you" (233–34).

Irene confronts her sons with their blithe trivialization of rape and their walking out on women they have impregnated; she tells her daughter that a good day of housework would give the latter some energy when she wakes up "feeling dead" (241). But in the end, before her final lyrical prayer of tolerance, called "The Black Sheep," Irene explodes in response to Buzz's nonchalant "what's for dinner?" She refuses to cook, and she can no longer bear the blame they all place on her for her husband's suicide, admitting that she keeps them all "emotionally tied" to her so that they will remain children when they go to her house, thereby rendering her "a mother and . . . not a widow for a few moments." Her final cry is that she does not want to be in real time but in emotional time (253). Absent her domestic and familial role—which has yielded little but blame—she can see nothing but a great abyss.

A preview article for a later Finley work called her "vision of domesticity . . . both haunting and daunting."[112] A review of the Los Angeles production of *Total Blame* praised it as "a healthy, truth-seeking play, full of concern for its characters—laughing at them, but not laughing them off."[113] Michael Feingold notes that "compassion is the root of Finley's art"; in this play, "[f]ar from attacking the notion of family, Finley simply implodes the naturalistic treatment of it, thereby getting rid of all the unhealthy ways in which a hackneyed image reinforces hackneyed social attitudes."[114] Here, certainly, is an instance of Varun

Begley's assertion that theatre's "inherent materialism . . . might be deployed against the status quo and its realist vernacular."[115] Cubism, imploded naturalism, and materialism as a weapon against the status quo are Finley's aesthetic arsenal in battling objectification. The 1990s solidified her already strong reputation as a sort of bad girl with good goals, at least regarding social critique.

The Theory of Total Blame, despite its clear links to iconic instances of kitchen sink realism and its plea for a truly realistic (read "honest") look at the psychodynamics of the so-called normal family, has not been included in American drama anthologies or revived. As the discussion of *Living Out* in the final chapter of this study shows, guilt and blame remain staples of motherhood in the nuclear family, where domestic labor rests squarely on mom's shoulders even when she is employed outside the home and dad is not.

DOMESTIC LABOR IN BLACK AND WHITE

Happy Ending, Douglas Turner Ward's 1965 one-act satire about the tribulations of two canny African American maids, Vi and Ellie, is a singular representation of what might be called domestic labor as a weapon. Ward's domestics, two sisters in their late thirties, use hyper-awareness and organizational smarts to scam expensive food and clothing from their clueless white employers and thereby support an extended family in high style. If the use of a short piece from the earliest part of the period covered in this chapter to speak to the entire three decades seems to ignore imagined shifts or additions, no spoiler alert is necessary to point out that in 2012 a new study showed domestic workers earned a median wage of ten dollars an hour with 23 percent making less than their state's minimum wage. An absence of health insurance, adequate pay, or even guaranteed meal breaks (sick leave would be out of the question) continue to define the landscape.[116] Vi and Ellie still have something to tell us.

Happy Ending was paired during its original run with a longer one-act, *Day of Absence*. Both share the theme of "the victory of the underdog."[117] *Day of Absence*, in which all the black citizens of a southern town disappear for twenty-four hours, revealing both white dependence on black labor — much of it domestic labor and caregiving — and the presence of black blood in prominent citizens previously passing but now also missing, was to become the more famous and frequently restaged of the pair.[118] But Faedra Carpenter considers *Happy Ending* "the more incendiary of the two . . . [as it] features black folks being openly disparaging of white people and clearly strategizing against them."[119] *Happy Ending* foreshadowed a principle that would guide the Negro Ensemble Company—formed in 1967 on the not-for-profit model with a grant from the Ford Foundation and Ward as its artistic director—the embrace of "more or less conventional forms" in the interest of reaching ordinary blacks not part of an educated cadre of intellectuals interested in the avant-garde.[120]

Happy Ending is set in the "spotless kitchen" of a modest Harlem apartment. Photographs taken of the original apartment show a design that faithfully fulfills the playwright's description of a "dazzling white refrigerator . . . a modern stove-range . . . [and] a kitchen sink."[121] The play starts as the two domestics are crying about an unnamed impending disaster. Suddenly their well-dressed, good-looking twenty-something nephew, Junie, bursts in. They reveal that the source of their woe is Mr. Harrison, their employer, threatening divorce over his wife's infidelity. Junie cannot believe his aunts fear the loss of something that is "only" a job, telling them to "Git another" and wondering "why you stagnate as domestics when you're trained and qualified to do something better and more dignified."[122]

Here begins the education of the character Ward said was based on himself, as the aunts elucidate the reality of their situation. Working as a practical nurse or a hairdresser is "too hard, the money ain't worth it and there's not much room for advancement," says Vi, offering an updated version of the attitude of late nineteenth- and early twentieth-century African American women, who defined themselves by their families, not the dead-end jobs to which they were confined.[123]

Vi and Ellie have raised children; they support Ellie's current husband (played by Ward in the original production) as well as Junie; and they help various relatives in the South. As Junie rebukes them and claims he needs no handouts, they subtly remind him of the steaks, squab, duck, and lobster available to him on demand, as well as the designer clothes and lavishly appointed bedroom he takes for granted. Ellie points out that while she scrubs, dusts, provides child care, answers the door, and takes out the garbage for her employers, "I also ORDER the food, estimate the credit, PAY the bills and BALANCE the budget."[124] Both her skills as housekeeper and child-care provider and her functioning in effect as chatelaine make possible the high-level consumer lifestyle within the otherwise modest Harlem tenement. By the end of the play, Junie grasps the reality of his situation, and the Harrisons telephone to say that they are staying together, hence the (doubly) happy ending.

One way to read the scales falling from Junie's eyes is to see him as a prototypical rebellious youth of the 1960s, oblivious to how his elders are underwriting his dropping out (Junie is supposedly looking for a job but for months has found nothing worthy of his self-proclaimed talents). One way to read Ellie and Vi is as stand-ins for housewives dependent upon their husbands' income and living the good life because, like Mr. Harrison, their spouses will "write . . . a check wit'out even looking."[125] One way to read *Happy Ending* and also *Day of Absence* is suggested in Michael Smith's *Village Voice* review but never explicitly named as instances of Aristophanic comedy. Smith notes that both plays begin with "a novel and arresting situation; then the bulk of the play is devoted to variations on it . . . finally interrupted by a deus ex machina . . . which removes the initial stimulus without resolving it."[126]

None of these characterizes the criticism of *Happy Ending*. Using words like "cheat and a heel," "stealing is wrong . . . unfair and immoral," and "crass and limited point of view,"[127] mainstream and a few alternative newspaper critics took Ward to task for crude dramaturgy and inconsistency. The blacks in *Day of Absence* were clearly taken advantage of; those in *Happy Ending* were "cheats." How could blacks — albeit downtrodden — be presented by a serious playwright as both? One might well ask how they could not, if Ward's goal was a multifaceted look at a real situation.

Here, Ward offers the possibility of a single playwright and even a single package of plays turning a (real) phenomenon over and over to see it in multiple (real) lights. That phenomenon is racism, of course, but racism made manifest in large part via representations of menial labor, including domestic labor. The domestic labor in *Happy Ending* is not performed but rather underwrites the actions and agon of the play. Without domestic labor there is no platform for subversions, no arena for enterprise, no avenue for agency. If the domestics are cheats, they succeed as such only because the employers are too lazy to see what is going on right under their noses. The master's tools are not used here to dismantle his house but to build a carbon copy for the servants, who seek no changes in the stacked deck called the real world—only a different hand with better cards for themselves.

Once again, as has been the case since the African American plays written in the 1910s and 1920s, women characters are able to have "spotless" homes, work outside those homes for money, and express a political consciousness. If that was a relatively new package for second-wave white women trying to "have it all," it remained a version of business as usual for their counterparts of color.

■ ■ ■

White women trying to have it all and their domestics of color made headlines in 1993. The scandal surrounding President Bill Clinton's nomination that January of Zoë Baird for US attorney general emerged from the disclosure that Baird and her husband, Yale Law School professor Paul Gewirtz, employed two illegal immigrants from Peru to work as nanny and chauffeur for their child and that the employers did not pay Social Security taxes on the employees' wages. The next month, when Clinton sought to nominate Judge Kimba Wood for attorney general, it was revealed that she, too, had hired an undocumented immigrant to look after her child. Although Wood had done so at a time when the practice was legal, and although she had paid Social Security taxes, the Baird and Wood revelations—collectively dubbed "Nannygate"—laid bare the class divisions between women who were able to employ domestic labor and the workers unable to earn legal status or benefits as domestics because their employers could "get away with it."

In the decades ahead, African American and Latina domestics would come to share stage time with their white employers, occupying central places in plays and musicals garnering major journalistic attention, playing to interracial audiences, and quickly showing up in drama classes. Audiences would be asked to see the unfairness of domestics' low wages, lack of bargaining power, double shifts, and unsympathetic spouses, and spectators would be asked to connect the behavioral, sociological, and economic dots. Between privileged whites and overworked domestics of color, one demographic lost ground in theatrical portrayals: the average Jill who would jettison *Good Housekeeping* for *Working Woman* in the 1980s[128]—the teacher, nurse, cashier, saleswoman, bookkeeper, factory worker, or secretary—largely disappeared from the stage. Domestic labor in drama would highlight money—the money that could relieve a woman of having to do it, that could allow her to perform only the creative parts of it, or that those employed for the less fun parts needed just to get by.

7   THE CLEAN HOUSE, OR CHANGE

1993–2005

Post-1990s Americans of all classes with access to television, the low-price mall store K-Mart, or magazine stands have been routinely confronted with the domesticity-fueled empire created by Martha Stewart, variously regarded as guru, goddess, monster, or joke. Stewart published her first book, *Entertaining*, in 1982. By 1999, there were a dozen more. By 2013 there were an additional several dozen, mostly featuring cooking, baking, gardening, entertaining, crafts, and decorating, but adding business management to the list in 2005 with *The Martha Rules*. Stewart has had her own magazine, television program, and radio show; now the upscale Macy's sells housewares bearing her name.

But, as food writer Molly O'Neill notes, "Like . . . the whole line of American women who systematized cooking and homemaking and created successful public personas from their private lives—Martha is about wishful thinking."[1] Journalist Margaret Talbot labeled Stewart "a kitchen-sink idealist."[2] Cultural journalist Anne Kingston calls Stewart "the perfect Type A proxy for an audience composed of women who arrived home exhausted from work to confront equally fatigued husbands, resentful children, meals that needed to be prepared, laundry that has to be washed, and homework that needed to be reviewed." Martha provided anesthetized relief from the daily grind. "Despising Martha became a way of focusing fury arising from a broad swath of modern frustrations induced by the high standards and commercial imperatives she represented."[3] The love/hate Martha population (72 percent of subscribers to *Martha Stewart Living* in 1996 were employed as managers or professionals),[4] juggling high expectations in the office and at home, also fits the profile of theatregoers willing to see plays about the frustrations of balancing domestic labor with career needs.

By 1993, a third wave of feminism had been named, and many of its proponents declared the overarching concerns of the second wave either passé or already solved or both.[5] However, as both feminist theory and the plays discussed here show, a national domestic labor problem of double shifts, underpaid household help, and no affordable child care persisted. In the years following Nannygate, five widespread cultural phenomena shaped domestic life and the plays dealing with it, although these phenomena hardly influenced all Americans responsible for housework in the same way. First, the robust economy that prevailed for the decade after Clinton's 1992 election brought prosperity to millions.[6] Second, beginning in the 1970s, there was a steady and large influx of immigrants, most Hispanic or Asian. By the 1990s, over fourteen million legal immigrants arrived annually in the United States.[7] Lisa Loomer's play *Living Out* (2003) puts the two previous phenomena in conversation, focusing on an immigrant nanny and her privileged white employer.

Third was a dramatic decrease in families headed by intact married couples. By 2000, the number of female-headed households with children had increased to 20 percent, and the number headed by intact married couples had fallen to 53 percent. Married couples rearing children were less than 25 percent of all households.[8] Fourth was the no-turning-back presence of women of all classes in the workforce. The number of American women working full-time rose from 14.8 million in 1967 (36.6 million men that year) to 41 million in 2002 (just under 50 million men). Women were 44 percent of all full-time American workers at the start of the new millennium.[9] Working poor women—several unmarried and a few with small children—are the subject of the play *Nickel and Dimed* (first presented in 2002). As the play states pointedly, their labor—in this context, domestic labor—is possibly the most frequently ignored facet of helping keep the prosperous consumer life intact for others. The play's female characters are both employees and responsible for child care and housecleaning in their own homes, which for one of the housecleaners and her kids is a motel room. Misunderstandings between families living under two very differing paradigms—two middle-class parents with mom at home vs.

single working-poor mom—are at work in *Caroline, or Change* (2003).

The fifth phenomenon, consumerism promulgated and (mis)understood as a form of self-improvement or activism, is nowhere so problematically summed up as in President George W. Bush's advice that New Yorkers begin recovering from the September 11, 2001, bombings by spending money on goods and entertainment. Martha Stewart's products and the aesthetic she promotes represent a facet of this consumption obsession. The final case study in this chapter, *The Clean House* (which premiered at South Coast Repertory in 2005), brings together several strands of discussion facilitated by an unpacking of the meaning—and meaninglessness—of domestic labor in the early twenty-first century. Cleaning in this play is presented as boring, comforting, personal, impersonal, irrelevant, and necessary in the context of paid employment, peace of mind, and impending death. It figures differently depending on the class, consumer expectations, and skill sets of its various women characters and invites a look at the consumption-as-satisfaction false consciousness regarding justice and fair play in the domestic labor realm.

Justice is the major theme in three of the plays discussed here and is, accordingly, much on the minds of those who put domestic labor at the forefront of their theatre work. The four plays include a musical, an unabashedly episodic panorama, "Greek" choruses, and bilingualisms. They do not feature middle-class women who might be considered in any way average or ordinary. The working women in these plays occupy two ends of a spectrum: the "haves" are writers, doctors, or lawyers; the "have nots" are working illegally as nannies, or they are maids or housecleaners doing extra shifts as waitresses or at low-end big-box stores and living in poverty. Nonworking wives have husbands who can both pay the bills and hire household help. The husbands of the employer wives are also writers, lawyers, doctors, and in one case a music teacher; the husbands of the domestics are generally absent, unemployed, or day laborers. The plays largely also do what realism—here despite many obvious aesthetic innovations—has always done best: they skirt the systemic in the name of the individual.

UPSTAIRS DOWNSTAIRS

In 1998, sociocultural critic/investigative journalist Barbara Ehrenreich began the research that would result in her 2001 nonfiction best seller, *Nickel and Dimed: On (Not) Getting By in America*.[10]

Ehrenreich went undercover as a minimum-wage worker for three months to learn firsthand about the economic realities of the lives of the working poor in the United States. Taking a job first as a waitress in a low-price restaurant in Florida, then as a housecleaner in Maine for a company much like Molly Maid, and finally as a clerk at a Minnesota Wal-Mart, she supplemented her meager income from these jobs with extra shifts cleaning motel rooms and working as a dietary aid at a nursing home. Ehrenreich learned that working even two jobs still leaves a vast swath of Americans one dead car battery away from disaster. Three of her jobs—housecleaning, waitressing, and caring for the elderly—are aspects of domestic labor that can either be purchased on a pay-as-you-go basis or outsourced.

Ehrenreich's book caught the attention of director Bartlett Sher of Seattle's Intiman Theatre, and Sher commissioned Joan Holden, resident playwright of the activist San Francisco Mime Theatre, to write a play based on *Nickel and Dimed.* The resulting piece is an almost perfect exercise in Brechtian drama. Written for six performers, it features several dozen characters, quickly shifting locales, and signs announcing workplaces and pay scales. As a waitress, Barbara—the only character played by a performer who does not undertake any other roles—makes $2.15 an hour plus tips. As a "Magic Maid" she earns $6.65 per hour, while employers pay $25 per hour per maid. At an Alzheimer's residential facility, where her weekend job is to serve meals to residents, she earns $7 an hour.

The play cuts back and forth among the various jobs and characters.[11] The playwright's first note in the published text reads "STYLE AND PACE: Epic/comic, not naturalistic, although the psychology is real."[12] The successful Intiman production moved quickly to Los Angeles's Mark Taper Forum to open the 2002–3 season. By 2006, the year the play was mounted in New York, it had enjoyed runs in professional and semiprofessional theatres in San Francisco; Minneapolis; Las Cruces, New Mexico; Cary, North Carolina; Austin, Texas; and Atlanta.[13] Since then it has been widely produced in colleges as far flung as Palo Alto, California (Foothill College); Milwaukee (Marquette University); and Hempstead, New York (Hofstra University).

Critical reception has been remarkably similar across productions. Reviewers recognized the play's straightforward delivery of "economic realities that most Americans prefer to ignore"[14] and its overarch-

Sharon Lockwood as Barbara in *Nickel and Dimed*, Intiman Theatre, Seattle, 2003.
Photo by Chris Bennion. Used by permission of Chris Bennion and the Intiman Theatre.

ing point that we need to stop "pretending that 'minimum wage' and 'living wage' mean the same thing."[15] Critics also assessed their experience of the play in terms of credible, sympathetic, mimetic performances, praising performers for making it "easy . . . to relate to the fictional protagonists as human beings,"[16] applauding such things as one actress's "humorous and moving take on the aging housekeeper,"[17] and using the garden-variety "personable" and "very convincing" as ways of approving illusionistic characterizations.[18] Almost all the critics used two intersecting but different realism axes to praise the work. The financial strictures of the working poor were recognized as inescapably factual (real), and credible impersonation was the index of truthful (real) acting.

Where the reviewers differ is in their assessments of how audiences—always understood to be a "we" different from the "they" being portrayed—might respond. A small number of critics also paid significant attention to dramaturgy, directing, and design. For instance, one review of the New York production, presented in a small theatre by the feminist 3Graces Theater Company, complained that the "production design overall seems to be battling with the small stage space.[19] Another, responding to the Austin, Texas, production gives with one hand and takes with the other, chiding Holden for the "dramatic thinness" of her script, which seems mostly "to want to educate its audience about the inequalities in our national economy" yet admitting that "focusing too closely on how *Nickel and Dimed* succeeds as a traditional play will blind one to its true purpose: to give voice to the people scraping by on $5, $6, $7 an hour."[20]

More significantly, critics recognize the challenge thrown down by *Nickel and Dimed* but offer varying responses about how it might most productively be received. In Seattle, critic Emily Hall wondered whether "the usual *Harper*'s-reading, NPR-listening liberals [will] congratulate themselves for having sat through something difficult, and then slip into the nights of their well-fed lives? How do you translate a play wrapped impenetrably in good intentions into actual policy change?" Hall sat next to Seattle's mayor the night she saw the play, and "although I wanted terribly much to ask him what he might do about poverty in Seattle, I didn't."[21]

Atlanta's Curt Holman found "condescending" the moment in the play when the house lights are brought up and audience members are directly asked whether they've ever "dehumanized" the working class. (Holden's script stipulates that this scene is optional, and some productions have chosen talk-back sessions after the performance or displays of photos of maids and waitresses in their lobbies rather than risk making audiences squirm.) Holman notes that "it's hard to tell if the play is trying to lay a guilt trip on anyone who's ever hired a house cleaner, or maybe coax someone to defend the dignity of honest labor."[22]

In *Nickel and Dimed*'s scene featuring both employer and housecleaning team, the character Rich Lady chides Barbara for cleaning a window with circular rather than perpendicular wipes. In the same scene, the Nanny tells the housecleaners which bathroom to use and that they may not have the air conditioning turned on because of the presence of the Rich Lady's baby, for whom it is deemed unhealthful. Condescension and the assumption of the housecleaners' incompetence are the governing tropes. Reviewer Jennifer Janviere sidestepped the larger political questions to conclude that "it reminds us of an important lesson that we sometimes forget in the daily bustle of our hectic lives; namely, to treat others with respect and empathy."[23]

Nickel and Dimed cries out for both changes in public policy and greater understanding, as we see a motel maid working in cheap sneakers, unable to pay for shoes with support, and eating a package of hot dog buns for lunch. Later, a mother of two very young children surreptitiously takes a forbidden break at her housecleaning job to telephone the older child, a toddler, at the motel room where she has locked him and his infant sister into the bedroom but out of the bathroom, for safety. The few dollars she had been paying an irresponsible sister-in-law to watch the children was money wasted, and we hear her instruct the little boy to use his potty seat and to change his sister's disposable diaper when she wakes up from her nap.

The play invites audiences to think as well as to feel, but it does not tell them what to do. This work goes farther than any other post-Depression play depicting domestic labor and the working poor to insist that laws, courtesy, awareness, and personal choices are available tools for change. For better or for worse, this is not news. There are no meaningful encounters staged between domestic worker and domestic employer, as the two classes of characters are segregated in dramas where their own worldviews are the optics offered as (incompatible) norms. The next two plays put worker and employer on the same stage at the same time, showing how domestic labor has neither a fixed meaning nor a fixed value, as one woman's drudgery is another's lifeline and yet another's escape route.

DOMESTIC LABOR IN BLACK AND WHITE AND BROWN

No other facet of domesticity has attached to it such high cultural stakes as mothering, and earlier chapters show that mothering as depicted in theatre can be smothering, either for the parent or the offspring, even if mothers who seek independence outside the home are usually returned there by the playwrights who spawned them, in the name of love or responsibility. By the 1990s a combination of backlash, nostalgia, marketing, and a realization that neither top-tier careers with brutal schedules nor repetitive pink-collar work was a panacea put homemaking back on the radars of women who could afford what was touted as "choice."[24] As early as 1988, *Good Housekeeping* magazine ran a series of ads targeting what it called the "New

Traditionalist." This fictional character, as Susan Faludi puts it, "gladly retreats to her domestic shell . . . [in] little more than a resurgence of the 1950s 'back-to-the-home' movement," both promulgated by magazines and merchandisers anxious about selling their wares to familiar markets.[25] New Traditionalists—there were six in the series—were working women (all white collar), but surrounded by and committed to their children.[26]

Mothering coupled with a retreat from public life and paid employment would recur as themes supposedly reflecting cultural trends right up to 2013, when Emily Matchar wrote *Homeward Bound: Why Women Are Embracing the New Domesticity*.[27] Between the 1988 *New Traditionalist* and 2013 *Homeward Bound* bookends, Lisa Belkin's 2003 *New York Times* article, "The Opt-Out Revolution"—which became a catch-phrase—and Claudia Wallis's 2004 cover story in *Time* magazine, "The Case for Staying Home: Why More Young Moms Are Opting Out of the Rat Race," explored women's desire for lives that are "less intense and more fulfilling."[28]

Journalists dutifully nodded to the fact that the MBAs, lawyers, and Ivy League graduates who were their interview subjects were not representative of all, or even "average," American women. Belkin's apologia was that her research cohort included women who were supposed to be the professional equals of men, noting that their choice to side-step the career fast track was "explosive." A decade after Belkin's high-profile piece, the *New York Times* did a follow-up, in which journalist Judith Warner looked at women who had "opted out" in the interest of more time for mothering and had come to regret it. While few wanted to return to high-stakes, pressure-cooker jobs, they felt a distinct loss of power and confidence, with many "troubled by the gender-role traditionalism that crept into their marriages once they gave up work," as they ceased to be their husbands' equals and were suddenly expected to have a gift for housework.[29]

By 2009 just under 64 percent of American mothers worked outside the home, with a third of these serving as the primary breadwinners for their families. In the same year, only 9 percent of people in dual-earner marriages said that they shared housework, child care, and income generation equally, with mothers in marriages with both spouses employed full-time doing 40 percent more child care and 30 percent more housework than the father.[30] Feminists on the left, who continue to worry about women's lack of status in the workplace and parity on the payroll, warn of the irreversible loss of income suffered by women who have children—even if they do not "opt out" of paid employment.[31] Those on the right, who favor the "option" of staying home, focus on our culture's refusal to recognize private child rearing as work that both benefits society at large (who else is supposed to do it?) and is assigned almost no financial value.[32] Because the United States is the only high-income country in the world without a required paid maternity leave, women who have children pay a "mommy tax" in the form of lost lifetime income, even if they take only minimal time off.[33] Both sides point to the emotional tug-of-war women face if they work for pay and have children.

Lisa Loomer's play *Living Out* sits at the intersection of these emotional and financial dilemmas, and it does so from the perspectives of both a privileged and a working-class mother. These are the two demographics most likely to include women who stay at home, in one case as a lifestyle choice facilitated by a high-earning husband and in the other a necessity and sometimes a cultural expectation, with limited financial resources and/or spousal machismo (regardless of ethnicity) as contributing reasons. Written in 2003, *Living Out* tapped into the "opt out" mood and also into the guilt and difficulties experienced by mothers of any class who enjoy their work outside the home but whose husbands and employers offer too little meaningful assistance with either housework or child care. The play complicates the binary—opt out or hire in vs. hire out—as both the main female characters like working, earn more than their husbands, and struggle with guilt over needing others to help with child care at home.

Living Out's upper-middle-class couple, Nancy and Richard Robin, have just had their first child and have moved from East Los Angeles to the expensive Santa Monica. Nancy is excited about returning to work as an entertainment lawyer; Richard is a public defender unwilling to "sell out" by taking a corporate position. The Robins hire Ana Hernandez, an undocumented woman from El Salvador who lives in East L.A. with her intermittently employed construction worker husband, Bobby, and their six-year-old son. An older son lives with a grandmother in El Salvador. Nancy's goals are a high-powered career and a "safe" neighborhood for her child. Ana's goals are earning enough money to bring her older son to the United States and moving to a "better" neighborhood. She also uses the word "safe" in the context of the schooling and health of her younger son, who has asthma and for whom she believes the air in East L.A. is detrimental.[34]

Nancy's uncertainty about mothering and her good intentions are contextualized via two other yuppie moms whose concerns run diaper bag designs, the evils of sugar, the pleasures of "mommy and me" classes, and the need to keep tabs on their children's nannies, about whose lives and cultures they are clueless. Ana's immigration concerns and understanding of white privilege are conveyed in scenes with two other Latina nannies, both savvy but themselves beset with ethnic prejudice. The yuppie mothers and the Latina nannies function as what are often called Greek choruses, and their scenes are funnier and less theatrically naturalistic than the ones set in the Robin and the Hernandez homes. The script states that these homes should occupy the same stage kitchen and living room with members of both households occupying the dramaturgically requisite areas as needed. Parallelism, in other words, is one of the play's concerns, something noted by several reviewers for several productions mounted between 2003 and 2011.[35]

One of the parallels is the stage time devoted to domestic labor in the women's respective homes and who performs it. Early in the play, immediately after Nancy has hired Ana, each woman talks to her husband, as both husbands kick back with the sports pages of their respective newspapers. Nancy folds the baby's laundry, although her job is more demanding and stressful than her husband's; Ana, although she has spent the day at a job interview and then buying groceries, is met by Bobby's requests that she prepare dinner, even though he is unemployed and has not spent the day at work. Ana brings him food. In later scenes taking place on days when both women have worked late, Bobby again requests that Ana make dinner; Richard declares he is going to order a pizza. Both women start scenes or cover awkward moments with bits of sweeping, "straightening up," putting away groceries, or making coffee (20, 31, 35, 37).

Unsurprisingly, as child care is the domestic labor motivating the play's action, child care is most of what Ana performs, albeit in brief spurts with an infant "played" by a stage prop; it is certainly the domestic labor most discussed. Unfailingly, the Robins' baby responds to Ana's ability to coo and comfort, which sometimes makes Nancy regretful or jealous.[36] In keeping with the parallel themes Ana is also anxious about leaving her young son with someone other than his parent; when Bobby finally lands a full-time job in act 2, Ana says, "I don't want somebody else watching my son" (44). Although the proposed caregiver is Bobby's sister, Ana objects that the sister is too young and the car she drives is unsafe.

The contrast between the child care *performed* (rocking, singing, leaving to change a diaper, cooing, holding, preparing a bottle) and the child care *discussed* is a good deal of what makes the play timely and pushes cultural buttons. One kind of child care is immediate, not related to education or expense, and probably recognized across most cultures. The other comes from the "opt out" playbook. In *Living Out*, the nonworking, well-to-do mothers cannot fathom having children if one cannot stay home with them (finances permitting), although they hire nannies and devote themselves to yoga and volunteer work. Nancy's anxiety and guilt emerge from being part of this economic cohort. Their concerns are about their children having the "right" activities, attention, foods, air quality, and safety (as understood by upper-middle-class parents).

These mothers are proponents of "intensive mothering," defined as a model of mothering that "tells us that children are innocent and priceless, that their rearing should be carried out primarily by individual mothers and that it should be centered on children's needs, with methods that are informed by experts, labor-intensive, and costly."[37] As Sharon Green observes in her article about Loomer's plays featuring conflicted mothers, "In contemporary cultural discourse 'good mothering,' [*sic*] and the ideology of intensive mothering have been conflated; the former is *defined* by practices of the latter, and . . . other parenting practices, [*sic*] are articulated as 'deviancy.'"[38] Ana enacts effective basic mothering, but her verbal discourse embraces intensive mothering. She understands the importance of appearing available to the employer's child at the expense of her own. Her cohort has instructed her to lie about having a child living with her in the United States. Well-to-do employers prefer nannies unhampered by children at home but experienced in raising children who have stayed behind in Latin America.

In Ana's double-bind mothering position, her nurturing skills are valued and will enable her to upgrade her own child's situation on the intensive mothering scale (by "enrichment" that can be purchased in the form of classes, activities, tutors, doctors, or lessons) even as she is unable to provide the basics at home. Basics alone, we are made to understand, are not enough, if the goal of (intensive) mothering is betterment. In the play's final scenes—called melodramatic by several reviewers—Ana's own child dies as the result of an asthma attack during a soccer game she misses because she has agreed to work overtime for the Robins. It is never made clear that her presence would have resulted in a trip to the "right" hospital on the "right" highway in the "right" kind of car, but clearly she feels tremendous guilt. At the end of the play she has left the Robins, who have decided to take care of their daughter themselves. She is seeking other employment, delaying bringing her older son to the United States, and questioning her abilities as a mother. The wedge between the ability to take care of a child well and the capacity for being a "good" (read "intensive") mother is palpable, but no reviewer remarked on it.

That Ana and Nancy want the same sorts of "betterment" for their children nods to what Linda Hirshman calls "the 'regime effect.'"[39] What is touted as "the best" by elites is emulated by those with less money, visibility, and clout as somehow good for them—or, at any rate, desirable—even when it entails retreating from public life to the realm of apple pie and play dates. The extent to which intensive mothering has become a norm shows up in the increased number of hours American mothers spend in primary child care, "defined as routine caregiving and activities that foster a child's well-being, such as reading and fully-focused play."[40] In 1975, stay-at-home mothers spent eleven hours a week on primary child care; by 2013 they spent roughly seventeen. Mothers employed outside the home in 1975 spent six hours on primary child care; their analogues in 2013 spent about eleven, making the present-day's employed mother's child care as time-consuming as that of her pre-intensive counterpart forty years ago.[41]

In *Living Out*, the elite "best" does include work outside the home as well as intensive mothering, an impossible combination except for those who can buy the latter and avoid guilt. That the latter is not necessarily "the best" is never interrogated, except perhaps by the nannies who laugh at the employer who gets crazed at the thought of her small child eating sugar but who hides candy bars in her drawers and relies on someone else to feed her offspring.

If the text stages an ideological conundrum in a country that purports to value mothering but refuses to pay for child care, the play in performance offers an interesting look at what persuades as "authentic" with "real people" who "come across as accurate."[42] In each of five productions examined here, Ana has been portrayed by an actress with a clearly Latina name (Zilah Mendoza in Los Angeles and New York; Isabel Ortega in San Francisco; Stephanie Diaz in Seattle; and Judy Rodriguez in Columbus, Ohio. The Greek chorus nannies were also played by actresses with Latina names.) Nancy, although clearly identified as Jewish in the text, was played in these respective productions by Amy Aquino, Kathryn Meisle, Rebecca Dines, Julie Briskman, and Charlesanne Rabensburg. While it is hard to locate ethnicity solely in last names, especially as some women still adopt their husbands' surnames upon marriage, the casting policy and reviews suggest that visible markers of ethnicity continue to be required for certain so-called minorities, while others have been "whitened" into a position of being able to be portrayed by capable performers of other cultural derivations than the one(s) scripted. "Reality" inheres in a one-to-one relationship between Latina performers and their roles, while characters and performers of other cultural and ethnic derivations are handled with more flexibility.[43]

Rather than a negative critique, this is an observation about continued anxiety and blind spots regarding recognition of "reality" (or truthfulness or accuracy) onstage and the ongoing tensions surrounding nontraditional casting. The audience at the matinee I attended in New York at Second Stage gasped at a quip about the impossibility of a family that pays a nanny well being Jewish. An analogous remark about Chinese employers caused not a ripple, and all of the lines delivered in Spanish appeared to go over the audience's heads. While non-matinee and West Coast or university audiences likely contain more Spanish-speaking spectators, all productions used identifiable Latinas as Latinas, suggesting a perception of credibility too susceptible to anxiety to leave to (mere?) acting. As with so many other productions examined in this study, multiple axes and indices of reality and the real, relating to script, environment, prices, products, affective credibility in casting, or "persuasive" performance collided in both the artistic decisions and the critical reception of *Living Out*. What no one questioned was the work—domestic labor largely in the form of parenting and provisioning food—that had to get done.

The domestic labor that has to get done in Tony Kushner and Jeanine Tesori's 2003 musical, *Caroline, or Change*, is determined by a combination of necessity and economic status. Put simply, no one wants her children to go without food, shoes, or dental care, but the maid—a single mother of four—pinches pennies on food and does laundry and cleaning for two families, while the mistress—married stepmother of one—only seems to shop for groceries and cook, enjoying daily household service for everything else and hiring additional help when there are three guests for a holiday dinner. Perhaps more than any other play in this study, *Caroline* portrays tension *within* a maid/mistress household, the difference *between* the households of the two, and how *historic distance* can deflect assessment of present-day problems.

The musical depicts a vertical axis within the home of a white employer—her realm at ground level in kitchen and living room and that of her African American maid below in the hot, humid basement/laundry room; a horizontal axis, as we see the two women in their own homes "across town" from each other; and a temporal axis, as the show is set forty years in the past but speaks the language of viewers enmeshed in their present-day world of a robust economy, the ordinary presence of women in the paid workforce, an unquestioned acceptance of consumerism as self-improvement, and a decrease in the number of two-parent homes in the United States.[44] That domesticity linked the women and that money, plain and simple—"not . . . Capital . . . but just by money, the meager stuff we work for and swap for bread and books and theater tickets," as Ashton Stevens said of *Awake and Sing* sixty-three years earlier—was the sticking point in the inequality equation were either wholly ignored (the domesticity) or regarded as a catalyst (the money) by most critics.[45]

Caroline is set in Lake Charles, Louisiana, the city where Kushner grew up, and is based on an incident from his own life.[46] Its dual focus is eight-year-old Noah Gellman—the Kushner stand-in—and his Jewish family's African American maid, Caroline Thibodeaux. Noah's mother has just died, and his father has remarried a woman Noah hates; the divorced Caroline is confronting the needs of her children, her aching knees, and her weekly pay, recognizing that although she is "mean and tough . . . / Thirty dollars ain't enough" (18). The boy is lonely; the maid is also lonely, uneducated, and in a frequently used adjective in the critical journalists' lexicon, dour. But her strength keeps Noah anchored, as he sings of Caroline being, from his perspective, the president of the United States and stronger than his (depressed and distant) dad.

The inciting factors for the play's crisis and resolution are the civil rights movement bundled with the Kennedy assassination and Noah's stepmother's decision to teach the boy the value of a nickel by letting Caroline keep any loose change left in his pants pockets when he chucks his clothes into the laundry hamper. A Chanukah gift of twenty dollars from Noah's grandfather ends up in the laundry room when the boy inadvertently leaves the bill in his pocket. Caroline, who has never liked taking a little boy's small change, decides that this time, with Christmas on the horizon, her own children, three of whom live at home, need a trip to the dentist, eyeglasses, some holiday presents, and, for the son stationed in Vietnam, a nice package of goodies.

Noah decides that, while contributing to Caroline's family may have made him feel important, the consumer opportunities the twenty will cost him are too great to give up. He slings an anti-black epithet; she replies with an anti-Jewish one. In her guilt and horror at her lack of charity toward a child—her employers' child—Caroline stays away from work for five days, finally deciding she must sacrifice her personal feelings to keep her nose to the grindstone and provide for her kids. She goes back to work, refusing both the change in Noah's pockets and the social change in the air. The show concludes as Caroline's outspoken fifteen-year-old daughter confesses to having helped topple a Civil War statue in town and vows to keep pushing for change, working with the courage she has acquired from her stoic and principled mother.

In this sung-through musical, also called, by various critics, a pop opera, a people's opera, and a chamber opera,[47] Jeanine Tesori's eclectic score draws on soul, gospel, Motown, klezmer, blues, and R&B, as well as on Jewish folk tunes and melodies inflected by slave labor motifs shaped by the repetitive physical tasks they were devised to accompany. The show was nominated for six Tony Awards, including Best Musical. Anika Noni Rose (playing Caroline's daughter, Emmie) won for Best Supporting Actress in a Musical. *Caroline* anthropomorphizes the washer, dryer, and radio that are its heroine's daily companions in the Gellmans' basement. Despite the creators' obvious goal of honoring the maid's life and her everyday world, some critics called the singing appliances "a fetish of personification" or a "flaw," and Caroline's dialogue with them "unusual and annoying."[48] They complained about the "ultra-drab basement laundry room," whining that "you can only listen to a song about doing the laundry for so long."[49] Some recognized the musical's "ability . . . to plumb and honor the ordinary," seeing it as "a slice-of-life drama," and "modest domestic story" that "strikes the right balance of realism and abstraction."[50]

Reviews were decidedly mixed, with David Hurst's very brief write-up summing up the standoff: "dazzling, yet distancing . . . fulfilling and frustrating."[51] Most focused on Kushner's handling of large political questions, on Caroline's entrapment, on Jewish-black relations, and on the relationship between Noah and Caroline. The *New Yorker*'s John Lahr encapsulated the script's obvious agon: "Caroline's economic necessity is played off against Noah's emotional needs." For Lahr, the musical is a triumph for "illuminating both worlds without condescending to either."[52]

But pairing Noah's and Caroline's worlds is pairing a child's-eye view with an adult's. *Caroline* keeps the younger generation racially segregated, except in Noah's fantasy of being part of Caroline's family.[53] I want to suggest that a fruitful place to look for insight about the Jewish-black tensions in the musical is in a comparison of the show's two mothers: Caroline and Rose, Noah's stepmother—two adults who do interact. Rose is the linchpin between Noah and Caroline, as she enlists Caroline's help in teaching Noah to pay attention to the money in his pockets and is tolerated but not liked by either Caroline or Noah.

Yet the two women characters bear some uncomfortable similarities, their differences of security and financial status notwithstanding. Both are mothers whose worlds revolve around housekeeping, cooking, parenting, and loneliness. Caroline bemoans the chaos into which her finances are thrown when she decides to serve her children meat twice in one week. Rose is extolled in song as a good cook by her new in-laws, and one of her encounters with Caroline involves her offering leftover stuffed cabbage with brisket for the maid's children, something Caroline turns down, as her children don't like cabbage. Rose's new husband acknowledges in a brief, sung soliloquy that he "cannot provide: / conversation, support, and a heart . . . Those all died" (97, ellipsis in original). Caroline left her abusive husband when he hit her, taking out on his wife his alcohol-fueled frustration at being unable to find work after serving in the military in World War II. She fantasizes that Nat King Cole will visit her and kiss her; she also hopes her husband might return (118).

Neither woman can imagine a life outside cooking, child care, and stuckness. While we are given more information about Caroline's backstory, Rose's suggests a middle-class white parallel to Caroline's lower-class black gendering. Caroline has no education and cannot imagine getting one; if Rose has a formal education, the show is silent on its nature or possible use. Caroline is stuck between economic necessity and personal fear, but Rose lives in the naturalist realm of "ongoing, nonlinear, repetitive motion . . . that has the distinctive effect of seeming also like a stuckness in place."[54] Her repetitive motion is hardly backbreaking or obsessive, but she seeks safety and security through shopping for groceries, supervising the maid, wanting a new dress, and worrying about Noah. Rose is in the fortunate position of being able to afford the consumer goods that offer freedom by "lightening of the domestic load through contrivance, technology, and the use of non-human, nonanimal power" (the washer and dryer are hers).[55] Yet she seems to have no interest in using her freedom except to minimize her own domestic labor.

Both women fear being without money; both have children who cannot wait to spend what little they are given on candy, comic books, sodas, or toys. Neither is at home in the world where she finds herself: Rose because it is the South and Caroline because it is a New South. (Caroline's friend Dotty, another maid, is attending night school, but Caroline disapproves of Dotty's ways, later admitting that she can barely read and can't afford to change.) Neither Rose nor Caroline sees herself as resourceful; both are defined by domesticity, whether they perform it for money or pay to have it done. Each clings to it relentlessly as a measure of her worth. In the show's final moments, Caroline returns to her job and Rose earns a modicum of Noah's trust, as he allows her to tuck him into bed for the first time.

Despite the singing appliances, musical eclecticism, and shifting locales, *Caroline, or Change* adheres to realism's "generic protocols for classifying, posing . . . and naming its subject matter,"[56] leading one critic to sum up the show's politics as asserting that "all Southern blacks are strong and wise and all Jewish liberals whiny and ineffectual."[57] I am hardly suggesting that this would have been a better piece of theatre if Rose had been limned as an incipient resistor of the feminine mystique squaring off with Caroline as a civil rights activist. Indeed, the latter function is given to Emmie, but tellingly, her fantasy future includes neither activism nor children but rather a car, a house where everything is new, a television in every room, "and my own telephone / and I live in my house / and I live in my house / by myself, all alone / and if I'm lonely, doesn't matter / I think they's worse than bein' lonely— / They's people who freeze / while they wait on their knees" (96).

If audiences for the original production were meant to read Emmie as the wave of the future, they were also in a position to assess that future, as it was the "now" of their viewing moment. Emmie craves consumerism and an absence of domestic obligation, and she likely plans to have someone else clean her big house, rather than—like her mother—work on her knees. Like Beneatha Younger of the 1959 *A Raisin in the Sun*, Emmie may or may not end up as an educated success, or even simply a solvent consumer. The challenge issued by *Caroline* is not to sympathize with its eponymous heroine in the context of the show's narrative. How could one not? Nor is it to accept that the next generation, embodied in Emmie, will get out. As Tonya Pinkins, the original Caroline, noted in an interview in 2004, "Realistically, the classism and racism were huge—and I'm not sure it has changed that much."[58] Classism and racism remain in place. Less dramatically but no less insidiously still in place is something asserted in *Caroline* by the embodied dryer: "Small domestic tragedies / bring strong women to their knees" (79). If the fictional Emmie did grow up to achieve a big house replete with televisions, phones, and no domestic responsibilities in 2004, she likely grew up to hire a contemporary who was not so lucky, and to do so at the culture's going rate: poverty wages.

LIFE AND DEATH IN THE CLEAN LANE

What might theatre say about domestic labor and feminism in a post-Fordist world where globalization, cross-class alliances, a desire to work hard for goals that are not wages, personal income, and high stakes for domestic cleanliness are all on the table? Sarah Ruhl's *The Clean House* throws all these into relief. The play features four women with radically differing relationships to housework and waged work, making it impossible to say that one or the other is better or more suitable to females, as none of the characters is fully happy or a fully responsible role model.

Lane, a doctor in her mid-fifties, is a workaholic who wears white and whose home—the main playing area—is all white. She hires Matilde, a twenty-seven-year-old Brazilian, to clean her house. Matilde hates cleaning, knowing that her calling is to follow in her parents' footsteps and write jokes. Lane's sister, Virginia, is a housewife for whom cleaning is a reason to get up in the morning; her marriage is boring, her husband is unable to father children, and she realized after majoring in Greek literature at Bryn Mawr that she could not be a critical writer because she has nothing to say. Virginia relishes domestic labor and covers for Matilde by cleaning Lane's house every day after finishing with her own. The fourth woman, sixty-seven-year-old Ana, originally from Argentina, is a terminally ill, glowing free spirit who lives in a small house with a barebones amount of unmatched furniture and a balcony overlooking the sea. Her beloved husband died thirty-six years earlier, and although she wanted children, she refused to have them until he stopped drinking, which he did, but too late. Her current lover is Lane's estranged husband, Charles.

The distinct positions regarding domestic labor bear analysis in light of what Kathi Weeks calls "the problem with work": Americans' worth and worthiness being defined by how they earn livings under capitalism and the possibility that we unquestioningly link purposefulness with job titles.[59] This problem isn't about actions undertaken to accomplish tasks. Rather, it is about capitalist economic systems that dominate our entire social unconscious and depend on the acceptance of waged labor as the *only* legitimate means of achieving human dignity, basic needs, moral worth, respect as a responsible citizen, and social standing.

In this scheme, non-wage-earning housewives still depend on a wage earner for sustenance, health care, social status, and respect, whether they are the income-producer's spouse or heir. After the family, the workplace is the primary source of sociality for most Americans, and the goal of good parenting is to give children the traits they will need to get jobs that enable them to match if not exceed their parents' class standing. Paid work outside the home is sometimes the requirement for welfare, ironically wreaking havoc on the home in the name of moral fortitude and responsible citizenship. Meanwhile, despite "the fact that [social] wealth is collectively not individually produced," the normative expectations remain intact, shoring up the imperative of "an individual responsibility [that] has more to do with the socially mediating role of work than its strictly productive function."[60] *The Clean House* offers a fascinating site to consider this nexus of values in relation to domestic labor.

In the play, Lane is a clear-cut spokeswoman for hierarchized paid labor, declaring, "I did not go to medical school to clean my own house."[61] Matilde is caught between needing income and her status as an immigrant, which means that she will most readily find it as a domestic even though her inclinations and talents lie elsewhere. She agrees to work part-time for Ana, partly because Ana is also uninterested in housework, therefore neither exceptionally fussy nor unwilling to engage on other terms with Matilde.[62] While we never see the interior of Ana's house, we know that it is not high-tech and all white; we also know that Ana treats Matilde as a friend and equal, as they pick apples and laugh together. Conceivably it is not housework itself that Matilde refuses but housework that will be subject to clinical judgment by an employer for whom its sterile performance is by an invisible servant.

The four women are thrown into direct contact in the second half of the play, when Charles leaves on a quest for an exotic plant reputed to have the power to arrest Ana's spreading cancer. Virginia goes into a rage at Lane's insults and trashes the white living room. Virginia's willingness to destroy her own work in the interest of "talking back" to her unfeeling sister opens the channel of communication between them. Lane, the doctor, accepts the task of caring for Ana in her last days and takes the dying woman into her own home. Virginia provides home-cooked meals and even homemade ice cream, and Lane has learned to ask for and accept help that is offered rather than purchased. Matilde finally assists Ana in dying, "killing" her with a joke, as Matilde's father had her mother.

The Clean House satisfies Helen Molesworth's two putatively non-congruent forms of feminist arts work—essentialist and identificatory.[63] There is female solidarity, as Virginia fantasizes about the days when women met together at public fountains to wash clothes and tell stories and observes that everyone living in separate, solitary houses is terrible. There is postmodernist distancing, as apples dropped from Ana's balcony fall into Lane's living room, and Matilde's dead parents, performed by the same actors who play Charles and Ana, dance through Lane's "real" house. And there are easy readings: Lane needs to learn compassion; Virginia needs to stop hiding; Ana is exceptional and seems to have an independent income, making her less a mimetic character with whom to identify than a fantasy to relish; and there are no children in sight, which means that characters' taking and representing clear stances is perhaps easier than it would be in the face of multiple unknown and mutable factors.

But reading the domestic labor, or its refusal, here as a problematization of paid work itself offers rich possibilities. Neither Lane nor Virginia is either fulfilled or willing to take a good look in the mirror, and for both the problems are a combination of work *and* domestic life. That the two WASPS come to greater awareness via two Latinas might also suggest that an infusion of an "other" culture (this one traditionally read as machismo and gendered) is worth a second look. A postwork reading offers more—and maybe more unsettling—ways of thinking about whether the Friedan/Child standoff is not better seen as a dance with two partners.

What is the difference between Virginia's and Matilde's cleaning of Lane's house? Lane asserts outright that she doesn't want to be cared for: she wants to pay a stranger. This has nothing to do with the labor or its use value but has everything to do with a wage system and a certain amount of consumerism for status. Matilde first sustains and then kills Ana with her company and, specifically, her jokes. Matilde is the one who offers work in the home that requires skills and would otherwise necessitate home-care workers. Palliative care is presented as a very real form of domestic labor that may be invisible to those thinking only of cleaning. After Ana dies, Lane is momentarily at sea. She has seen many deaths in a hospital context but considers closing the deceased's eyes and washing the body to be nurses' tasks. When Lane undertakes these tasks, she is both situating herself lower on the capitalist wage scale and conflating professional and domestic work. She is also, of course, recognizing the latter as real, and necessary, work.

The Clean House does not offer answers, but it asks important questions. Domestic labor is the "Mrs." of professional or even blue-collar work. Women who imagine replacing one with the other still find themselves trafficking in the same currency—constrained by capitalism, with its disregard for the value of domestic labor unless one pays for it—albeit with the expectation that the coin will always land on the other side. People who do both kinds of work generally realize that neither is without some predictability and some comfort. Depictions of domestic labor in theatre have generally been recognized as facets of kitchen sink realism—a causality-driven, often recuperative genre. This play references truthfulness without full reliance on realism in either the literary sense or as a defining feature of the mise-en-scène.

The Friedan/Child pas de deux is still with us. Most American women perform some domestic labor and find some parts of it fulfilling, other parts boring and demanding. Only the most privileged in our era of dual-income households can opt to "stay home," and those who claim to find satisfaction doing so often have household help for the least interesting and most physically taxing aspects of housework. Creating complicated dishes for a party one is hosting or making Halloween costumes for children is simply more pleasurable if one is not also responsible for scrubbing out the bathtub, washing the windows, pretreating the laundry, and cleaning the kitty litter box. But the gourmet dinner, the inventive costume, and the immaculately kept decorated home can be very rewarding endeavors. And participation in the paid workforce is often what gives the woman who performs domestic labor a place among an adult cohort involved in public concerns beyond at-home parties, sparkling bathrooms, and children's costumes. Performance is a place to play with these paradoxical pluralities.

NOTES

INTRODUCTION

1 John Guare, *The War against the Kitchen Sink: Collected Works, Volume I* (Lyme, NH: Smith and Kraus, 1996). In his introduction, Guare scorns the sentimentality and closure he associates with plays featuring "the dreaded living room with a dreaded kitchen sink spouting water" (viii).

2 J. L. Styan, *Modern Drama in Theory and Practice* (Cambridge: Cambridge University Press, 1981), 1:149. Amy Dempsey points out that Kitchen Sink School was the name given by critic David Sylvester in an article in 1954 to a group of British painters whose work depicted "drab, unheroic scenes of post-war austerity, the commonplace subject-matter of daily life: cluttered kitchens, bombed-out tenements and backyards." *Art in the Modern Era: A Guide to Styles, Schools, and Movements* (New York: Harry N. Abrams, 2002), 199.

3 William Demastes, "Preface: American Dramatic Realisms, Viable Frames of Thought," in *Realism and the American Dramatic Tradition*, ed. Demastes (Tuscaloosa: University of Alabama Press, 1996), ix.

4 See Dorothy Chansky, *Composing Ourselves: The Little Theatre Movement and the American Audience* (Carbondale: Southern Illinois University Press, 2004).

5 Ethan Mordden, *All That Glittered: The Golden Age of Drama on Broadway 1919–1959* (New York: St. Martin's Press, 2007).

6 Sarah Ruhl, *The Clean House* (New York: Samuel French, 2007), 8.

7 Warren Susman, Introduction, in *Culture and Commitment 1929–1945*, ed. Susman (New York: George Braziller, 1973), 2.

8 Carol Shields, Pulitzer Prize–winning Canadian novelist, quoted in her obituary, by Christopher Lehmann-Haupt, *New York Times*, 18 July 2003, A19.

9 Here I am piggybacking on the work of Nancy Chodorov in *The Reproduction of Mothering: Psychoanalysis and the Sociology of Gender*, 2nd ed., with a new preface (Berkeley: University of California Press, 1999), 3, x. Chodorow uses psychoanalysis, especially objects-relation theory to "provide . . . a systemic, structural account of socialization and social reproduction" that goes beyond instrumentalist ideas of example or instruction or pressures. In the preface and afterword to the 1999 edition, Chodorov acknowledges the limitations of foundational psychoanalytic theory for accounting for the experiences of all women (especially lesbians) and all parents, especially with more women in the workforce than was the case when she undertook her original research. Nonetheless, even in 2015, the dynamics she describes are

readily recognizable. The family setup she assumes (a working father much away from home and primary child-rearing responsibilities handled by a mother in a private house rather than, say, communal care) was by far and away the primary one for at least the first two-thirds of the period in this book. Most significantly, for my work, is her observation that "[t]he reproduction of women's mothering is the basis for the reproduction of women's location and responsibilities in the domestic sphere" (208). Chodorow arrives at the same conclusion of many nonpsychoanalytic social critics: children and adults would enjoy and respect themselves and each other more if parenting were not gendered and if heterosexuality were not linked to a psychology that devalues the female and tamps down on male expressivity.

10 See Clayton Hamilton, "Organizing an Audience," *Bookman* 34 (October 1911): 161–66; Edwin Carty Ranck, "What Is a Good Play?" *Theatre* 30, no. 221 (July 1919): 24–25; Thomas H. Dickinson, *The Case of American Drama* (Boston: Houghton Mifflin, 1915), 128; Richard Butsch, *The Making of American Audiences: From Stage to Television, 1750–1990* (New York: Cambridge University Press, 2000), 80, chaps. 5, 9; and Susan Jonas and Suzanne Bennett, "New York State Council on the Arts Theatre Program Report on the Status of Women: A Limited Engagement?," January 2002, accessed 8 April 2015, http://www.womenarts.org/nysca-report-2002/. The 2002 NEA *Survey of Public Participation in the Arts* (www.arts.gov) reveals that 60 percent of American theatregoers are women.

11 Newspapers in small North American cities in the 1930s offered some notable exceptions to this rule of thumb.

12 Arlie Hochschild, *The Second Shift* (New York: Avon Books, 1989); Linda Hirshman, "Homeward Bound," *American Prospect* 16, no. 12 (December 2005): 20–26.

13 Betty Friedan, *The Feminine Mystique* (1963; repr., New York: Dell Publishing, 1974). Julia Child and Friedan both claimed a place in American consciousness around the same time; both created serious, if competing, domestic legacies in the American households actual and staged. This duality is a guiding theme of chapter 5.

14 See Pam Morris, *Realism* (New York: Routledge, 2003); Demastes, *Realism and the American Dramatic Tradition*; Brenda Murphy, *American Realism and American Drama, 1880–1940* (Cambridge: Cambridge University Press, 1987); Georg Lukács, "Realism in the Balance," and Bertolt Brecht, "Against Georg Lukács," both in *Aesthetics and Politics* (London: NLB, 1977).

15 Lukács, "Realism in the Balance," 34.

16 Brecht, "Against Georg Lukács," 81, 82.

17 Morris, *Realism*, 23.

18 Ibid., 85.

19   Brian Richardson, "Introduction: The Struggle for the Real—Interpretive Conflict, Dramatic Method, and the Paradox of Realism," in Demastes, *Realism and the American Dramatic Tradition*, 1–17, at 3.

20   Morris, *Realism*, 4.

21   Ibid., 94.

22   William Demastes sums up the charges against realism's tyranny as stemming "from the conclusion that realism is a structurally unambitious, homogeneous, tunnel-visioned form, its every product churning out the same fundamental message and denying creation of a more open, pluralistic theatre." *Realism and the American Dramatic Tradition*, ix.

23   Morris, *Realism*, 140.

24   Jeffrey H. Richards, "Politics, Playhouse, and Repertoire in Philadelphia, 1808," *Theatre Survey* 46, no. 2 (November 2005): 219.

25   Harvey, quoted in Morris, *Realism*, 144.

26   Justin Lewis, "The Meaning of Things; Audiences, Ambiguity, and Power," in *Viewing, Reading, Listening: Audiences and Cultural Reception*, ed. Jon Cruz and Justin Lewis, 19–32 (Boulder, CO: Westview Press, 1994), quotes on 27, 29, 26.

27   Tracy C. Davis, "Questions for a Feminist Methodology in Theatre History," in *Interpreting the Theatrical Past: Essays in the Historiography of Performance*, ed. Thomas Postlewait and Bruce McConachie (Iowa City: University of Iowa Press, 1989), 37–58, quote on 66.

28   Lewis, "The Meaning of Things," 20.

29   Robert F. Gross, "Servant of Three Masters: Realism, Idealism, and 'Hokum' in American High Comedy," in Demastes, *Realism and the American Dramatic Tradition*, 71–90, at 73.

30   William W. Demastes, *Beyond Naturalism: A New Realism in American Theatre* (Westport, CT: Greenwood Press, 1988), 3. The second quote is from Eric Bentley, in ibid.

31   Phillip B. Zarrilli, Bruce McConachie, Gary Jay Williams, and Carol Fisher Sorgenfrei, *Theatre Histories: An Introduction* (New York: Routledge, 2006), 333. McConachie wrote the section in which these observations appear.

32   Jennifer Fleissner, *Women, Compulsion, Modernity: The Moment of American Naturalism* (Chicago: University of Chicago Press, 2004).

33   Ibid., 9.

34   Ibid., 22.

35   Ibid., 31.

36   The best books on the history of domestic labor in the United States are Susan Strasser, *Never Done: A History of American Housework* (New York: Henry Holt, 1982, with a new preface in 2000); and Ruth Schwartz Cowan,

More Work for Mother: The Ironies of Household Technology from the Open Hearth to the Microwave (New York: Basic Books, 1983). See also the entry on kitchens in Andrew F. Smith, ed., *The Oxford Encyclopedia of Food and Drink in America* (Oxford: Oxford University Press, 2004), 2:10–17; and Christine Rosen, "Are We Worthy of Our Kitchens?," *New Atlantis, a Journal of Technology and Society* 11 (Winter 2006): 75–86.

37   Cowan, *More Work for Mother*, 29–30.

38   Ibid., 99. Phyllis Palmer adds richly to this discussion by parsing data for the 1920–45 period. By discounting the very poor, farms, and the homes of full-time domestic workers themselves, Palmer constructs a compelling picture of educated and urban households having—for the last time in US history— a rather high percentage of domestic help. For example, studies in the late 1920s of members of the American Association of University Women showed that half the membership had full-time help. Even among the less wealthy and high school educated, day help one or more times a week was quite common. *Domesticity and Dirt: Housewives and Domestic Servants in the United States, 1920–1945* (Philadelphia: Temple University Press, 1989), 8.

39   Amy Bentley, introductory remarks to "Sweetness, Gender, and Power: Rethinking Sidney Mintz's Classic Work," a panel at the Women, Men, and Food: Putting Gender on the Table conference at the Radcliffe Institute for Advanced Study, Cambridge, MA, April 13, 2007.

40   Strasser, *Never Done*, 99.

41   Ibid., 86, 102.

42   Sutton Vane, *Outward Bound* (New York: Liveright, 1924), 152.

43   See Ann Douglas, *The Feminization of American Culture* (New York: Alfred A. Knopf, 1977); Barbara Welter, "The Cult of True Womanhood: 1820–1860," *American Quarterly* 18 (Summer 1966): 151–74; Cowan, *More Work for Mother*, chaps. 2, 3; and Strasser, *Never Done*, chap. 10.

44   Catharine E. Beecher, *A Treatise on Domestic Economy for the Use of Young Ladies at Home, and at School* (Boston: Marsh, Capen, Lyon, and Webb, 1841), 282–83, 367–69. In 1869, the same dishwashing instructions were repeated in Catharine E. Beecher and Harriet Beecher Stowe, *The American Woman's Home: or, Principles of Domestic Science* (New York: Arno Press and *New York Times*, 1971) with an added paragraph about the sink. It "should be scalded out every day, and occasionally with hot lye." Dishcloths should be "put in the wash every week," and there should be three, graded by levels of the greasiness of the items for which they were used (371–72).

45   Lydia Maria Child, *The American Frugal Housewife* (1832; repr., Sandwich, MA: Chapman Billies, n.d.), 16.

46   Strasser, *Never Done*, 105.

47   Cowan, *More Work for Mother*, 61.

48 Jane Smiley, "It All Begins with Housework," in *Consuming Desires: Consumption, Culture, and the Pursuit of Happiness,* ed. Roger Rosenblatt (Washington, DC: Island Press, 1999), 155–72, quote on 163.

49 See Laura Shapiro, *Perfection Salad: Women and Cooking at the Turn of the Century* (New York: Henry Holt, 1986).

50 Martin Flavin, *The Criminal Code,* in *The Best Plays of 1929–30 and the Year Book of the Drama in America,* ed. Burns Mantle (New York: Dodd, Mead, 1931), 79. The play was made into a 1931 film directed by Howard Hawks and featuring a pre-*Frankenstein* Boris Karloff.

51 Cowan, *More Work for Mother,* 42.

52 Sherrie A. Inness, *Dinner Roles: American Women and Culinary Culture* (Iowa City: University of Iowa Press, 2001), 98.

53 David M. Katzman, *Seven Days a Week: Women and Domestic Service in Industrializing America* (New York: Oxford University Press, 1978), 273.

54 Nelson Lichtenstein, *State of the Union: A Century of American Labor* (Princeton, NJ: Princeton University Press, 2003).

55 For an evolving understanding of the American Dream, see Lawrence R. Samuel, *The American Dream: A Cultural History* (Syracuse, NY: Syracuse University Press, 2012).

56 Rosen, "Are We Worthy of Our Kitchens?," 75–86.

57 William Haefeli, cartoon, "I don't care if everyone else is getting one . . . ," *New Yorker,* 2 June 2003, 101.

58 Inness, *Dinner Roles,* 12.

59 Cowan, *More Work for Mother,* 100–101.

60 Langston Hughes's 1935 play *Mulatto* occupies a kind of transitional place in this genealogy. It ran on Broadway for a year and has a domestic setting with an African American housekeeper as a central character. The play is, however, the tragedy of her son, the "illegitimate" offspring of her employer. Here I want to keep the focus on domestic workers as the characters whose own stories and ideas motivate the action of the play.

61 Lewis, "The Meaning of Things," 19.

62 Wilella Waldorf, drama critic for the *New York Post* from 1941 to 1946, is a case in point.

63 Obviously viewing these images at home is only "free" following the purchase of the means of delivery, but these technologies are also available at no charge in public venues and sometimes are unavoidable.

64 Jennifer Scanlon, *Inarticulate Longings: The "Ladies' Home Journal," Gender, and the Promises of Consumer Culture* (New York: Routledge, 1995).

65 See Mary Ellen Zuckerman, *A History of Popular Women's Magazines in the United States, 1792–1995,* Contributions in Women's Studies, Number 165 (Westport, CT: Greenwood Press, 1998).

66 Roland Marchand, *Advertising the American Dream: Making Way for Modernity, 1920–1940* (Berkeley: University of California Press, 1985). Present-day "difference" is addressed largely in terms of color but not by consumer choices, at least in the mainstream media.

67 Kathleen Anne McHugh's wonderful *American Domesticity: From How-to Manual to Hollywood Melodrama* (New York: Oxford University Press, 1999) does precisely that.

68 Susan Bennett, "Theatre/Tourism," *Theatre Journal* 57, no. 3 (October 2005): 407–28.

69 David Savran, *Highbrow/Lowdown: Theater, Jazz, and the Making of the New Middle Class* (Ann Arbor: University of Michigan Press, 2009), esp. chap. 7. One might argue that Bennett's arriving late to the commercial theatre party precisely underscores Savran's point about "serious" critics and scholars needing to eschew the commercial, even as he points out that mostly, in American drama, that is where all aspirations, by virtue of financial necessity, basically lead.

70 Roger Angell, introduction to "The First Decade 1925–1934," in *The Complete Cartoons of the "New Yorker,"* ed. Robert Mankoff (New York: Black Dog & Leventhal, 2004), 13.

71 Ross, quoted in Faye Hammill and Karen Leick, "Modernism and the Quality Magazines," in *The Oxford Critical and Cultural History of Modernist Magazines*, vol. 2, *North America 1894–1960*, ed. Peter Brooker and Andrew Thacker (Oxford: Oxford University Press, 2012), 176–96, quote on 185.

72 "Conventional" is how Hammill and Leick summarize the *New Yorker*'s taste writ large.

73 Soyica Diggs Colbert, *The African American Theatrical Body: Reception, Performance, and the Stage* (Cambridge: Cambridge University Press, 2011), 33.

74 See Dorothy Chansky, "Burns Mantle and the American Theatregoing Public," in *Theatre History Studies* 31, no. 1 (2011): 51–66.

75 Sixteen percent of the American population lived in dwellings with electric lights in 1912 vs. 63 percent in 1927. Gwendolyn Wright, *Building the Dream: A Social History of Housing in America* (New York: Pantheon, 1981), 208.

CHAPTER ONE

1 Jesse Lynch Williams, *Why Marry?* (New York: Charles Scribner's Sons, 1920), 135.

2 Ibid., 146.

3 See Mordden, *All That Glittered*.

4   See Chansky, *Composing Ourselves*; and Maurice Browne, "The Temple of a Living Art," Chicago Little Theatre, 1914.

5   Quoted in Alfred Bernheim, *The Business of the Theatre: An Economic History of the American Theatre, 1750–1932* (1932; repr., New York: Benjamin Blom, 1964), 102.

6   Harvey Levenstein, *Revolution at the Table: The Transformation of the American Diet* (New York: Oxford University Press, 1988), 147–60.

7   See Shapiro, *Perfection Salad*.

8   Levenstein, *Revolution at the Table*, 148–50.

9   Douglas McDermott, "The Theatre and Its Audience," in *The American Stage: Social and Economic Issues from the Colonial Period to the Present*, ed. Ron Engle and Tice L. Miller (New York: Cambridge University Press, 1993), 14–15.

10 See Chansky, *Composing Ourselves*; and Savran, *Highbrow/Lowdown*.

11 See Ronald H. Wainscott, *The Emergence of the Modern American Theater 1914–1929* (New Haven, CT: Yale University Press, 1997), chap. 6.

12 Savran, *Highbrow/Lowdown*, chap. 7, and "The Canonization of Eugene O'Neill," *Modern Drama* 50, no. 4 (Winter 2007): 565–81.

13 Katzman, *Seven Days a Week*, 51–53, 115–17, 130–34.

14 Levenstein, *Revolution at the Table*, 183–93.

15 See Christina Simmons, *Making Marriage Modern: Women's Sexuality from the Progressive Era to World War II* (Oxford: Oxford University Press, 2009), 122–38.

16 See Robert E. Humphrey, *Children of Fantasy: The First Rebels of Greenwich Village* (New York: John Wiley & Sons, 1978); Leslie Fishbein, *Rebels in Bohemia: The Radicals of The Masses, 1911–1917* (Chapel Hill: University of North Carolina Press, 1982); and Susan Glaspell, *The Road to the Temple* (New York: Frederick A. Stokes, 1927), 235–36.

17 Christine Stansell, *American Moderns: Bohemian New York and the Creation of a New Century* (New York: Henry Holt, 2000), 160–61.

18 Arnold Goldman, "The Culture of the Provincetown Players," *Journal of American Studies* 12, no. 3 (1978): 303.

19 Helen Deutsch and Stella Hanau, *The Provincetown: A Story of the Theatre* (New York: Russell & Russell, 1931), 19–21.

20 Katzman, *Seven Days a Week*, 67, 68, 70, 72, 73.

21 Ibid., 223–24, 13–14, 240, 55.

22 Donna R. Gabaccia, *We Are What We Eat: Ethnic Food and the Making of Americans* (Cambridge, MA: Harvard University Press, 1998), 99–102; Levenstein, *Revolution at the Table*, 146; Leslie Brenner, *American Appetite: The Coming of Age of a National Cuisine* (New York: HarperCollins, 2000), 89.

23 Shapiro, *Perfection Salad*, 168, 190.

24 Ibid., 112.

25 John Dewey, "The School and the Life of the Child," in *The School and Society*, by Dewey (Chicago: University of Chicago Press, 1907), chap. 2, 56–58, accessed 14 March 2015, http://www.brocku.ca/MeadProject/Dewey/Dewey_1907/Dewey_1907b.html.

26 See J. Ellen Gainor, *Susan Glaspell in Context: American Theater, Culture, and Politics 1915–48* (Ann Arbor: University of Michigan Press, 2001), 91.

27 Lynn D. Gordon, *Gender and Higher Education in the Progressive Era* (New Haven, CT: Yale University Press, 1990), 2.

28 Ibid., 197, 163; see also Paula S. Fass, *The Damned and the Beautiful: American Youth in the 1920s* (New York: Oxford University Press, 1977). "Seven Sisters" refers to a group of elite, private women's liberal arts colleges in the Northeast. Radcliffe merged with Harvard in 1999; Bryn Mawr and Vassar are now coeducational. The others—Smith, Mount Holyoke, Wellesley, and Barnard—are still women's colleges. The "sister" designation denotes the parallel status of these schools to men's Ivy Leagues at the time the term came into use in the 1920s.

29 Shapiro, *Perfection Salad*, 185.

30 Ibid., 187.

31 Cheryl Black, *The Women of Provincetown, 1915–1922* (Tuscaloosa: University of Alabama Press, 2002), 49, 62–63, 108–11, 131–32, 136–44.

32 Alice Gerstenberg, *Ten One-Act Plays* (New York: Brentano's, 1921).

33 Shapiro, *Perfection Salad*, 222–27.

34 Cora M. Winchell, "For the Homemaker: Homemaking as a Phase of Citizenship," *Journal of Home Economics* 14 (January 1922): 30, 31, 32, 33 (italics in original).

35 Strasser, *Never Done*, 235.

36 Mrs. Max West, "If Not Why Not," *Journal of Home Economics* 12 (August 1920): 344, 345.

37 Katzman, *Seven Days a Week*, 146.

38 Christopher Morley, *Thursday Evening*, in *Contemporary One-Act Plays of 1921 (American)*, ed. Frank Shay (Cincinnati: Stewart Kidd, 1922), 455–85. Page numbers are from this edition.

39 Katzman, *Seven Days a Week*, 114.

40 Glenna Matthews, *"Just a Housewife": The Rise and Fall of Domesticity in America* (New York: Oxford University Press), 192–93.

41 Amy Koritz discusses the situation of women like Laura in *Culture Makers: Urban Performance and Literature in the 1920s* (Urbana: University of Illinois Press, 2009), 14, 46–48, 56–62.

42 Simplex Ironer ad, 1918 (#22,821 in New York Public Library picture collection).

43 Ed Schiffer, "'Fable Number One': Some Myths about Consumption," in *Eating Culture*, ed. Ron Scapp and Brian Seitz (Albany: State University of New York Press, 1993), 292.

44 Richardson, "Struggle for the Real," 3; and Morris, *Realism*, 4.

45 Mary Burrill, *Aftermath* (1919), and Alice Dunbar-Nelson's *Mine Eyes Have Seen* (1918), both in *Zora Neale Hurston, Eulalie Spence, Marita Bonner, and Others: The Prize Plays and Other One-Acts Published in Periodicals*, ed. Jennifer Burton (New York: G. K. Hall, 1996). Angelina Weld Grimké, *Rachel* (1916), in *Strange Fruit: Plays on Lynching by American Women*, ed. Kathy A. Perkins and Judith L. Stephens (Bloomington: Indiana University Press, 1998). Later examples include Willis Richardson, *Compromise* (1925), in *The New Negro: Voices of the Harlem Renaissance*, ed. Alain Locke (New York: Atheneum, 1992); and Georgia Douglas Johnson, *A Sunday Morning in the South*, in *The Plays of Georgia Douglas Johnson* (Urbana-Champaign: University of Illinois Press, 2006).

46 Mary Burrill, *They That Sit in Darkness* (1919), in *Black Theatre U.S.A*, ed. James V. Hatch and Ted Shine (New York: Free Press, 1996).

47 Jacqueline Jones, *Labor of Love, Labor of Sorrow: Black Women, Work, and the Family, from Slavery to the Present* (New York: Vintage Books, 1986), 134.

48 Anthony M. Platt, introduction to *The Negro Family in the United States*, by E. Franklin Frazier (1939; repr., Notre Dame, IN: University of Notre Dame Press, 2001); Nazera Sadiq Wright, "Black Girls and Representative Citizenship," in *From Bourgeois to Boojie: Black Middle-Class Performances*, ed. Vershawn Ashanti Young with Bridget Harris Tsemo (Detroit, MI: Wayne State University Press, 2011), 91–109.

49 Koritha Mitchell, *Living with Lynching: African American Lynching Plays, Performance, and Citizenship, 1890–1930* (Urbana: University of Illinois Press, 2011), 31.

50 Burton, *The Prize Plays*.

51 W. E. B. Du Bois, "The Talented Tenth," in *The Negro Problem: A Series of Articles by Representative Negroes of To-Day* (New York: James Pott, 1903).

52 Dunbar-Nelson, *Mine Eyes Have Seen*, in Burton, *The Prize Plays*. Page numbers are from this edition.

53 See Jones, *Labor of Love, Labor of Sorrow*, chap. 5; and Cheryl Lynn Greenberg, *"Or Does It Explode?": Black Harlem in the Great Depression* (New York: Oxford University Press, 1991), chap. 1.

54 It would become an organ of the Communist Party of America in 1922 and

merged with two other publications to form *The Workers' Monthly* in 1924. For a history of the publication and access to all issues, see http://www.marxists.org/history/usa/culture/pubs/liberator/.

55 See Montgomery Gregory's essay "The Drama of Negro Life," in *The New Negro: Voices of the Harlem Renaissance*, ed. Alain Locke, introduction by Arnold Rampersad (New York: Atheneum, 1972), which is discussed at greater length in the next chapter. See also Chansky, *Composing Ourselves*, chap. 6.

56 Burrill, *Aftermath*, in Burton, *The Prize Plays*. Page numbers are from this edition.

57 As Mitchell phrases it, "[T]he household is 'castrated' and its head removed." *Living with Lynching*, 37.

CHAPTER TWO

1 Ruth Schwartz Cowan, "Two Washes in the Morning and a Bridge Party at Night: The American Housewife between the Wars," in *Decades of Discontent: The Women's Movement, 1920–1940*, ed. Lois Scharf and Joan M. Jensen (Westport, CT: Greenwood Press, 1983), 177–96; see also Rayna Rapp and Ellen Ross, "The 1920s: Feminism, Consumerism, and Political Backlash in the United States," in *Women in Culture and Politics: A Century of Change*, ed. Judith Friedlander, Blanche Wiesen Cook, Alice Kessler-Harris, and Carroll Smith-Rosenberg (Bloomington: Indiana University Press, 1988), 52–61.

2 The *Best Plays* series was started in 1919. It was and still is issued annually.

3 Most domestic plays, certainly from the 1920s, have family relations and issues at their heart. Tom Scanlan notes the wider variety of topics and genres among late nineteenth- and early twentieth-century European dramatists and points out that even home-centered domestic plays (e.g., those by Chekhov, Ibsen, or Shaw) are far more likely to include an extended circle of people beyond the nuclear family typifying the American play. *Family, Drama, and American Dreams* (Westport, CT: Greenwood Press, 1978), 5–6.

4 Guy Bolton, *Chicken Feed* (New York: Samuel French, 1924), 17.

5 The computation was done by salary.com using the ten jobs that most closely match the multiple jobs mothers do at home. (A short list includes day-care center teacher, housekeeper, janitor, and van driver.) A mother who works for wages outside the home and then returns to do a second shift "earns" $76,184 at home. Dory Devlin, "What Is a Mother's Work Really Worth?," 9 May 2009, accessed 15 March 2015, http://www.workitmom.com/articles/detail/7458/what-is-a-mothers-work-really-worth.

6   Channing Pollock, *The Fool*, typescript (New York Public Library for the Performing Arts [NYPLPA], Special Collections 1923), 1-30-31, call number NCOF+ (Pollock, C., "Fool," New York, 1923).

7   Bruce A. McConachie, "Using the Concept of Cultural Hegemony to Write Theatre History," in Postlewait and McConachie, *Interpreting the Theatrical Past*, 50, 48.

8   Barbara Ehrenreich, *Fear of Falling: The Inner Life of the Middle Class* (New York: Harper Perennial, 1990), 11.

9   Eugene O'Neill, *Beyond the Horizon*, in *Eugene O'Neill: Early Plays*, ed. and introduction by Jeffrey H. Richards (New York: Penguin Books, 2001), 191. Page numbers are from this edition.

10   O'Neill detractors and supporters alike note the homosocial world of many of his plays. Jeffrey H. Richards observes that "the woman is more symbol than being . . . a divisive force between two male friends—not someone with autonomy or integrity" (xv). Virgil Geddes calls *Beyond the Horizon* "essentially a story of men. . . . [W]hen [the women] speak . . . it is little more than woman's version of the man's situation." *The Melodramadness of Eugene O'Neill* (Brookfield, CT: The Brookfield Players, 1934), 21. Arthur Gelb, an O'Neill biographer, described *Horizon* in a review of a 1962 revival as "the tragedy of two brothers" and Ruth as a "shallow, disillusioned girl." "Theater: Native Tragedy: 'Beyond the Horizon' Given in Milwaukee," *New York Times*, 26 October 1962.

11   Compare Tom Scanlan's argument about the centrality of domesticity for O'Neill in "Eugene O'Neill and the Drama of Family Dilemma," in *Family, Drama, and American Dreams*, 83–125.

12   Alexander Woollcott snorted at the "draperies (painted in the curiously inappropriate style of a German post card)." Review of *Beyond the Horizon*, *New York Times*, 4 February 1920.

13   See Ronald Wainscott's detailed description of the remaining evidence of the original production in *Staging O'Neill: The Experimental Years, 1920–1934* (New Haven, CT: Yale University Press, 1988), 16–24.

14   See Fleissner, *Women, Compulsion, Modernity*, discussed here and in chapter 1.

15   Farm journal columnist Nellie Kedzie Jones, quoted in Strasser, *Never Done*, 38–40.

16   "Tragedy of Great Power at Morosco," *New York World*, 4 February 1920, 13.

17   Alexander Woollcott, quoted in Wainscott, *Staging O'Neill*, 27.

18   Strasser, *Never Done*, 61.

19   Wainscott, *Staging O'Neill*, 27.

20   Burns Mantle, "'Beyond the Horizon' Food for the O'Neills," *New York Daily*

News, 2 December 1926; Percy Hammond, "Mr. O'Neill's 'Beyond the Horizon' Revived Skillfully by the Actors' Theater," *New York Tribune*, 1 December 1926.

21 Katharine Zimmermann, "Actors Theatre Revives 'Beyond the Horizon,'" *New York World-Telegram*, 1 December 1926.

22 Joel Pfister, *Staging Depth: The Politics of Psychological Discourse* (Chapel Hill: University of North Carolina Press, 1995).

23 See Fleissner, *Women, Compulsion*, 9, 22, 31.

24 White sauces were popular accompaniments to savory foods in the 1920s, and canned ingredients were marketed and purchased with a vengeance. See Sylvia Lovegren, *Fashionable Food: Seven Decades of Food Fads* (Chicago: University of Chicago Press, 2005), 3, 15.

25 Milk toast was a popular "comfort food" for children, the elderly, and the ill; it consists of pieces of toast in a bowl covered with hot milk or cream and possibly pats of butter.

26 Zona Gale, *Miss Lulu Bett*, in *Plays by American Women 1900–1930*, ed. Judith E. Barlow (New York: Applause Theatre Books, 1985), 93.

27 Review of *Miss Lulu Bett* , Rochester (NY) *Herald*, 23 September 1921.

28 Paul R. Martin, review of *Miss Lulu Bett*, Chicago *Journal of Commerce and Financial Times*, 22 October 1921.

29 Fay Templeton Patterson, "Miss Lulu Bett at the Pitt," *Pittsburgh Leader*, 11 January 1922.

30 See, for example, "Planning Springtime Dinners for the Business Woman Housewife," in Mabel Jewett Crosby's "Better Housekeeping" section of *Ladies' Home Journal*, April 1925; see also Palmer, *Domesticity and Dirt*, 33.

31 "The Editor Goes to the Play," *The Theatre*, November 1928, 46.

32 Ibid.

33 Ronald Wainscott, *The Emergence of the Modern American Theater 1914–1929* (New Haven, CT: Yale University Press, 1997), 92.

34 See Jennifer Parent, "Arthur Hopkins' Production of Sophie Treadwell's *Machinal* (1928)," *Drama Review* 26, no. 1 (T93) (Spring 1982): 91.

35 Sophie Treadwell, *Machinal*, in Barlow, *Plays by American Women 1900–1930*. Page numbers are from this edition.

36 Treadwell, quoted in Julia A. Walker, *Expressionism and Modernism in the American Theatre: Bodies, Voices, Words* (Cambridge: Cambridge University Press, 2005), 215.

37 "The Editor Goes to the Play," 46; see also Wainscott, *Emergence of the Modern American Theater*, 138.

38 See Proctor and Gamble's ad for Ivory soap flakes in *Ladies' Home Journal*, March 1925, 2.

39 Maxwell Anderson, *Gypsy*, typescript (NYPL-PA Special Collections, 1927),

2–7, call number NCOF+ (Anderson, M. Gypsy). Page numbers are from this typescript.

40 Robert Garland, "Maxwell Anderson's Latest Has Its Latest at Klaw," *New York Evening Telegram*, 16 January 1929, 8.

41 Burns Mantle, Introduction, *The Best Plays of 1928–29* (New York: Dodd, Mead, 1929), v–vi.

42 Richard Lockridge, "Vagrancies and Verities," *New York Sun*, 15 January 1929.

43 This is not to say that mothers disappear from domestic plays. But in later work they are more likely to be the central characters or the mothers of *male* protagonists or the wives of protagonists. Often they are dead before the play starts. Marsha Norman's *'night, Mother* (1983) is a significant exception.

44 Rapp and Ross, "The 1920s," 55.

45 Ibid., 59.

46 *Variety*, review of *The Show-Off*, 7 February 1924; Leo A. Marsh, "'The Show-Off' Opens at the Playhouse," *New York Telegraph*, 6 February 1924; "The New Play" (review of *The Show-Off*), *New York World*, 6 February 1924.

47 Michael Smith, "Theatre Journal," *Village Voice*, 14 December 1967, 40.

48 Irene Backalenick, "Intriguing '20s Comedy Is Cautionary Tale for the '90s," *Westport News*, 11 December 1996.

49 Foster Hirsch, *George Kelly* (Boston: Twayne Publishers, 1975), 18, 21.

50 Ibid., 34.

51 See Warren Susman, "Culture and Civilization: The Nineteen-Twenties," in *Culture as History: The Transformation of American Society in the Twentieth Century*, by Susman (New York: Pantheon), 105–21; Scanlon, *Inarticulate Longings*; Janice Williams Rutherford, *Selling Mrs. Consumer: Christine Frederick and the Rise of Household Efficiency* (Athens: University of Georgia Press, 2003). See also Koritz, *Culture Makers*, esp. the introduction, chap. 2.

52 Ruth Schwartz Cowan, *More Work for Mother: The Ironies of Household Technology from the Open Hearth to the Microwave* (New York: Basic Books, 1985), 89.

53 The pages of the *Ladies' Home Journal* capture this mix; see Mabel Jewett Crosby's April 1925 article in *Ladies' Home Journal* featuring a week's worth of menus for the "business woman housewife"; the Corona typewriter ad in *Ladies' Home Journal*, March 1925, 203; and the typewriter ad in *Ladies' Home Journal*, January 1929, 115.

54 Robert and Helen Merrell Lynd foregrounded the uneven adoption of modern appliances in their study of American life in Muncie, Indiana, in 1925; see Robert S. Lynd and Helen Merrell Lynd, *Middletown: A Study in Mod-*

ern American Culture (1929; repr., New York: Harcourt Brace Jovanovich, 1956), 176, 175.

55 George Kelly, *The Show-Off: A Transcript of Life in Three Acts* (New York: Samuel French, 1924), 13.

56 It is also a collage of classes even by traditional standards: the father is a machinist; one daughter employs a maid, while the other works as a secretary; the two sons-in-law have very different incomes but eat at the same restaurant.

57 Hirsch, *George Kelly*, 67.

58 Mel Gussow, "A Lout, but a Lout Who Means Well," review of *The Show-Off*, *New York Times*, 6 November 1992, C3.

59 For the role of higher education in "selling" domesticity, see Fass, *The Damned and the Beautiful*; and Lynn D. Gordon, *Gender and Higher Education in the Progressive Era* (New Haven, CT: Yale University Press, 1990).

60 Christine Frederick, *Selling Mrs. Consumer* (New York: The Business Bourse, 1929). Page numbers are from this edition.

61 Fewer marriages took place in the New England and mid-Atlantic states between 1924 and 1927 than in any other region of the country. These were areas with major cities, theatres, and higher percentages of college-educated women than in almost any other in the United States at the time. See *Statistical Abstract of the United States* for 1926, accessed 16 March 2015, http://www2.census.gov/prod2/statcomp/documents/1926-02.pdf, 21–26; and 1929, http://www2.census.gov/prod2/statcomp/documents/1929-02.pdf, 92.

62 Frederick made a career of urging women to find satisfaction in efficient and creative homemaking, an irony not lost on her biographer. See Rutherford, *Selling Mrs. Consumer*, 60, 66, 79, 147.

63 See Fass, *The Damned and the Beautiful*; and Scanlon, *Inarticulate Longings*.

64 Mary Drake McFeely, *Can She Bake a Cherry Pie? American Women and the Kitchen in the Twentieth Century* (Amherst: University of Massachusetts Press, 2000), 47.

65 Arthur Richman, *Ambush* (New York: Duffield, 1922), 3.

66 Ibid., 128.

67 On class differences in views of paid work and domesticity, see Robert W. Smuts, *Women and Work in America* (New York: Schocken Books, 1971), 137.

68 Lee Wilson Dodd, *The Changelings* (New York: E. P. Dutton, 1924), 146.

69 Maxwell Anderson, *Saturday's Children* (New York: Longmans, Green, 1927), 127.

70 The honorable mention plays were not published in the magazine. *Blue*

Blood was brought out later in 1926 by Appleton-Century (New York) and was included in Frank Shay's *Fifty More Contemporary One-Act Plays* in 1928.

71 Locke, *The New Negro.*

72 Ibid., 159.

73 Mitchell, *Living with Lynching*, 12; see also Claire M. Tylee, "Womanist Propaganda, African-American Great War Experience, and Cultural Strategies of the Harlem Renaissance: Plays by Alice Dunbar-Nelson and Mary P. Burrill," *Women's Studies International Forum* 20, no. 1 (1997): 153–63, quote on 161.

74 See Judith L. Stephens, introduction to *The Plays of Georgia Douglas Johnson: From the New Negro Renaissance to the Civil Rights Movement* (Urbana: University of Illinois Press, 2006).

75 Ibid., 7.

76 Russell, 1990, quoted in Tylee, "Womanist Propaganda," 155.

77 Page references are to the script published in Stephens, *Plays of Georgia Douglas Johnson* (2006).

78 Tera W. Hunter, *To 'Joy My Freedom: Southern Black Women's Lives and Labors after the Civil War* (Cambridge, MA: Harvard University Press, 1997), 48.

79 Frazier, *The Negro Family in the United States*, 186. See also Robert C. Morris, *Reading, 'Riting, and Reconstruction: The Education of Freedmen in the South, 1861–1870* (Chicago: University of Chicago Press, 1976), chap. 3.

80 Jones, *Labor of Love, Labor of Sorrow*, 98, 112.

81 Ibid., 142–46. See also Morris, *Realism.*

82 Psyche A. Williams-Forson, *Building Houses out of Chicken Legs: Black Women, Food, and Power* (Chapel Hill: University of North Carolina Press, 2006).

83 Janice Bluestein Longone, introduction to Mrs. Malinda Russell, *A Domestic Cookbook* (Ann Arbor, MI: William L. Clements Library, 2007), ix.

84 Ibid., 32.

85 *The Buckeye Cookbook: Traditional American Recipes as Published by the Buckeye Publishing Co. in 1883* (New York: Dover Publications, 1975). Originally published as *Practical Housekeeping: A Careful Compilation of Tried and Approved Recipes* (Minneapolis: Buckeye Publishing, 1883).

86 Shapiro, *Perfection Salad*, 144–45.

87 Andrew F. Smith, "Mayonnaise," in *Oxford Encyclopedia of Food and Drink in America*, vol. 2 (New York: Oxford University Press, 2004), 62.

88 See Helen McCully, *The French Have a Word for It: Mayonnaise: Recipes from Some of the World's Greatest Chefs and the Kitchens of Best Foods*

(Westchester, IL: Best Foods Division of Corn Products Company, 1967 [Hellmann's and Best Foods are registered trademarks of Corn Products Company]).

89 Liambean, "Mayonnaise Recipe and Many Variants," accessed 17 March 2015, http://liambean.hubpages.com/hub/Mayonnaise-and-many-variants.

90 Johnson, *Blue Blood*, 66–67.

91 See Du Bois, "The Talented Tenth."

92 For a study of rape as the tacitly understood shared heritage among African American women, see Noliwe M. Rooks, *Ladies' Pages: African American Women's Magazines and the Culture That Made Them* (New Brunswick, NJ: Rutgers University Press, 2004).

CHAPTER THREE

1 Frederick Lewis Allen, *Since Yesterday: The 1930s in America, September 3, 1929 to September 3, 1939* (1940; repr., New York: Harper & Row, 1972), 250–52.

2 For histories of 1930s plays, see Christopher Bigsby, *A Critical Introduction to Twentieth-Century American Drama* (Cambridge: Cambridge University Press, 1982); Anne Fletcher, "Reading across the 1930s," in *A Companion to Twentieth-Century American Drama*, ed. David Krasner (Oxford: Blackwell, 2005), 106–26; Brenda Murphy, *American Realism and American Drama, 1880–1940* (Cambridge: Cambridge University Press, 1987); Barbara Melosh, *Engendering Culture: Manhood and Womanhood in New Deal Public Art and Theater* (Washington, DC: Smithsonian Institution Press, 1991); Hallie Flanagan, *Arena* (New York: Duell, Sloan & Pearce, 1940); Harold Clurman, *The Fervent Years: The Story of the Group Theatre and the Thirties* (New York: Hill & Wang, 1957); Helen Krich Chinoy, *The Group Theatre: Passion, Politics, and Performance in the Depression Era*, ed. Don B. Wilmeth and Milly S. Barranger (New York: Palgrave Studies in Theatre and Performance History, 2013); Morgan Himelstein, *Drama Was a Weapon: The Left-Wing Theatre in New York, 1929–1941* (New Brunswick, NJ: Rutgers University Press, 1963); and Daniel Friedman and Bruce McConachie, *Theatre for Working Class Audiences in the United States, 1830–1980* (Westport, CT: Greenwood, 1985).

3 Harvey Levenstein, *Paradox of Plenty: A Social History of Eating in Modern America* (New York: Oxford University Press, 1993), 60–61.

4 Robert Cooley Angell, *The Family Encounters the Depression* (Gloucester, MA: Peter Smith, 1936), 15.

5 See reviews of *Her Master's Voice* in Burns Mantle, *New York Daily News*, 24 October 1933; and John Anderson, *New York Evening Journal*, 24 October 1933.

6   Henry T. Murdock, "Domestic Comedy by Clare Kummer Reopens Chestnut," *Philadelphia Ledger*, 3 October 1933.

7   The play focuses on the value of government price supports under the Agricultural Adjustment Administration. See "Agricultural Adjustment Act," United States History, accessed 17 March 2015, http://www.u-s-history.com/pages/h1639.html; "Farmers and the New Deal," History Learning Site, accessed 17 March 2015, http://www.historylearningsite.co.uk/New_Deal_farmers.htm; and Allen, *Since Yesterday*, 116–17, 122, 166, 187, 203–4.

8   Elmer Rice, *We, the People* (New York: Coward-McCann, 1933), 73–74.

9   Ibid., 72.

10   Allen, *Since Yesterday*, 6. By 1933, the price of a radio had dropped to forty-seven dollars, but the family in the play was clearly in dire straits by then. See "Radio in the 1930's," Zenith Stratosphere, accessed February 19, 2015, http://www.radiostratosphere.com/zsite/behind-the-dial/radio-in-1930.html.

11   Percy Hammond, review of *We, the People*, *New York Herald Tribune*, 23 January 1933.

12   Robert Garland, "'We, the People' Paints Nation's Ills, but Offers No Cure," *New York Telegram*, 23 January 1933.

13   Winifred Wandersee, *Women's Work and Family Values, 1920–1940* (Cambridge, MA: Harvard University Press, 1981), 97.

14   Harriet Bradley Fitt, "In Praise of Domesticity," in *College Women and the Social Sciences* (New York: John Day, 1934), quoted in Susan Ware, *Holding Their Own: American Women in the 1930s* (Boston: Twayne, 1982), 67.

15   Edith Isaacs, "Swords into Plowshares: Broadway in Review," *Theatre Arts Monthly* 18, no. 3 (May 1934): 323.

16   Harold Clurman, Introduction, in *"Waiting for Lefty" and Other Plays*, by Clifford Odets (New York: Grove Press, 1979), ix.

17   The line is from *Awake and Sing*, 95. All references to this play and to *Waiting for Lefty* are from Odets, *"Waiting for Lefty" and Other Plays*.

18   Regarding Americans' preference for dramaturgically predictable and sentimental/realist modes *even in activist theatre* of the 1930s, see Ilka Saal, *New Deal Theater: The Vernacular Tradition in American Political Theater* (New York: Palgrave Macmillan, 2007).

19   Leonardo Da Benci, "The Hardest Hitting . . . ," *Bridgeport* (CT) *Sunday Herald*, 14 April 1935, 6.

20   "Human rights" is from an interview with Odets quoted by Richard Pack in Pack's press release for the New Theatre League, "Boston Bans 'Waiting for Lefty' Play Called 'Un-American.'" Document is undated but was stamped by the New York Public Library as received on April 8, 1935. It is in the "Waiting for Lefty" clippings file. Extended quote is in Edwin A.

Gross, "Left-Wing Drama Comes of Age: An Interview with Clifford Odets," in *Critical Review*, New York University Heights College, June 1935, 42 (italics in original).

21 Clurman, Introduction, xi.

22 Harold Clurman, *The Fervent Years: The Story of the Group Theatre and the Thirties* (1945; repr., New York: Hill & Wang, 1957), 141.

23 Ibid., 119.

24 Odets was not alone in this; see Chinoy, *The Group Theatre*, 216 and chap. 12.

25 Christopher J. Herr, *Clifford Odets and American Political Theatre* (Westport, CT: Praeger, 2003), chap. 3. "Misogyny" is on 83.

26 Ibid., 75.

27 McHugh, *American Domesticity*, 113.

28 *Censored! A Record of Present Terror and Censorship in the American Theatre* (New York: New Theatre League, 1935), 25.

29 Ruth Vasey, *The World according to Hollywood 1918–1939* (Madison: University of Wisconsin Press, 1997), 102.

30 Gross, "An Interview," 44; Ashton Stevens, "Finds Fever in Odets Labor Melo Despite Bumps and Lulls," *Chicago American*, 27 May 1935.

31 Levenstein, *Paradox of Plenty*, 13, 14.

32 Ibid., chaps. 1, 2.

33 Ibid., 33.

34 See, for instance, "Eating to Keep Well," *Ladies' Home Journal*, January 1934, 30.

35 Sheila M. Rothman, *Woman's Proper Place: A History of Changing Ideals and Practices, 1870 to the Present* (New York: Basic Books, 1978), 186.

36 A present-day reader might be forgiven for wondering why all the fuss about the play's communism if she had read it in the long-existing anthology *Six Plays by Clifford Odets*, reissued as *"Waiting for Lefty" and Other Plays*. The original play, published in February 1935 in *New Theatre*, included a scene specifically advocating communism; it was replaced in the later version of the play with one with an antifascist spin. The substitution also removes from the play the sole female character who is a career woman.

37 Esther Lowell, "You're Telling <u>Me</u>!," *Working Woman*, 30 January 1934, 11.

38 See Sadie Van Veen, "Unemployed Women Raise Voices," *Working Woman*, February 1934, 6; Sasha Small, "Life *a la* Ladies Home Journal," July 1934, 10, 15; and Small, "The Rosy Road to Romance or, Short Cuts to Happiness," *Working Woman*, November 1934, 13, 15.

39 Dolores Hayden, *Redesigning the American Dream: Gender, Housing, and Family Life* (New York: W. W. Norton, 2002), 34.

40 Ibid., 113.

41 On attempts to collectivize housework, see Dolores Hayden, *The Grand Domestic Revolution: A History of Feminist Designs for American Homes, Neighborhoods, and Cities* (Cambridge, MA: MIT Press, 1981).

42 Lois Scharf, *To Work and to Wed: Female Employment, Feminism, and the Great Depression* (Westport, CT: Greenwood Press, 1980), 137.

43 Quoted in Mary Elizabeth Pidgeon, introduction to *Employed Women under N.R.A. Codes*, Bulletin of the Women's Bureau [of the Department of Labor] (Washington, DC: US Government Printing Office, 1935), 1. This was reprinted in 1975 by Da Capo Press (New York) with *Women in the Economy of the United States of America*, also by Pidgeon (Washington, DC: US Department of Labor, 1937).

44 Scharf, *To Work and to Wed*, 112.

45 William H. Chafe, *The Paradox of Change: American Women in the 20th Century* (New York: Oxford University Press, 1991), 116.

46 Scharf, *To Work and to Wed*, 104.

47 Pidgeon, *Employed Women under N.R.A. Codes*, 39.

48 Gallup, quoted in Chafe, *The Paradox of Change*, 116.

49 Burns Mantle, "Two New Plays Very Radical in Tendencies," *Erie* (PA) *Dispatch Herald*, 7 April 1935.

50 "History-Making Plays," review of *Three Plays by Clifford Odets*, *New Masses*, 2 July 1935, 39.

51 Max Sien, "Current New York Stage Is Powerful," *Cincinnati Post*, 19 June 1935.

52 Edwin F. Melvin, "A View of 'Lefty' and His Affairs," *Boston Evening Transcript*, 16 April 1935; "The World of Books," *Springfield* (MA) *Republican*, 12 July 1935.

53 Walter D. Hickman, "'Waiting for Lefty' Is Masterpiece of Theater," *Indianapolis Times*, 1 July 1935.

54 Robert Garland, "Group Scores Again in 'Awake and Sing,'" *New York World Telegram*, 20 February 1935; "Double Bill at Longacre Tonight," New York *Herald Tribune*, 26 March 1935. The department stores Macy's and Gimbels were located, respectively, at 34th Street between Sixth Avenue and Broadway and at 34th Street and 5th Avenue. The reference to people living south of 34th Street means below the stylish Upper East Side or the residential, middle-class West End Avenue and Riverside Drive.

55 D. Freeman, "Action Is Not Confined to the Stage," New York *Herald Tribune*, 14 April 1925.

56 As they discuss finances, it is clear that the son earns $16 a week and turns $11 over to the family; the uncle sends a $5 check weekly to provide for the grandfather; the father and daughter work full-time as a haberdashery clerk and a typist. If the latter two earn, say, $15 and $9 respectively, the family's

annual income would be $2,080 at a time when about $1,200 was average. When the daughter marries, she disparages the $21 weekly her husband earns, and her immediate family replaces her income by taking in a boarder.

57   Gove Hambidge, "Make the Diet Fit the Pocketbook," *Ladies' Home Journal*, May 1934, 44.

58   Ashton Stevens, "Stevens Reads Odet's [*sic*] Shrill 'Awake and Sing!' to Find a New Bronx Cheer," *Chicago American*, 15 May 1935.

59   Ellen Schiff, *Awake and Singing New Edition: Six Great American Jewish Plays* (New York: Applause, 2003), 183.

60   Stevens, "Stevens Reads Odet's Shrill 'Awake and Sing!'"

61   "History-Making Plays," 39.

62   Lowell, "You're Telling Me!," 11.

63   See Beth Bailey, *From Front Porch to Back Seat: Courtship in Twentieth-Century America* (Baltimore: Johns Hopkins University Press, 1988); and Karen Anderson, *Wartime Women: Sex Roles, Family Relations, and the Status of Women during World War II* (Westport, CT: Greenwood Press, 1981).

64   McHugh, *American Domesticity*, 156.

65   Producer/director David Belasco (1853–1931) was famous for photographic mimeticism in his settings.

66   See Fleissner, *Women, Compulsion*.

67   Eugene O'Neill's *The Iceman Cometh*, one of whose central characters is the bartender Harry Hope, was published in 1940, but it is unlikely that Kingsley knew about O'Neill's play.

68   "Box Office Now Open," *New York Times*, 26 November 1939.

69   John Mason Brown, "Sidney Kingsley Stages 'The World We Make,'" *New York Post*, 21 November 1939.

70   Richard Watts Jr., "Escape into Life" (review of *The World We Make*), *New York Herald Tribune*, 21 November 1939.

71   Richard Lockridge, "'The World We Make,' with Margo, Opens at the Guild Theater," *New York Sun*, 21 November 1939.

72   Sidney B. Whipple, "The World We Make, a Play of Realism," *New York World Telegram*, 21 November 1939.

73   "New Play in Manhattan" (review of *The World We Make*), *Time*, 4 December 1939.

74   Bernard Simon, "But Is It Real?," *Brooklyn Daily Eagle*, 3 December 1939.

75   John Mason Brown, "The Question of Sidney Kingsley's Realism," in the column "Two on the Aisle," *New York Post*, [1939].

76   "New Play in Manhattan."

77   Arthur Pollock, "Sidney Kingsley Meets in 'The World We Make' a Story

That Is More Than a Match for His Scenery," unsourced clipping (NYPL-LC Special Collections), *The World We Make* clippings file.

78 Sidney Kingsley, "The Mantle of Belasco," *New York Times*, 17 December 1939.

79 Simon, "But Is It Real?"

80 Sidney Kingsley, *The World We Make*, typescript (NYPL-PA Special Collections), 1-3-21 to 22.

81 Dixie Tighe, "First Lady Attends 'World We Make'," unsourced clipping (NYPL-LC Special Collections), *The World We Make* clippings file.

82 Sara M. Evans, *Born for Liberty: A History of Women in America* (1989; repr., New York: Simon & Schuster, 1997), 207.

83 Palmer, *Domesticity and Dirt*, 131.

84 The 75 percent figure is from *Black Theatre U.S.A.: The Early Period* (New York: Free Press, 1996), 266. The play is published in *Black Theater, U.S.A.: Forty-Five Plays by Black Americans 1847–1974*, ed. James V. Hatch, consultant Ted Shine (New York: Free Press, 1974), 656–57.

85 Joseph McLaren, *Langston Hughes: Folk Dramatist in the Protest Tradition, 1921–1943* (Westport, CT: Greenwood Press, 1997), chap. 3.

86 Arnold Rampersad, *The Life of Langston Hughes, Volume I: 1902–1941, I, Too, Sing America* (New York: Oxford University Press, 2002), 356–67.

87 See Donald Bogle, *Toms, Coons, Mulattoes, Mammies, and Bucks: An Interpretive History of Blacks in American Films*, 4th ed. (New York: Continuum, 2001), 57–66.

88 See Lori Harrison-Kahan, *The White Negress: Literature, Minstrelsy, and the Black-Jewish Imaginary* (New Brunswick, NJ: Rutgers University Press, 2011), 120–21; Jane Caputi, "'Specifying' Fannie Hurst: Langston Hughes's 'Limitations of Life,' Zora Neale Hurston's *Their Eyes Were Watching God*, and Toni Morrison's *The Bluest Eye* as 'Answers' to Hurst's *Imitation of Life*," *Black American Literature Forum* 24, no. 4 (Winter 1990): 697–716, at 700–702; and Daniel Itzkovitz's introduction to his edition of the novel *Imitation of Life* (Durham, NC: Duke University Press, 2004).

89 Caputi points out that in earlier correspondence from Hughes to Hurst, Hughes praised *Imitation of Life*, perhaps trying to radicalize her and hoping she would accept his invitation to a writer's congress; she did not.

90 Kimberly Wallace-Sanders, *Mammy: A Century of Race, Gender, and Southern Memory* (Ann Arbor: University of Michigan Press, 2008), 60–62.

91 A short list includes George S. Kaufman and Edna Ferber's *Stage Door* (1936); Kaufman and Hart's *You Can't Take It with You* (1936); and S. N. Behrman's *No Time for Comedy* (1939).

92 Jones, *Labor of Love, Labor of Sorrow*, 199.

93 Greenberg, *Or Does It Explode?*, 78–79.

94 Karen L. Cox, *Dreaming of Dixie: How the South Was Created in American Popular Culture* (Chapel Hill: University of North Carolina Press, 2011). See also Roland Marchand, *Advertising the American Dream*.

95 Wallace-Sanders, *Mammy*, 67.

96 Rampersad, *Life of Langston Hughes*, 365.

97 Richardson, "Struggle for the Real," 3.

98 Jeffrey H. Richards, "Politics, Playhouse, and Repertoire in Philadelphia, 1808," *Theatre Survey* 46, no. 2 (November 2005): 219.

CHAPTER FOUR

1 The best single source is Albert Wertheim's *Staging the War: American Drama and World War II* (Bloomington: Indiana University Press, 2004).

2 Quoted in Anderson, *Wartime Women*, 87.

3 Donald Albrecht, ed., *World War II and the American Dream: How Wartime Building Changed a Nation* (Cambridge, MA: MIT Press, 1995).

4 Joseph Fields and Jerome Chodorov, *My Sister Eileen* (New York: Random House, 1941), 50.

5 See Harriet Hyman Alonso, *Robert E. Sherwood: The Playwright in Peace and War* (Amherst: University of Massachusetts Press, 2007).

6 Robert E. Sherwood, *There Shall Be No Night* (New York: Charles Scribner's Sons, 1941), 96. Page numbers are from this edition.

7 Florence Ryerson and Colin Clements, *Harriet* (New York: Charles Scribner's Sons, 1943). Page numbers are from this edition.

8 Louis Kronenberger, "Miss Hayes as Mrs. Stowe," *New York Newspaper "PM,"* 4 March 1943.

9 Burton Rascoe, "Helen Hayes Triumphs as Uncle Tom's Author," *New York World-Telegram*, 4 March 1943.

10 Wilella Waldorf, "Helen Hayes Back in Crinolines as Harriet Beecher Stowe," *New York Post*, 4 March 1943. Waldorf was a regular *Post* drama critic for the half decade until her death in 1946.

11 John Van Druten, *I Remember Mama* (1944; repr., New York: Dramatists Play Service, 1972). Page numbers are from the 1972 edition.

12 Burns Mantle, ed., *Best Plays of 1944–45* (New York: Dodd, Mead), 67.

13 Mordden, *All That Glittered*, 176–77.

14 "Lutefisk," accessed 8 April 2015, http://en.wikipedia.org/wiki/Lutefisk; "Lye-Soaked Lutefisk: The Heart and Soul (and Frenzy) of a Norwegian Dinner," Sodium Hydroxide, 2008, accessed 20 March 2015, http://sodium-hydroxide.com/lye-soaked-lutefisk-the-heart-and-soul-and-frenzy-of-a-norwegian-dinner/.

15 Levenstein, *Paradox of Plenty*, viii, 28–29, 45.

16 Rose Franken, *Outrageous Fortune* (New York: Samuel French, 1944). Page numbers are from this edition.

17 William Hurlbut, *Bride of the Lamb* (New York: Boni & Liveright, 1926).

18 Rachel Crothers, *As Husbands Go* (New York: Samuel French, 1931), 157.

19 Robert E. Sherwood, *The Rugged Path*, typescript (NYPL-LC special collections, 1945), call number NCOF + (Sherwood, R. E., Rugged Path). Page numbers are from this typescript.

20 On juvenile delinquency during World War II, see Anderson, *Wartime Women*, 96–101.

21 Elsa Shelley, *Pick-Up Girl* (New York: Dramatists Play Service, 1943). Page numbers are from this edition.

22 Research by the Women's Bureau of the Department of Labor in 1954 revealed no statistical correlation between juvenile delinquency and the employment of mothers. See Alice Kessler-Harris, *Out to Work: A History of Wage-Earning Women in the United States* (New York: Oxford University Press, 1982), 304.

23 Garson Kanin, *Born Yesterday* (New York: Dramatists Play Service, 1946), 51.

24 David M. Kennedy, *Freedom from Fear: The American People in Depression and War, 1929–1945* (New York: Oxford University Press, 1999), 779.

25 Quoted in Maureen Honey, "Remembering Rosie: Advertising Images of Women in World War II," in *The Home-Front War: World War II and American Society*, ed. Kenneth Paul O'Brien and Lynn Hudson Parsons (Westport, CT: Greenwood Press, 1995), 98.

26 Maxwell Anderson, *Storm Operation* (Washington, DC: Anderson House, 1944), 119.

27 This situation occupies exactly a single line of dialogue in Moss Hart's 1943 *Winged Victory*.

28 Moss Hart, *Winged Victory* (New York: Random House, 1943), 172.

29 Maxwell Anderson, *The Eve of St. Mark* (Washington, DC: Anderson House, 1942), 13.

30 The National Theatre Conference, started in 1931, brought together representatives from educational and professional theatre; see August Staub, "The National Theatre Conference: The First Seventy-Five Years, 1931–2006," October 2008, accessed 22 March 2015, http://www.nationaltheatre conference.org/wp-content/uploads/2014/01/ntc-history-book.pdf.

31 Bailey, *From Front Porch to Back Seat*, 42–43.

32 Ferdinand Lundberg and Marynia F. Farnham, *Modern Woman: The Lost Sex* (New York: Harper & Brothers, 1947). Page numbers are from this edition.

33 Beth Bailey notes that between 1940 and 1959, the percentage of girls be-

tween fourteen and seventeen who were married grew by one-third (*From Front Porch to Back Seat*, 43).

34 See, for example, James Thurber and Elliott Nugent's *The Male Animal* (1940); Samson Raphaelson's *Jason* (1942); Norman Krasna's *Dear Ruth* (1944); and Lillian Hellman's *Another Part of the Forest* (1946).

35 Sophie Treadwell, *Hope for a Harvest* (New York: Samuel French, 1942), 16.

36 Rose Franken, *Soldier's Wife* (New York: Samuel French, 1945). All page numbers are from this edition.

37 Burton Rascoe, "New Franken Play Is Sign She Should Write Less," *New York World-Telegram*, 5 October 1944; and Lewis Nichols, "Miss Franken Touches Slightly on the War, and Much on Love, in 'Soldier's Wife,'" *New York Times*, 5 October 1944.

38 See Yvonne Shafer, "Rose Franken," in *American Women Playwrights, 1900–1950* (New York: Peter Lang, 1995), 102–20.

39 John Chapman, "'Soldier's Wife' a Delightful Little Comedy of a Home-Front Crisis," *New York Daily News*, 5 October 1944.

40 A favorable review of a 2006 revival at New York's Mint Theatre noted that "the kitchen sink realism takes the various plot complications to a definitive finale," thereby locating "kitchen sink realism" not in the household details but in a tidy emplotment—something most of the original reviewers found lacking. Elyse Sommer, *"Soldier's Wife,"* a *CurtainUp* Review, 16 February 2006, accessed 8 April 2015, http://www.curtainup.com/soldierswife.html.

41 See *Tennessee Williams: Notebooks*, ed. Margaret Bradham Thornton (New Haven, CT: Yale University Press, 2006), 433.

42 Albert Wertheim, *Staging the War: American Drama and World War II* (Bloomington: Indiana University Press, 2004), 270–71.

43 Blanche might have stayed at a hotel, but she wants to be near family—in a domestic setting. In any case, there would be no play without an insistence on a cramped, "improper" domestic space.

44 Clifford E. Clark Jr., "Ranch-House Suburbia: Ideals and Realities," in *Recasting America: Culture and Politics in the Age of Cold War*, ed. Lary May (Chicago: University of Chicago Press, 1989), 171–91, quote on 185.

45 See Philip C. Kolin, *Confronting Tennessee Williams's "A Streetcar Named Desire": Essays in Critical Pluralism* (Westport, CT: Greenwood Press, 1993); and John S. Bak, "Criticism on *A Streetcar Named Desire*: A Bibliographic Survey, 1947–2003," *Cercles* 10 (2004): 3–32.

46 Mark Royden Winchell, "The Myth Is the Message, or Why *Streetcar* Keeps Running," in *Confronting Tennessee Williams's A Streetcar Named Desire: Essays in Critical Pluralism*, ed. Philip C. Kolin (Westport, CT: Greenwood Press, 1993), 133–45.

47 Herbert Blau, *The Dubious Spectacle: Extremities of Theater, 1976–2000* (Minneapolis: University of Minnesota Press, 2002), 205.

48 Winchell, "The Myth Is the Message," 142.

49 Elaine Tyler May, *Homeward Bound: American Families in the Cold War Era* (New York: Basic Books, 1999), 51.

50 Jessamyn Neuhaus, "The Way to a Man's Heart: Gender Roles, Domestic Ideology, and Cookbooks in the 1950s," *Journal of Social History* 32, no. 3 (1999): 529–55, at 541, 542.

51 Matthews, *"Just a Housewife,"* 196.

52 Neuhaus, "The Way to a Man's Heart," 546.

53 Mari Jo Buhle, *Feminism and Its Discontents: A Century of Struggle with Psychoanalysis* (Cambridge, MA: Harvard University Press, 2000), 174–79.

54 See Winchell, "The Myth Is the Message," 136.

55 Daniel Mendelsohn, "Victims on Broadway II," *New York Review of Books*, 9 June 2005, 32.

56 Ward Morehouse, "New Hit Named Desire," *The Sun*, 4 December 1947; Brooks Atkinson, "First Night at the Theatre" (review of *A Streetcar Named Desire*), *New York Times*, 4 December 1947; Robert Coleman, "Desire Streetcar in for Long Run," *Daily Mirror*, 4 December 1947; Louis Kronenberger, "A Sharp Southern Drama by Tennessee Williams," *PM Exclusive*, 5 December 1947; Morehouse, "New Hit Named Desire"; William Hawkins, "Streetcar a Fine Play of Clashing Emotions," *New York World-Telegram*, 4 December 1947; Atkinson, "First Night at the Theatre."

57 Ward Morehouse, "'On Whitman Avenue' Naïve and Obvious, Weakest of Race-Problem Plays," *The Sun*, 9 May 1946; William Hawkins, "Play Hits Out at Race Prejudice: 'On Whitman Avenue' Is Tense, Well Acted Treatment of Problem," *New York World-Telegram*, 9 May 1946.

58 Robert Garland, "'Whitman Avenue' Presented at Cort," *New York Journal American*, 9 May 1946; Howard Barnes, "Rocky Street," *New York Herald Tribune*, 9 May 1946; Hawkins, "Play Hits Out"; "overacting" in Louis Kronenberger, "A Vital Theme Is Ill Handled," *PM Exclusive*, 10 May 1946, and Lewis Nichols, "The Play," *New York Times*, 14 May 1946.

59 Garland, "'Whitman Avenue' Presented at Cort."

60 Maxine Wood Finsterwald, *On Whitman Avenue*, typescript (NYPL-PA Special Collections), 1-1-24, call number NCOF + p.v. 306. Page numbers are from this typescript.

61 The specific references suggest that the unnamed midwestern city is Detroit, where the opening of the Sojourner Truth housing development (intended for blacks and probably the referent for the fictional Nat Turner project) resulted in violence in 1942 and 1943; see Albrecht, *World War II and the*

American Dream, 108–14. Also, the Wayne County Board of Supervisors authorized a threefold expansion of the airport in 1944.

62   See Wertheim, *Staging the War*, 262–70.

CHAPTER FIVE

1   May, *Homeward Bound*.

2   See also Clark, "Ranch-House Suburbia," 185.

3   May, *Homeward Bound*, 86.

4   Regarding women who did not fit the stereotypes and popular publications not insisting women belonged *only* in the home, see Joanne Meyerowitz, ed., *Not June Cleaver: Women and Gender in Postwar America, 1945–1960* (Philadelphia: Temple University Press, 1994).

5   Ibid., 21.

6   Ibid., 194.

7   Bruce McConachie, *American Theatre in the Culture of the Cold War: Producing and Contesting Containment, 1947–1962* (Iowa City: University of Iowa Press, 2003).

8   Contrast David Savran's readings of key Cold War–era plays in *Communists, Cowboys, and Queers: The Politics of Masculinity in the Work of Arthur Miller and Tennessee Williams* (Minneapolis: University of Minnesota Press, 1992, 13).

9   Martin Halliwell, *American Culture in the 1950s* (Edinburgh: Edinburgh University Press, 2007), 4, 3.

10   Ibid., 9.

11   McConachie, *American Theatre in the Culture of the Cold War*, 13.

12   Cheryl Black, in her plenary talk at the III Cádiz Conference on American Drama and Theatre (May 2009), concluded a discussion of modern plays in which women commit murder by reading an excerpt from Arthur Miller's "Tragedy and the Common Man," inviting auditors to substitute feminine pronouns for all the masculine ones in the original text. Affective and effective, it was also bracing for being a new exercise.

13   Kathleen Collins, *Watching What We Eat: The Evolution of Television Cooking Shows* (New York: Continuum, 2009) 45, 25. Collins's sources are US Census Bureau's *Statistical Abstract of the United States: 2003* and its mini-historical statistics concerning "Selected Communications Media: 1920 to 2001." Lynn Spigel points out that television was not a viable reality for most Americans until 1955, as a Federal Communications Commission freeze on station allocation meant that most areas of the nation outside the Northeast had only one station (or none). See *Make Room for TV: Television and the Family Ideal in Postwar America* (Chicago: University of Chicago Press, 1992), 32.

14 Ibid., 4.

15 A short list of the era's blockbuster musicals also includes *Bells Are Ringing*; *Brigadoon*; *Finian's Rainbow*; *Guys and Dolls*; *Gypsy*; *The King and I*; *Kiss Me, Kate*; *My Fair Lady*; *Pajama Game*; *The Sound of Music*; *South Pacific*; and *West Side Story*.

16 Jack Poggi, *Theater in America: The Impact of Economic Forces 1870–1967* (Ithaca, NY: Cornell University Press, 1968); Wendell Stone, *Caffe Cino: The Birthplace of Off-Off-Broadway* (Carbondale: Southern Illinois University Press, 2005); David Crespy, *Off-Off Broadway Explosion: How Provocative Playwrights of the 1960s Ignited a New American Theater* (New York: Back Stage Books, 2003); and Stephen J. Bottoms, *Playing Underground: A Critical History of the 1960s Off-Off-Broadway Movement* (Ann Arbor: University of Michigan Press), esp. chaps. 1, 2.

17 Jackson Lears, "A Matter of Taste: Corporate Cultural Hegemony in a Mass-Consumption Society," in May, *Recasting America*, 38–57, quote on 41.

18 Ibid., 50, 51. E. Franklin Frazier takes to task the African American population that embraced the very same values in *Black Bourgeoisie: The Rise of a New Middle Class in the United States* (New York: Collier Books, 1962); and see Louis Peterson's 1954 play *Take a Giant Step* for an expression of the dominant values set in a well-off black family.

19 Samuel, *The American Dream*, 43.

20 Elizabeth C. Cromley, "Transforming the Food Axis: Houses, Tools, Modes of Analysis," *Material History Review* 44 (Fall 1996): 8–23.

21 A third zone, the private zone, was for sleeping and private family activities. See also Cindy R. Lobel, *Urban Appetites: Food and Culture in Nineteenth-Century New York* (Chicago: University of Chicago Press, 2014), chap. 5.

22 Cromley, "Transforming the Food Axis," 18.

23 Ibid., 19.

24 Arthur Miller, *Death of a Salesman* (New York: Viking Press, 1958), 11. Page numbers are from this edition.

25 Linda Kintz, "The Sociosymbolic Work of Family in *Death of a Salesman*," in *Approaches to Teaching Miller's "Death of a Salesman*," ed. Matthew C. Roudané (New York: Modern Language Association, 1995), 102–14, at 105.

26 Jo Mielziner, *Designing for the Theatre: A Memoir and a Portfolio* (New York: Atheneum, 1965), 25.

27 Miller's script used "apartment houses," and Mielziner uses "tenement buildings" (ibid., 25, 35).

28 Ibid., 46.

29 Arnold Aronson, "The Symbolist Scenography of Arthur Miller," in *Arthur Miller's America*, ed. Enoch Brater (Ann Arbor: University of Michigan Press, 2005), 78–93, quote on 89–90.

30 Ibid., 89.

31 L. Bailey McDaniel, "Domestic Tragedies: The Feminist Dilemma in Arthur Miller's *Death of a Salesman*," in *Arthur Miller's "Death of a Salesman*," ed. Eric J. Sterling (Amsterdam: Rodopi, 2008), 21–32, quotes on 23, 27.

32 See Fleissner, *Women, Compulsion*, and discussion in introduction.

33 Barbara Penner, "Rehearsing Domesticity: Postwar Pocono Honeymoon Resorts," in *Negotiating Domesticity: Spatial Productions of Gender in Modern Architecture*, ed. Hilde Heynen and Gülsüm Baydar (London: Routledge, 2005), 103–20.

34 Kintz, "The Sociosymbolic Work of Family in *Death of a Salesman*," 106.

35 Peter Levine (quotes from interview with Miller), "'Attention Must Be Paid': Arthur Miller's *Death of a Salesman* and the American Century," in *The "Salesman" Has a Birthday: Essays Celebrating the Fiftieth Anniversary of Arthur Miller's "Death of a Salesman*," ed. Stephen A. Marino (Lanham, MD: University Press of America), 45–52, quotes on 48, 50.

36 William Inge, *Four Plays* (New York: Grove Press, 1958). Page numbers are from this edition.

37 Douglas, quoted in Cromley, "Transforming the Food Axis," 13.

38 See Jessamyn Neuhaus, "The Way to a Man's Heart: Gender Roles, Domestic Ideology, and Cookbooks in the 1950s," *Journal of Social History* 32, no. 3 (1999): 529–55.

39 Erika Endrijonas, "Processed Foods from Scratch: Cooking for a Family in the 1950s," in *Kitchen Culture in America: Popular Representations of Food, Gender, and Race*, ed. Sherrie A. Inness (Philadelphia: University of Pennsylvania Press, 2000), 157–73, quote on 169.

40 See Lydia Martens, "Feminism and the Critique of Consumer Culture, 1950–1970," in *Feminism, Domesticity, and Popular Culture*, ed. Stacy Gillis and Joanne Hollows (New York: Routledge, 2009), 33–48. In fairness to Lola, it would not be until 1953 that the market for consumer goods ended its period of backlogged postwar demand and entered a period of fierce advertising competition for manufacturers. See Penny Sparke, *As Long as It's Pink: The Sexual Politics of Taste* (Halifax, Canada: Press of the Nova Scotia College of Art and Design, 2010, 132).

41 Hobe Morrison, "Play on Broadway: *Come Back Little Sheba*," *Variety*, n.d., 58; and John Chapman, "Mr. Blackmer and Miss Booth Earn Big Cheers in Moody 'Little Sheba,'" *New York Daily News*, 16 February 1950.

42 Quoted in Jeff Johnson, *William Inge and the Subversion of Gender* (Jefferson, NC: McFarland, 2005), 37.

43 "Tina's" recipe on the allrecipes.com website calls for three cups of day-old bread cubes, chicken broth, cream of mushroom soup, melted butter, and a mere two tablespoons each of chopped celery and chopped onion.

"When I want comfort food, this is the one that I turn to." Accessed 12 October 2013, http://allrecipes.com/Recipe/Stuffed-Pork-Chops-I/Detail .aspx?prop24=RD_RelatedRecipes.

44 Levenstein, *Paradox of Plenty*, 117.

45 Ibid., 119.

46 Quoted in ibid., 130.

47 Ibid., 140.

48 Martin Halliwell's *American Culture in the 1950s*, part of a decade-by-decade series published by Edinburgh University Press, is the last to have a discrete chapter with "theatre" or "drama" in its title. Later decades' mentions of plays (far fewer) are subsumed in chapters with "performance" as the dominant term. The point is also clear in the title of Ethan Mordden's book *All That Glittered: The Golden Age of Drama on Broadway 1919–1959*.

49 Seabrook paraphrased in Gad Guterman, "Field Tripping: The Power of *Inherit the Wind*," *Theatre Journal* 60, no. 4 (December 2008): 568.

50 As Roland Barthes observes, food "is a system of communication, a body of images, a protocol of usages, situations, and behavior." "Toward a Psychosociology of Contemporary Food Consumption," in *Food and Culture: A Reader*, ed. Carole Counihan and Penny Van Esterik (New York: Routledge, 1997), 21.

51 Exceptions include Langston Hughes's *Mulatto* (1935) and Dorothy and DuBose Heyward's *Mamba's Daughters* (1939), in each of which the playwright resolves the major dramatic question with a murder. The plays discussed in this chapter bring black domestics in line with white women to the extent that their struggles are not handled as material for which the police and the undertaker need to be summoned.

52 Certainly George C. Wolfe's "The Last Mama-on-the-Couch Play," arguably the most memorable sketch in his searing 1986 satire *The Colored Museum*, skewers the long-suffering matriarch figure.

53 In calling the 1950 character's world pre–mass commodity, I am drawing on Michael Kammen's notion of "commercial culture," which he also calls proto-mass culture (PMC). See *American Culture, American Tastes: Social Change and the 20th Century* (New York: Basic Books, 1999), 49, 167.

54 Some audience members were surely familiar with the 1946 novel, as McCullers had become a celebrity after the publication of the 1940 *The Heart Is a Lonely Hunter*.

55 To offer just a smattering of examples of how much the domestic landscape writ large changed, in the twenty years between 1940 and 1960, housing units in the forty-eight United States lacking bathtub or shower fell from 39 to 12 percent (William E. Leuchtenburg, *A Troubled Feast: American Society since 1945* [Boston: Little, Brown, 1973], 63). While the 1959 model

kitchen featured at the US exhibition in Moscow featured a washer/dryer, a dishwasher, exhaust fan, electric stove, and numerous other gadgets, a mere fifteen years earlier, in 1944, 23 percent of respondents to a *McCall's* magazine survey still cooked with wood, coal, or kerosene, while 25 percent had no access to hot water. Note that these are literate women—almost certainly white—who could afford the magazine. See Ruth Oldenziel, "Exporting the American Cold War Kitchen: Challenging Americanization, Technological Transfer, and Domestication," in *Cold War Kitchen: Americanization, Technology, and European Users*, ed. Ruth Oldenziel and Karin Zachmann (Cambridge, MA: MIT Press, 2009), 315–40, at 328.

56 See Noliwe M. Rooks, *Ladies' Pages: African American Women's Magazines and the Culture That Made Them* (New Brunswick, NJ: Rutgers University Press, 2004), 109–110; and Zuckerman, *A History of Popular Women's Magazines*, 119.

57 See, for instance, John Mason Brown, "Plot Me No Plots," reprinted from the *Saturday Review* of 28 January 1950, in *Critical Essays on Carson McCullers*, ed. Beverly Lyon Clark and Melvin J. Friedman (New York: Simon & Schuster Macmillan, 1996), 45–48. Jerry Gaghan's review in the *Philadelphia News*, 23 December 1949, labeled the play written "in the currently-favored plotless style."

58 Carson McCullers, *The Member of the Wedding: A Play*, introduction by Dorothy Allison (1951; repr., New York: New Directions/Penguin, 2006), 52. Hereafter *Member* (play).

59 Viral meningitis usually runs its course. Bacterial meningitis is frequently lethal if untreated. In 1945, the year the play and source novel are set, penicillin was not yet commercially available.

60 *Member* (play), 118.

61 Ibid.

62 Lester Polakov, *We Live to Paint Again* (New York: Logbooks Press, 1993).

63 Carson McCullers, *The Member of the Wedding* (Cambridge, MA: Riverside Press, 1946), 5. Hereafter *Member* (novel).

64 Ibid.

65 Ibid., 71.

66 Ibid., 4.

67 See Vernon Rice, "A Changed and Unchanged Waters," *New York Post*, 4 January 1950, 56.

68 *Member* (novel), 109.

69 *Member* (play), 7.

70 Trudier Harris, *From Mammies to Militants: Domestics in Black American Literature* (Philadelphia: Temple University Press, 1982), 15.

71 *Member* (play), 98.

72 To cite just one example, when Frankie's father drags her out of the honeymoon car and tells Berenice to "take charge of her," the stage direction reads *"Frankie flings herself on the kitchen chair and sobs with her head in her arms on the kitchen table"* (99). With no other room, table, or chairs in sight, these directions reinforce the inescapability of the kitchen but also its reliability in time of emotional need.

73 Oldenziel, "Exporting the American Cold War Kitchen," 323–24.

74 Lux, a product of the Lever company, started as laundry soap flakes in 1899. Its toilet soap advertising campaign of the 1920s "inspired countless . . . other toiletries to add the new look of glamour into their advertising." Juliann Sivulka, *Soap, Sex, and Cigarettes: A Cultural History of American Advertising* (Boston, MA: Wadsworth/Cenage Learning, 2012), 158. See also Stefan Schwarzkopf's study of the repositioning of Lux as an international soap brand, "Discovering the Consumer: Market Research, Product Innovation, and the Creation of Brand Loyalty in Britain and the United States in the Interwar Years," *Journal of Macromarketing* 29, no. 1 (March 2009): 8–20.

75 *Member* (play), 51.

76 Ibid., 57.

77 See Victoria E. Johnson, *Heartland TV: Prime Time Television and the Struggle for U.S. Identity* (New York: New York University Press, 2008).

78 Morris, *Realism*, 85.

79 Waters re-created her stage role on the screen in 1952, as did co-stars Julie Harris and Brandon DeWilde.

80 Carol Channing, in *Broadway: The American Musical* (2004), a six-part television documentary directed by Michael Kantor.

81 Nearly thirty-five hundred African Americans were lynched in the United States between 1882 and 1968. In 1918 Representative Leonidas Dyer, a Republican from St. Louis, introduced an antilynching bill in Congress. See "NAACP History: Anti-lynching Bill," accessed 28 March 2015, http://www.naacp.org/pages/naacp-history-anti-lynching-bill. It passed in the House of Representatives, but filibusters in the Senate in 1922, 1923, and 1924 finally killed it. The problem remained sufficiently serious, especially in the South, that the Costigan-Wagner Bill was drafted in the Senate in 1934 to make lynching a federal crime and thus take it out of state administration. It was defeated. See Alexander Tsesis, *We Shall Overcome: A History of Civil Rights and the Law* (New Haven, CT: Yale University Press, 2008), 178–80.

82 Ethel Waters, with Charles Samuels, *His Eye Is on the Sparrow, an Autobiography by Ethel Waters* (1951; repr., London: Jazz Book Club, 1958), 207–8.

83 Stephen Bourne, *Ethel Waters: Stormy Weather* (Lanham, MD: Scarecrow Press, 2007), 44.

84 Bourne's research uncovers the fact that Louise Anderson was eighteen when she gave birth to Ethel in 1896, not, as Waters writes in *Sparrow*, age twelve in 1900.

85 See, for example, Gaghan, review of *The Member of the Wedding*, *Philadelphia News*, 23 December 1949; and Edith H. Miller, "A Review of the Play about the Little Girl Who Thought She Could Be a Member of the Wedding," *Clarksburg News*, 25 May 1950. See also Kimberly Wallace-Sanders, *Mammy: A Century of Race, Gender, and Southern Memory* (Ann Arbor: University of Michigan Press, 2008).

86 "Christlike" is from Alice Hughes, "A Woman's New York," for King Features Syndicate, typed for release January 13, 1950 (NYPLPA Special Collections); "earthy" is from the caption under Al Hirschfeld's cartoon, *New York Times*, 30 July 1950, front page, arts section; "Old Testament agelessness" is from William Hawkins, "Novice Calmly Steals the Show," 14 January 1950 (unsourced clipping, NYPLPA Special Collections); "mystic heritage" is from Louise Mace, the column "Stage and Screen News," "Here and There in the Theaters," in *Springfield* (MA) *Republican*, 5 February 1950.

87 John Beaufort, "'The Member of the Wedding' on Broadway," *Christian Science Monitor*, 14 January 1950; Brooks Atkinson, "Three People: 'The Member of the Wedding' Superbly Acted by an Excellent Company," *New York Times*, 15 January 1950, X1.

88 Waters's lesbian relationship with Ethel Williams in the 1920s was not revealed in her autobiography. Stephen Bourne discusses it in his biography.

89 Louise Mace, "Here and There in the Theaters."

90 See Brooks Atkinson, "The Theatre: 'A Raisin in the Sun,'" *New York Times*, 12 March 1959; John Beaufort, "'Raisin in the Sun' a Thoughtful Comedy about Believable People: Many Achievements Noted in Miss Hansberry's Play," *Christian Science Monitor*, 21 March 1959; Frank Aston, "'Raisin in Sun' Is Moving Tale," *New York World Telegram and The Sun*, 12 March 1959; John McClain, "'A Raisin in the Sun' Gives a 'Wonderful Emotional Evening,'" *New York Journal American*, 12 March 1959; Whitney Bolton, "'Raisin in the Sun' Tops; Poitier Is Superb," *New York Morning Telegraph*, 8 March 1959.

91 Amiri Baraka, "'Raisin in the Sun's' [*sic*] Enduring Passion," *Washington Post*, 16 November 1986; Michael Anderson, "A Landmark Lesson in Being Black," *New York Times*, 7 March 1999; Felicia R. Lee, "Deferred Dreams That Resonate across Decades," *New York Times*, 17 February 2008, sec. 2, 19; Ben Brantley, "No Rest for the Weary: 'Raisin in the Sun' Brings Denzel Washington Back to Broadway," *New York Times*, 4 April 2014, C1.

92 Lorraine Hansberry, *A Raisin in the Sun* (New York: Vintage Books, 1994), 22. Page numbers are from this edition.

93 Lorraine Hansberry, "Willie Loman, Walter Younger, and He Who Must Live," *Village Voice*, 12 August 1959, 7–8.

94 Steven R. Carter, *Hansberry's Drama: Commitment amid Complexity* (Urbana: University of Illinois Press, 1991), 62.

95 Louis Kronenberger, "The Season on Broadway," *Best Plays of 1958–1959* (New York: Dodd, Mead, 1959), 16.

96 Leuchtenburg, *A Troubled Feast*, 74.

97 Cited in Samuel, *The American Dream*, 67.

98 See Soyica Diggs Colbert, *The African American Theatrical Body: Reception, Performance, and the Stage* (Cambridge: Cambridge University Press, 2011), 40–47; and Kristin L. Matthews, "The Politics of 'Home' in Lorraine Hansberry's *A Raisin in the Sun*," *Modern Drama* 51, no. 4 (Winter 2008): 556–78.

99 Matthews, "The Politics of 'Home,'" 561.

100 Colbert, *African American Theatrical Body*, 46.

101 Ibid., 34.

102 See *Reimagining "A Raisin in the Sun": Four New Plays*, ed. Rebecca Ann Rugg and Harvey Young (Evanston, IL: Northwestern University Press, 2012). The plays to which I refer appear in this anthology: Robert O'Hara's *Etiquette of Vigilance* and Bruce Norris's *Clybourne Park*.

103 Albee, *The American Dream*, in *The Collected Plays of Edward Albee*, vol. 1, *1958–1965* (New York: Overlook Duckworth, 2004). Pages are from this edition.

104 Crespy, *Off-Off-Broadway Explosion*, 30.

105 See ibid.; and Matthew C. Roudané, *Understanding Edward Albee* (Columbia: University of South Carolina Press, 1987), 59.

106 Brian Way, "Albee and the Absurd: *The American Dream* and *The Zoo Story*," reprinted in *Edward Albee: Modern Critical Views*, ed. Howard Bloom (New York: Chelsea House Publishers, 1987), 14.

107 Roudané, *Understanding Edward Albee*, 58.

108 Michael E. Rutenberg, *Edward Albee: Playwright in Protest* (New York: Drama Book Specialists, 1969), 67.

109 Margaret Benston, "The Political Economy of Women's Liberation" (1969), in *The Politics of Housework*, ed. Ellen Malos (Cheltenham, UK: New Clarion Press, 1985), 100–109, quote on 102.

110 Quoted in Kathi Weeks, *The Problem with Work: Feminism, Marxism, Antiwork Politics, and Postwork Imaginaries* (Durham, NC: Duke University Press, 2011), 126 (italics in original).

111 Lundberg and Farnham, *Modern Woman*.

112 Thomas R. Dash, "'The American Dream' Vivid, Satiric Comic Strip," *Women's Wear Daily*, 25 January 1961; Howard Taubman, "Albee's *The*

American Dream," 25 January 1961, *New York Times*, and "On Stage" in Long Island *Newsday*, 1 February 1961, 9C; Dash, "'The American Dream' Vivid, Satiric Comic Strip"; and Whitney Bolton, "Provocative Double Bill at York Theater," *Daily Telegraph*, 26 January 1961.

113 Roudané, *Understanding Edward Albee*, 52.

114 Wylie, quoted in Matthews, *"Just a Housewife,"* 201, 202, 207.

115 "How to Keep His Dinner Warm," ST Lyrics, accessed 8 April 2015, http://www.stlyrics.com/lyrics/howtosucceedinbusinesswithoutreallytrying/happytokeephisdinnerwarm.htm. Music and lyrics by Frank Loesser.

116 Margalit Fox, "Betty Friedan, Who Ignited Cause in 'Feminine Mystique,' Dies at 85," *New York Times*, 5 February 2006.

CHAPTER SIX

1 Leuchtenburg, *A Troubled Feast*, 106. See also Sharon Monteith, *American Culture in the 1960s* (Edinburgh: Edinburgh University Press, 2008).

2 See Geraldine Bedell, "Why We Love Those Wise Big Women," *New Statesman* (London), 8 May 2000, 22; Sparke, *As Long as It's Pink*, 146; and Gail Collins, *When Everything Changed: The Amazing Journey of American Women from 1960 to the Present* (New York: Little, Brown, 2009), 24, passim. See Joanne Meyerowitz, "Beyond the Feminine Mystique: A Reassessment of Postwar Mass Culture, 1946–1958," *Journal of American History* 79 (March 1993): 1455–82, for a reappraisal.

3 Dana Polan, *Julia Child's "The French Chef"* (Durham, NC: Duke University Press, 2011), 25.

4 See Monteith, *American Culture in the 1960s*; Bruce J. Schulman, *The Seventies: The Great Shift in American Culture, Society, and Politics* (New York: Free Press, 2001); Graham Thompson, *American Culture in the 1980s* (Edinburgh: Edinburgh University Press, 2007); for a transcript of the Civil Rights Act, see http://www.ourdocuments.gov/doc.php?doc=97&page=transcript; and Collins, *When Everything Changed*.

5 See Meyerowitz, "Beyond the Feminine Mystique"; and Martens, "Feminism and the Critique of Consumer Culture," 33–47.

6 Ironically, perhaps, Childs's way of imagining domestic satisfaction also involved her "disidentifying with the housewife." Joanne Hollows, "The Feminist and the Cook: Julia Child, Betty Friedan and Domestic Femininity," in *Gender and Consumption: Domestic Cultures and the Commercialisation of Everyday Life*, ed. Emma Casey and Lydia Martens (Aldershot, Hampshire, UK: Ashgate, 2007), 33–38, at 34, 36, 43. Hollows's citation is from Friedan, *The Feminine Mystique*, 244–45.

7 See Joseph Wesley Zeigler, *Regional Theatre: The Revolutionary Stage* (New

York: Da Capo Press, 1973); and Julius Novick, *Beyond Broadway: The Quest for Permanent Theatres* (New York: Hill & Wang, 1968.)

8 See James M. Harding and Cindy Rosenthal, eds., *Restaging the Sixties: Radical Theaters and Their Legacies* (Ann Arbor: University of Michigan Press, 2006); and Harry J. Elam Jr., *Taking It to the Streets: The Social Protest Theater of Luis Valdez and Amiri Baraka* (Ann Arbor: University of Michigan Press, 2001).

9 The NEA was also a major source of support for mainstream regional theatres whose work would prove a forum for serious work challenging some facets of a predictable status quo. See Dick Netzer, *The Subsidized Muse: Public Support for the Arts in the United States* (London: Cambridge University Press, 1978); and Mark Bauerlein, with Ellen Grantham, *National Endowment for the Arts: A History, 1965–2008* (Washington, DC: National Endowment for the Arts, 2009), accessed 14 March 2015, http://purl.access .gpo.gov/GPO/LPS113863.

10 The only program receiving more money was the Federal/State Partnership—the program guaranteeing grants to state arts councils, some of whose monies also went to theatre, making theatre the biggest winner in government funding in the late 1960s (compiled from NEA *Annual Reports* and reported in Netzer, *The Subsidized Muse*, 65). For a full list, see Charles Christopher Mark, *Reluctant Bureaucrats: The Struggle to Establish the National Endowment for the Arts* (Dubuque, IA: Kendall / Hunt Publishing, 1991), 221–26.

11 Jack Morrison, *The Rise of the Arts on the American Campus* (New York: McGraw-Hill, 1973), 10–11.

12 The four decided to challenge the decency clause recommended by Congress. Their case went to the Supreme Court, which upheld the decency clause in 1998.

13 Susan Faludi, *Backlash: The Undeclared War against American Women*, 15th anniversary ed. (New York: Random House, 2006), 53.

14 Ibid., 98.

15 Ibid., 7.

16 The first issue was an insert in *New York* magazine; *Ms.* began independent publication in 1972.

17 Only a single reviewer—a woman—noted that Edna has gone *back* to work, i.e., that she has been employed for wages before. See Florence Johnson, "Simon's Play a 'Laugh- a-Minute'" (review of *The Prisoner of Second Avenue*), New Haven *Journal-Courier* (New York Public Library for the Performing Arts, *The Prisoner of Second Avenue* clippings file, n.d.). The script makes clear that Edna worked as a secretary in the past (35).

18   Tom Donnelly, "An Upbeat View of Lindsay's Inferno?," unsourced clipping (NYPLPA, Billy Rose Collection), *Prisoner of Second Avenue* clippings file, 52.

19   Susan Koprince, *Understanding Neil Simon* (Columbia: University of South Carolina Press, 2002), 59.

20   Critic Martin Gottfried made this point in his review of *The Prisoner of Second Avenue*, *Women's Wear Daily*, 15 November 1971, 14. Otis L. Guernsey Jr. called Simon "the Molière of our era" in "The Season in New York," his introductory essay to *The Best Plays of 1971–1972* (New York: Dodd, Mead), 18.

21   Alice Kessler-Harris, *Out to Work: A History of Wage-Earning Women in the United States* (New York: Oxford University Press, 1982), 317, 318.

22   Rachel Bowlby, foreword to *A Concise Companion to Realism*, ed. Matthew Beaumont (Chichester, UK: Wiley-Blackwell, 2010), xviii.

23   Richard Coe, "Neil Simon's 'Prisoner,'" *Washington Post*, 20 October 1971, D9.

24   Richard J. Scholem, review of *The Prisoner of Second Avenue*, typescript, Greater New York Radio Theatre, aired November 5, 1971 (NYPL-PA Special Collections, *The Prisoner of Second Avenue* clippings file).

25   Leo Mishkin, "Neil Simon Does It Again" (review of *The Prisoner of Second Avenue*), *New York Morning Telegraph*, 15 November 1971.

26   George Oppenheimer, "Too Many Laughs" (review of *The Prisoner of Second Avenue*), *New York Newsday*, 12 November 1971. Brendan Gill, "Laughing When It Hurts" (review of *The Prisoner of Second Avenue*), *New Yorker*, 20 November 1971, 111.

27   "Do Thin Walls a Comedy Make?" (review of *The Prisoner of Second Avenue*), *Village Voice*, 18 November 1971.

28   John Quinn, "Minority Report: A Dim View of Simon," *New York Daily News*, 21 November 1971.

29   Clayton Riley, "Neil Simon: He Keeps 'em Giggling," *New York Times*, 19 December 1971, sec. D, 5.

30   Herbert Blau, *Reality Principles: From the Absurd to the Virtual* (Ann Arbor: University of Michigan Press, 2011), 121. Page numbers for later quotations are from this edition.

31   Neil Simon, *The Prisoner of Second Avenue* (New York: Random House, 1972), 15. All page numbers are from this edition.

32   Richard Natale, unsourced clipping (NYPL-PA, Billy Rose Collection), *Prisoner of Second Avenue* clippings file.

33   Sara Rath, "Casseroles," in Smith, *Oxford Encyclopedia of Food and Drink in America*, 1:194.

34   Irma S. Rombauer, Marion Rombauer Becker, and Ethan Becker, *The Joy of Cooking* 75th anniversary ed. (New York: Scribner, 2006), 205.

35   Hobe Morrison, review of *The Prisoner of Second Avenue*, *Variety*, 17 November 1971, 88; and Clive Barnes, "Stage: Creeping Paranoia and Crawling Malaise" (review of *The Prisoner of Second Avenue*), *New York Times*, 12 November 1971, 55.

36   Quoted in Richard Natale, unsourced clipping (NYPLPA, Billy Rose Collection), *Prisoner of Second Avenue* clippings file.

37   "Women's Earnings as a Percentage of Men's, 1951–2011, infoplease, accessed 19 February 2015, http://www.infoplease.com/ipa/A0193820.html.

38   Israel Horovitz, *Park Your Car in Harvard Yard*, in *Israel Horovitz: Collected Works*, volume 2, *New England Blue: Plays of Working-Class Life* (Portland, ME: Smith & Kraus, 1995). All page numbers are from this edition. The play was presented as early as 1986 in Gloucester, Massachusetts.

39   Mart, "*Park Your Car in Harvard Yard*" (review), *Variety*, 11 June 1986, 88; Frank Rich, "Robards and Ivey as Head and Heart" (review of *Park Your Car in Harvard Yard*), *New York Times*, 8 November 1991, accessed 9 January 2013, http://www.nytimes.com/1991/11/08/theater/review-theater-robards -and-ivey-as-head-and-heart.html; Alvin Klein, "Westport Stages, 'Park Your Car,'" *New York Times*, 6 September 1992, sec. 13 (Connecticut ed.), 18; William A. Raidy, "Dying Teacher Receives Valuable Lesson in Living" (review of *Park Your Car in Harvard Yard*), New Jersey *Star Ledger*, 8 November 1991, 59; John Beaufort, "Play by Israel Horovitz Tells a Tale of Opposites," *Christian Science Monitor*, 21 November 1991, 12.

40   Nancy Folbre, *The Invisible Heart: Economics and Family Values* (New York: New Press, 2001), 66.

41   Ibid., 67.

42   Ibid., 252.

43   Martha Rosler, "For an Art against the Mythology of Everyday Life," in *Decoys and Disruptions: Selected Writings, 1975–2001* (Cambridge, MA: MIT Press, 2004), 7.

44   Martha Rosler and Jane Weinstock, "Interview with Martha Rosler," *October* 5, no. 17 (Summer 1981): 90.

45   Ibid., 89.

46   Rolser, "For an Art against the Mythology," 8.

47   Helen Molesworth, "House Work and Art Work," in *Art after Conceptual Art*, ed. Alexander Alberro and Sabeth Buchmann (Cambridge, MA: Generali Foundation and MIT Press, 2006), 66–84, quote on 79.

48   See Brecht, "Against Georg Lukács," 82.

49   Quotes are from Rosler and Weinstock, "Interview," 97, 85, 86.

50 Molesworth, "House Work and Art Work," 79.

51 Weeks, *The Problem with Work*, 130.

52 Ibid.

53 Ibid., 137.

54 "Toasters at Risk Once Again," *New York Times*, 22 Oct 1999, E2.

55 Stephen J. Bottoms, *Playing Underground: A Critical History of the 1960s Off-Off-Broadway Movement* (Ann Arbor: University of Michigan Press, 2004), 105–9.

56 Stephen J. Bottoms, *The Theatre of Sam Shepard: States of Crisis* (Cambridge: Cambridge University Press, 1998), 17.

57 Ibid., 29, 267, 188.

58 Sam Shepard, *True West*, in *Sam Shepard: Seven Plays* (New York: Bantam Books, 1986), 3. All page numbers are from this edition.

59 Brian Richardson, "The Struggle for the Real—Interpretive Conflict, Dramatic Method, and the Paradox of Realism," in Demastes, *Realism and the American Dramatic Tradition*, 1–17, quote on 13.

60 Clive Barnes, "Shepard's 'West' Retains Its Truth" (review of *True West*), *New York Post*, 8 August 1983, 21.

61 For an extended argument, see William Kleb, "Worse Than Being Homeless: *True West* and the Divided Self," in *American Dreams: The Imagination of Sam Shepard*, ed. Bonnie Marranca (New York: Performing Arts Journal Publications, 1981), 117–25.

62 John Heilpern, "One Slob Loser, One Golden Boy, and the Death of the Family," *New York Observer*, 27 March 2000, p. 23.

63 Toast functions as sacrament, according to critic Richard Christiansen in "Myth vs. Reality: A True Portrayal in 'True West,'" *Chicago Tribune*, 29 June 1982, sec. 2, 7.

64 T. E. Kalem, "City Coyotes Prowling the Brain" (review of *True West*), *Time*, 5 January 1981.

65 *True West* began life at San Francisco's Magic Theatre, where Shepard was playwright-in-residence from the mid-1970s to the early 1980s. It opened at the New York Shakespeare Festival Public Theatre at the end of 1980 with actors Tommy Lee Jones and Peter Boyle. Controversy surrounding the last-minute departure of director Robert Woodruff coupled with Shepard's 1979 Pulitzer for *Buried Child* guaranteed the production a lot of attention, although much of it turned out to be negative. *True West* was revived at Chicago's Steppenwolf Theatre in 1982 in a production picked up for a commercial production in New York that earned rave reviews for actors Gary Sinise and John Malkovich. A revival on Broadway in 2000 featured Philip Seymour Hoffman and John C. Reilly alternating as the brothers.

66   Jack Kroll, "California Dreaming" (review of *True West*), *Newsweek*, 5 January 1981.

67   Stanley Crouch, "American Perfection" (review of *True West*), *Village Voice*, 2 November 1982.

68   Jonathan Kalb, "*True West*," *New York Press*, 22–28 March 2000, sec. 2, 17.

69   Lynda Hart, *Sam Shepard's Metaphorical Stages* (Westport, CT: Greenwood Press, 1987), 96.

70   Martin Tucker, *Sam Shepard* (New York: Continuum, 1992), 139.

71   Kleb, "Worse Than Being Homeless," 120, 122.

72   Frank Rich, "Stage: Shepard's 'True West,'" *New York Times*, 24 December 1980, C9.

73   Interview with Robert Coe, *New York Times Magazine*, quoted in Ellen Oumano, *Sam Shepard: The Life and Work of an American Dreamer* (New York: St. Martin's Press, 1986), 137.

74   Dan Isaac, "Brothers Grim" (review of *True West*), *Other Stages*, 1 January 1981, 4.

75   Sheila Rabillard, "Shepard's Challenge to the Modernist Myths of Origin and Originality: *Angel City* and *True West*," in *Rereading Shepard*, ed. Leonard Wilcox (New York: St. Martin's Press, 1993), 71–96.

76   Ibid., 86.

77   Sy Syna, *News World*, 1 April 1983. *New York*'s John Simon saw a play that "reeks of observed and comprehended reality" (11 April 1983). David Richards noted "dialogue . . . representing the leaner end of realism" (*Washington Post*, 15 April 1983). Gerald Nachman saw a play "darkly amusing and real" ("Out, Brief Candle," *San Francisco Chronicle*, 8 September 1983); and Frank Rich declared it "[a] totally realistic play" (*New York Times*, 1 April 1983). Michael Feingold hedged his critical bets with "Not a great play, it is nonetheless a real one, with a real sense of how people live—and perhaps wish they didn't—in America right now" ("And Suicide Is Confession," *Village Voice*, 12 April 1983). At the opposite end of the spectrum, Clive Barnes quoted the ending of *A Doll House* to make his own point: "'People don't do things like that.' It is an observation that I think could very well apply to *'night, Mother*" ("'night, Mother' Is a Long Day's Night," *New York Post*, 1 April 1983). UPI's Glenne Currie found it "unconvincing" ("Play about Suicide Not Broadway Material," UPI typescript, 1 April 1983 [NYPLPA Special Collections, *'night, Mother* clippings file]). And shortly after the play became available for production outside New York, a critic of a 1986 Chicago production could start a review with a statement that for him the play had always been "basically unbelievable" (Richard Christiansen, "'Mother' as Good as It Can Be," *Chicago Tribune*, 1 March 1986.)

78 Marsha Norman, *'night, Mother* (New York: Hill & Wang, 1983), 3. All quotes are from this edition.

79 A design scheme as well as performers' inflections in the Broadway production led to the idea of the locale as both southern and ugly and without taste. Allan Wallach identified the setting as a house "on the outskirts of a city in the American South" (*Newsday*, 1 April 1983, 19); Brendan Gill put it in the "Sun Belt" (*New Yorker*, 11 April 1983, 109); Douglas Watt guessed "someplace in the South, judging from speech patterns and the author's Louisville background" (*New York Daily News*, 1 April 1983). Designer Heidi Landesman made clear that "[t]he environment has to be unbelievably depressing but in such a way that the audience sees it, but Thelma and Jessie don't" (Susan Lieberman, "*'night, Mother*," *Theatre Crafts* 19, no. 5 [May 1985]: 22, 46, quote on 22). These choices and impressions seem to contravene the playwright's desire, although "real" people in a "particular part of the country" cannot rule out the South as a choice.

80 A respondent quoted in Suzanne Bennett and Susan Jonas's much-cited 2002 study, "Report on the Status of Women: A Limited Engagement?," noted that women were always regarded by audiences and readers as "specific" and not "universal," no matter what they undertook or represented in a play. The report was prepared for the New York State Council for the Arts Theatre Program and reflected three years of research.

81 See Robert Brustein, "Don't Read This Review!," *New Republic*, 2 May 1983; and Frank Rich, "Theater: ''Night, Mother' at Harvard," *New York Times*, 12 January 1983.

82 Stéphanie Genz, "'I Am Not a Housewife, but . . .': Postfeminism and the Revival of Domesticity," in Gillis and Hollows, *Feminism, Domesticity, and Popular Culture*, 49–62, quote on 59.

83 See *'night, Mother* at the Theatre on Film and Tape (TOFT) section of the NYPLPA.

84 Douglas Watt, "''night, Mother': A Study of a Suicide," New York *Daily News*, 1 April 1983.

85 Michael Feingold, "And Suicide Is Confession" (review of *'night, Mother*), *Village Voice*, 12 April 1983; and Howard Kissel, Review of *'night, Mother*, *Women's Wear Daily*, 1 April 1983.

86 Christiansen, "'Mother' as Good as It Can Be"; Allan Wallach, "When 'night means 'bye" (review of *'night, Mother*), *Newsday*, 1 April 1983; Barnes, "''night, Mother' Is a Long Day's Night."

87 Sy Syna, "Woman Seeks Release in Absorbing 'Mother,'" *News World*, New York, 1 April 1983; Nachman, "Out, Brief Candle."

88 Brustein, "Don't Read This Review!," and Rich, "Theater: ''Night, Mother' at Harvard"; Michael Feingold, "And Suicide Is Confession" (review of *'night,*

Mother), *Village Voice*, 12 April, 1983; John Beaufort, "Grim Drama Is 1983 Winner of Pulitzer Prize," *Christian Science Monitor*, 22 April 1983. Frank Rich reversed himself between the Harvard opening in January and the transfer to Broadway in April 1983, switching his assessment to "homey, appointed with the right appliances, conventionally tasteful" until the lights come up and reveal it to be "antiseptic." Heidi Landesman designed the production for both venues.

89 Humm, "'night, Mother," *Variety*, 6 April 1983.

90 Gerald Weales, "Really 'Going On': Marsha Norman's Pulitzer Winner," *Commonweal*, 19 June 1983, 370–71.

91 Jenny S. Spencer, "Norman's *'night, Mother*: Psycho-drama of Female Identity," *Modern Drama* 30, no. 3 (September 1987): 364–75, quote on 370.

92 Dolan makes this point in *The Feminist Spectator as Critic* (Ann Arbor: University of Michigan Press, 1988), chap. 2.

93 Linda Kintz, *The Subject's Tragedy: Political Poetics, Feminist Theory, and Drama* (Ann Arbor: University of Michigan Press, 1992), chap. 2, 220–21.

94 William S. Demastes, "Jessie and Thelma Revisited: Marsha Norman's Conceptual Challenge in *'night, Mother*," *Modern Drama* 36 (1993): 109–19, quote on 114.

95 Ibid., 117, 11 (italics in original).

96 Varun Begley, "Objects of Realism: Bertolt Brecht, Roland Barthes, and Marsha Norman," *Theatre Journal* 64 (2012): 353, 346, 338–39.

97 Ibid., 339, 344.

98 *'night, Mother*, 51.

99 Begley, "Objects of Realism," 352.

100 Fleissner, *Women, Compulsion*, 9.

101 Ivone Margulies, *Nothing Happens: Chantal Akerman's Hyperrealist Everyday* (Durham, NC: Duke University Press, 1996), 5. See also chap. 3, "The Equivalence of Events: *Jeanne Dielman, 23 Quai du Commerce, 1080 Bruxelles*."

102 Jenny Spencer discusses this phenomenon.

103 Norman, *'night, Mother*, 82.

104 Ben Highmore, *Everyday Life and Cultural Theory: An Introduction* (New York: Routledge, 2002), 2, 3.

105 Lynda Hart, "Motherhood according to Karen Finley: *The Theory of Total Blame*," in *A Sourcebook of Feminist Theatre and Performance: On and beyond the Stage*, ed. Carol Martin (New York: Routledge, 1996), 108–19, quotes on 113, 111.

106 Michael Feingold, Editor's Note, *The Theory of Total Blame*, in *Grove New American Theater*, ed. Michael Feingold (New York: Grove Press, 1993), 219. All quotes to Finley, *The Theory of Total Blame*, are from this edition.

107 Craig Bromberg, "No Yams in Karen Finley's 'Long Day's Journey' for the '90s," *Los Angeles Times*, 30 November 1989, accessed 13 August 2013, articles. latimes.com/print/1989-11-30/entertainment/ca-451_1_performance-art.

108 The use of chocolate to cover her body served as a protest against objectification and domestic violence. Karen Finley, quoted in Lynn Beavis, "Performance Art, Censorship, and Psychoanalysis: Theorizing the Outrageous Acts of Karen Finley," master's thesis, Concordia University, Montreal, 2003, 76.

109 Karen Finley, "A Suggestion of Madness," in *A Different Kind of Intimacy: The Collected Writings of Karen Finley* (New York: Thunder's Mouth Press, 2000), 63.

110 *The Theory of Total Blame* premiered at The Kitchen in New York in 1988; it was performed at the RAPP Art Center in New York's East Village in June 1989; at the Pyramid Arts Center, Rochester, New York, in October 1989; and at LACE (Los Angeles Contemporary Exhibitions) in November and December 1989. The description of Irene appears both in Hart, *Winged Victory*, 111, and in "Karen Finley, the Ultimate Black Sheep," RJN, accessed 1 August 2013, www.rjn.stumble.com/old_site/KAREN.HTML. Salvation Army observation is from Dan Sullivan, "'Total Blame': A Performance-Art Virago Turns Playwright," *Los Angeles Times*, 2 December 1989, accessed 14 August 2013, http://articles.latimes.com/1989-12-02/entertainment/ca -198_1_karen-finley.

111 Hart, *Winged Victory*, 114.

112 A. D. Amorosi, Critic Pick, "Karen Finley," *Philadelphia Citypaper*, 20–27 November 1997, accessed 14 August 2013,http://archives.citypaper.net /articles/112097/pick.finley.shtml?print=1.

113 Sullivan, "'Total Blame.'"

114 Feingold, Editor's Note, 219.

115 Begley, "Objects of Realism," 339, 344.

116 "A Troubling Portrait of Domestic Work," *New York Times* Editorial, 3 December 2012, A28. The 2012 report, by Nik Theodore, associate professor of urban policy at the University of Illinois at Chicago, and Linda Burnham, research director of the National Domestic Workers Alliance, shows that African American housecleaners earn an average of $10.89 per hour. *Home Economics: The Invisible and Unregulated World of Domestic Work* (New York: National Domestic Workers Alliance, 2012), accessed 29 March 2015, http://www.domesticworkers.org/pdfs/HomeEconomicsEnglish.pdf.

117 Sheila Rush, Introduction to *Two Plays by Douglas Turner Ward* (New York: Third Press, 1966).

118 Mance Williams, *Black Theatre in the 1960s and 1970s* (Westport, CT: Greenwood Press, 1985), 152. Ward freely acknowledged the influence of Genet's *The Blacks*. See Rush, Introduction to *Two Plays*, x–xi.

119 Faedra Chatard Carpenter, "Douglas Turner Ward's Play on Whiteness: *Day of Absence* on America's Public Stages," plenary talk given at the American Society for Theatre Research conference, Nashville, TN, November 3, 2012.

120 Williams, *Black Theatre*, 158. For a history of the NEC, see Errol G. Hill and James V. Hatch, *A History of African American Theatre* (New York: Cambridge University Press, 1993), 395–97.

121 Douglas Turner Ward, *"Happy Ending" and "Day of Absence"* (New York: Dramatists Play Service, 1994), 7. All quotes are from this edition. Photographs are in the Bert Andrews Collection at the Schomburg Center for Research in Black Culture, New York Public Library.

122 Ibid., 13, 15, 16.

123 Jones, *Labor of Love, Labor of Sorrow*, 134.

124 Ward, *Happy Ending*, 17.

125 Ibid.

126 Michael Smith, review of *Happy Ending* and *Day of Absence*, *Village Voice*, 18 November 1965.

127 Herbert Kupferberg, "Negro Plays—Sparks, but No Real Fire" (review of *Happy Ending* and *Day of Absence*), *New York Herald Tribune*, 16 November 1965; Martin Gottfried, "'Happy Ending'—'Day of Absence,'" *Women's Wear Daily*, 16 November 1965; Smith, review of *Happy Ending* and *Day of Absence*.

128 Faludi, *Backlash*, 106–7.

CHAPTER SEVEN

1 "But What Would Martha Say?" *New York Times Magazine*, 16 May 1999; 145–46, reprinted in Harriet Sigerman, ed., *The Columbia Documentary History of American Women Since 1941* (New York: Columbia University Press, 2003), 569–72.

2 Margaret Talbot, "Les Très Riches Heures de Martha Stewart," *New Republic*, 13 May 1996, accessed 28 May 2013, http://www.newrepublic.com/article/110547/les-tr%C3%A8s-riches-heures-de-martha-stewart.

3 Anne Kingston, *The Meaning of Wife* (New York: Farrar, Straus and Giroux, 2004), 67.

4 Talbot, "Les Très Riches Heures."

5 See Astrid Henry, *Not My Mother's Sister: Generational Conflict and Third-Wave Feminism* (Bloomington: Indiana University Press, 2004).

6 See William H. Chafe, *The Rise and Fall of the American Century: The United States from 1890–2009* (New York: Oxford University Press, 2009), chap. 12.

7 Ibid., 281.

8 Ibid., 283.

9   United States Census Bureau, "Women in the Work Force," 2009, accessed 3 April 2015, http://www.census.gov/newsroom/pdf/women_workforce _slides.pdf.

10 Barbara Ehrenreich, *Nickel and Dimed: On (Not) Getting by in America* (New York: Henry Holt, 2001).

11 This is a departure from the form of the book, which presents the three state sojourns one at a time.

12 Joan Holden, *Nickel and Dimed* (New York: Dramatists Play Service, 2005), 4. All page numbers are from this edition.

13 This is a representative list and not meant to be definitive.

14 Curt Holman, "The Wages of Fear: Nickel and Dimed Plays Tourist below the Poverty Line," *Creative Loafing Atlanta*, 10 May 2006, accessed 3 June 2013, http://clatl.com/atlanta/the-wages-of-fear/Content?oid=1258389.

15 Alan R. Hall, "Justice Theater Project Review: *Nickel and Dimed* Dramatizes Life among the 'Working Poor,'" *CVNC: An Online Arts Journal in North Carolina*, 22 November 2004, accessed 3 June 2013, http://cvnc.org /article.cfm?articleId=226.

16 Jennifer Janviere, "*Nickel and Dimed*: A Review," *Communicate: The Diederich College of Communication Blog*, 24 February 2010, accessed 3 June 2013, http://diederich.marquette.edu/COC/nickelanddimed-022010.aspx.

17 Andrea Stevens, "Evoking Lives Struggling to Exist on Bare Minimums," *New York Times*, 11 October 2006, accessed 3 June 2013, http://theater .nytimes.com/2006/10/11/theater/reviews/11nick.html?_r=0.

18 Richard Connema, "Theatreworks Production of *Nickel and Dimed* Is an Excellent Social Diatribe," 14 September 2003, accessed 3 June 2013, Talkin broadway.com, http://www.talkinbroadway.com/regional/sanfran/s377 .html.

19 Loren Noveck, "Nickel and Dimed," Nytheatre.com review, 6 October 2006, accessed 3 June 2013, http://www.nytheatre.com/Review/loren-noveck -2006-10-6-nickel-and-dimed.

20 Robert Faires, "Nickel and Dimed," *Austin Chronicle*, 15 April 2005, accessed 3 June 2013, http://www.austinchronicle.com/arts/2005-04-15/266715/.

21 Emily Hall, Review of *Nickel and Dimed*, *The Stranger*, 8–14 August 2002, accessed 18 June 2013, http://www.thestranger.com/seattle/theater-review -revue/Content?oid=11598.

22 Holman, "The Wages of Fear."

23 Janviere, " Nickel and Dimed: A Review."

24 In 2005 Linda Hirshman blasted privileged women who "chose" to opt out of the workplace and be housewives, locating the "real glass ceiling . . . at home." "Homeward Bound," *American Prospect* 16, no. 12 (December 2005): 20–26.

25 Faludi, *Backlash*, 70.

26 Marcy Darnovsky, "The New Traditionalism: Repackaging Ms. Consumer," *Social Text* 29 (1991): 72–91, at 79.

27 Emily Matchar, *Homeward Bound: Why Women Are Embracing the New Domesticity* (New York: Simon and Schuster, 2013).

28 Lisa Belkin, "The Opt-Out Revolution," *New York Times Magazine*, 26 October 2003, accessed 20 August 2013, http://www.nytimes.com/2003/10/26/magazine/the-opt-out-revolution.html?pagewanted=all&src=pm; and Claudia Wallis, "The Case for Staying Home," *Time*, 22 March 2004, accessed 20 August 2013, http://www.time.com/time/magazine/article/0,9171,993641,00.html. Quote is from Belkin.

29 Judith Warner, "Ready to Rejoin the Rat Race?," *New York Times Magazine*, 11 August 2013, 29.

30 Sheryl Sandberg, *Lean In: Women, Work, and the Will to Lead* (New York: Alfred A. Knopf, 2013), 23, 106–7.

31 See Leslie Bennetts, *The Feminine Mistake: Are We Giving Up Too Much?* (New York: Hyperion, 2007); and Hirshman, "Homeward Bound."

32 See Ann Crittenden, *The Price of Motherhood: Why the Most Important Job in the World Is Still the Least Valued* (2001; repr., New York: Henry Holt, 2010).

33 Tara Siegel Bernard, "In Paid Family Leave, U.S. Trails Most of the Globe," *New York Times*, 22 February 2013, accessed 3 April 2015, http://www.nytimes.com/2013/02/23/your-money/us-trails-much-of-the-world-in-providing-paid-family-leave.html?_r=0. "Mommy tax" is used throughout Crittenden's book and first defined on page xii.

34 Lisa Loomer, *Living Out* (New York: Dramatists Play Service, 2005), 26. Page numbers are from this edition.

35 See Margo Jefferson, "'Upstairs, Downstairs,' with Nanny-Cam Running," *New York Times*, 1 October 2003, accessed 25 August 2013, http://www.nytimes.com/2003/10/01/theater/theater-review-upstairs-downstairs-with-nanny-cam-running.html; and Robert Hurwitt, "'Living Out' Straddles Race, Class Divide," *SFGate*, 16 October 2004, accessed 25 August 2013, http://www.sfgate.com/bayarea/article/REVIEW-Living-Out-straddles-race-class-divide-2716954.php.

36 Ibid., 20, 24, 54, 57.

37 Sharon Hays, *The Cultural Contradictions of Motherhood* (New Haven, CT: Yale University Press, 1996), 21.

38 Sharon Green, "What Does It Take to Be a Good Mother? Contemporary Motherhood Ideology and the Feminist Potential of Lisa Loomer's Dramaturgy," *Journal of Dramatic Theory and Criticism* 28, no. 1 (Fall 2013): 7.

39 Hirshman, "Homeward Bound," 26.

40 Sheryl Sandberg, *Lean In*, 134.

41 Ibid.

42 See Jerry Kraft, "*Living Out*," in Aisle Say Seattle, accessed 25 August 2013, http://www.aislesay.com/WA-LIVINGOUT.html; and Elyse Sommer, "*Living Out*, A *CurtainUp* Review," accessed 25 August 2013, http://www.curtainup.com/livingoutny.html (both use "real people"); and Margaret Quamme, "'Living Out': Play Probes Tension between Mother, Nanny," 28 October 2011, *Columbus Dispatch*, accessed 22 August 2013, http://www.dispatch.com/content/stories/arts/2011/10/28/review-living-out.html.

43 See Warren Hoffman, *The Great White Way: Race and the Broadway Musical* (New Brunswick, NJ: Rutgers University Press, 2014), esp. chaps. 3, 5, concerning the problems of evolving racial and ethnic categorization and identity in US culture and on the stage. The invention and flexibility of "white ethnicity" is particularly apropos here (156). The subject is superbly historicized by Matthew Frye Jacobson in *Whiteness of a Different Color: European Immigrants and the Alchemy of Race* (Cambridge, MA: Harvard University Press, 1999).

44 For a discussion of the changes, see Stephanie Coontz, "The New Instability," *New York Times*, 26 July 2014 accessed 3 April 2015, http://www.nytimes.com/2014/07/27/opinion/sunday/the-new-instability.html?_r=0.

45 Stevens, "Stevens Reads Odet's [*sic*] Shrill 'Awake and Sing!'"

46 Tony Kushner, *Caroline, or Change* (New York: TCG, 2004), xi. All page numbers are from this edition.

47 See reviews by Adam Feldman, "Caroline, or Change," *Time Out New York*, 4 December 2003, 155; and Irene Backalenick, "Caroline, or Change," *Backstage*, 5 December 2003, 56.

48 Jeremy McCarter, "Maid in America," *New York Sun*, 3 May 2004, 16; Barry Bassis, "Tony Kushner's Latest Makes Music of Troubled Past," *New York Resident*, 26 January 2004, 27; Linda Armstrong, " 'Change' Works on Broadway," *New York Amsterdam News*, 6–12 May 2004, 21. Several critics reviewed the show when it opened at the Public Theatre in November 2003 and again when it moved to Broadway in May 2004. I draw from both sets of reviews here.

49 David Noh, "Tony Kushner's Pretentious Political Correctness: The Dawn of the Unmusical," *New York Blade*, 5 December 2003, 23; Charles Gross, "A Dry Idea," *a.m. New York*, 7 May 2004, 22.

50 John Lahr, "Underwater Blues," *New Yorker*, 8 December 2003, 123; Randy Kandel, "Caroline, or Change," *Show Business*, 19 May 2004, 12; Michael Phillips, "Too 'High-Hat' for a Tony?," *Chicago Tribune*, 8 February 2004, sec. 7, 8; McCarter, "Maid in America."

51 David Hurst, "Caroline or Change," *Next*, 14 May 2004, 40.

52 Lahr, "Underwater Blues," 124.

53 Critic Margo Jefferson argues that authorial sympathies stack the deck in Noah's favor, portrayal of the child's inner life revealing growth and the maid's lack thereof conveying stuckness. "The Power and Pitfalls of Children in the Plot," *New York Times*, 3 February 2014, accessed 3 April 2015, http://www.nytimes.com/2004/02/03/theater/critic-s-notebook-the-power-and-pitfalls-of-children-in-the-plot.html.

54 Fleissner, *Women, Compulsion*, 9.

55 Smiley, "It All Begins with Housework," 163.

56 Morris, *Realism*,140.

57 Terry Teachout, "When the Watchword Is Safety First," *Wall Street Journal*, 5 December 2003, W15.

58 Simi Horwitz, "Tonya Pinkins: Affecting Change," *Backstage*, 22 January 2004, accessed 3 April 2015, http://www.backstage.com/news/tonya-pinkins-affecting-change/.

59 Weeks, *The Problem with Work*.

60 Ibid., 6–8.

61 Ruhl, *The Clean House*, 8.

62 Ibid., 52.

63 Helen Molesworth, "Work Stoppages: Mierle Laderman Ukeles' Theory of Labor Value," *Documents* 10 (Fall 1997): 19–23.

INDEX

Numbers in italics refer to illustrations.